# DEATH OF AN EDITOR

# Death of an Editor

*The Caillaux Drama*

PETER SHANKLAND

Foreword by
The Rt Hon Sir Michael Havers QC

WILLIAM KIMBER   LONDON

First published in 1981 by
WILLIAM KIMBER & CO. LIMITED
Godolphin House, 22a Queen Anne's Gate,
London, SW1H 9AE


© Peter Shankland, 1981

ISBN 0-7183-0248-6

Typeset by Grove Graphics, Tring
and printed and bound in Great Britain by
The Garden City Press Limited,
Letchworth, Hertfordshire SG6 1JS

*To my wife Marion*
*with gratitude*
*for many happy years*

# Contents

# List of Illustrations

# Acknowledgements

I should like to thank my friend Peter Fraser for suggesting I should write about Joseph Caillaux – I have found it a most interesting and rewarding subject. The staffs of the London Library, the British Library and the Institut Français du Royaume Uni have been helpful and obliging, and Mrs Frances Rabin has brought books for me from Paris which were invaluable.

I am delighted that Sir Michael Havers, QC, MP, continuing our happy association, has offered to write a foreword, and it has been a pleasure to work once again with Mr Peter Kimber and his associates.

PETER SHANKLAND

# Foreword

by

## The Rt Hon Sir Michael Havers, QC

It has been asserted by a German newspaper, the *Kölnischer Zeitung*, that if Henriette Caillaux had not shot the editor of *Le Figaro* the first world war would not have broken out: because of her rash deed, the one man who could and would have prevented it was driven from office. This was Joseph Caillaux who had presided over the destinies of France with brilliant success during the Agadir Crisis of 1911 and inaugurated a policy of peaceful co-operation between France and Germany. This is not a claim that can be dismissed lightly. Some things appear to have been inevitable, but others should not have happened. Why was *Le Figaro* able to wage a campaign of calumny so bitter that a distracted woman could find no redress but to shoot the editor? It is clear that the laws of libel were unable to protect a citizen against an appalling and vindictive campaign.

No doubt it was the recognition of this fact which accounted for the acceptance of the verdict by our own journals *The Nation* and *The Daily Telegraph* as probably the right one.

Judge Swan of the United States Court of General Sessions, interviewed about this case by *The New York Times*, said it brought into relief as perhaps no other case had done the difference between French and American systems of administering criminal law. He found much to admire in the French system: he thought the preliminary investigation by the Examining Magistrate with legal training, to whom every citizen was obliged by law to give any information in his possession, preferable to an investigation by police and detectives: he praised the speed and facility with which the jury were selected; on the other hand, while admitting that the rules of evidence in the American courts were too narrow and exclusive, he was amazed that in the trial of Henriette Caillaux there seemed to be no rules at all: witnesses were encouraged to talk about themselves, about their emotions, about what other people, not present, had told them, and were allowed to indulge in heated political arguments. He remarked particularly that 'the brother of the dead man was permitted to testify to what the deceased would have done had the defendant made a request to him, thereby judging the mind of his dead brother as affected by a possible state of facts.'

No doubt Judge Swan was right in saying that nine tenths of the evidence would have been ruled out as irrelevant or inadmissible in an American court – as it would have been in an English court – but for the historian it is intensely revealing: we get to know the accused and the witnesses intimately, although I would dread a trial conducted in this way in the United Kingdom.

At the trial which is described in this fascinating book, the witnesses do indeed 'tell the whole truth' (and sometimes a great deal more than the truth!). They express themselves in a way that would have been impossible if the case had been tried in England, they talk without restraint of their deepest emotions, of their loves with tenderness and of their hatreds in glowing torrents of invective. Again and again foreign observers who were present commented that this trial was more dramatic and more exciting than any play in any of our theatres, and this effect was heightened by the participation of the audience who reacted emotionally to the speakers: there were even shouts for an encore when Maître Chenu addressed a resounding appeal to the gallery! Frequently the proceedings became disorderly, even riotous at times when the audience disputed among themselves and split up into warring factions. It is interesting to reflect how the whole tenor of trials in most countries has changed over the last fifty years. I suspect that Marshall Hall would not have achieved his great victories with a modern jury.

The second trial dealt with in this book, that of Caillaux before the Senate for Correspondence with the Enemy, was wholly political and his condemnation wholly unjust. Although he was rehabilitated in his own country and his sentence annulled, his name still carries a stigma in other countries which I hope this book will help to remove.

Caillaux was no traitor, and he was no defeatist. It is even a mistake to say he was a pacifist in our sense of the term. He wanted peace, he worked for peace and went to great lengths to secure it, but he also took wise measures for the defence of his country, far wiser than those of his fanatically Nationalist opponents. While dealing effectively with the immediate situation he looked far beyond it and tried to remove the sources of the evils which afflicted Europe.

The hatred of his enemies was directed not so much against Caillaux personally as against Caillaux the chief representative and embodiment of the Republican form of government they were attempting to destroy. Thus his fortunes were at their lowest ebb while the *Bloc National* was in power during the World War and after, and he was able to stage his remarkable come-back after the elections of May 1924. The man compels admiration for his courage and tenacity as well as for his integrity and for the breadth and independence of his vision.

It is time that the whole story was analysed and properly recorded; this book has brilliantly achieved this aim.

# CHAPTER ONE

# Prelude to Tragedy

Joseph Caillaux looked like an Englishman's idea of a typical Frenchman: he was a dandy, small and erect, always impeccably dressed in frock-coat, striped trousers and white spats, and he wore a monocle. He never seemed to change or to grow any older because, from an early age, he was almost completely bald, and he remained so. He had great charm, was voluble in conversation, impatient, quick-tempered and liable to become excited and say more than he had intended. He never hesitated in his speech: every word was clearly enunciated: the thoughts he expressed were as clear as the outline of his cocky little figure. When he made his first appearance in the Chamber of Deputies in 1898, at the age of thirty-one, he was as much the delight of the cartoonists as he would have been in England.

He started his political career with considerable advantages because he had inherited a comfortable fortune – a million francs – and his father, a noted engineer, had been Minister of Public Works in the government of 1875 which drafted and established the constitution of Third Republic. All his life he had heard politics discussed round the family dinner table. His father, while restraining his impetuousness, encouraged him to make a career in politics and suggested he should stand as parliamentary candidate for the district of Mamers, in the Sarthe, where the family was well-known: the present deputy, a Royalist, Monsieur de la Rochefoucauld, Duc de Doudauvent, was old enough to retire. Caillaux therefore called upon the Duke and asked if he might succeed him. The Duke, who had held the seat for twenty-five years, didn't welcome this suggestion: 'I'll succeed myself!' he exclaimed, 'and I should not like you to stand against me.' Caillaux therefore withdrew.

Some time after this rather ingenuous move he was invited by the opposite party, the Republicans, to be their candidate for the seat. At first he refused because he didn't wish to stand against the

Duke who had been an acquaintance of his father's, but seventeen days before the election he allowed himself to be persuaded to change his mind. He canvassed the district on his bicycle and won the seat by a comfortable majority. His opponents were indignant and never forgave him. They had looked upon him as one of themselves and, relying on his original statement that he didn't intend to stand, the Duke had not troubled to canvas in person.

In the Chamber he quickly made friends with Poincaré, Briand and Barthou of his own generation, and was soon on good terms with the redoubtable Georges Clemenceau, known as the Tiger because of his ruthless attacks on anyone who stood in his way on the road to power. The eminent statesman Waldeck-Rousseau took a liking to him and warned him about his friends: 'Poincaré', he said, 'has a stone in place of a heart . . . ' and he recalled what Gambetta had said: 'Where Clemenceau has set his foot the grass never grows again . . . ' but Caillaux took no notice and went with Poincaré, each with a mistress, to study the museums in Naples.

Nearly all his colleagues had spent their lives in politics or in the law or journalism, whereas he had spent the last ten years in the department of the Inspector General of Finances, travelling about the country checking the accounts of government offices and the railways. Consequently he had become an expert, and he frequently had opportunities to address the Chamber on questions of Public Revenue. He was a persuasive speaker, his arguments were measured and reasonable, he had a pleasant voice with a metallic ring in it when it rose to a climax. Waldeck-Rousseau on becoming Prime Minister in 1899 appointed him Minister of Finance. In a single year he had become a man of importance.

He had told his constituents, who were mostly small farmers, agricultural labourers, shopkeepers and craftsmen, that he would introduce a fairer system of taxation because at present many of the rich made no contribution at all, which he thought unjust; and that his foreign policy would be to work for the peace of Europe, starting with a reconciliation between France and Germany, because he did not believe that the ordinary people in either country were possessed of the desire to stab or shoot each other. These two main lines of policy he followed undeviatingly from the beginning to the end of his career. He could not have done anything more calculated to arouse against him the hatred of powerful sections of the community: the rich, who owned the big newspapers and could manipulate public opinion, did not want to be taxed; and the foreign policy of France, strongly influenced by the aggressive Nationalist and Royalist parties, was based on the idea of revenge on Germany for the humiliating defeat of 1870 and the loss of Alsace-Lorraine.

The first task he undertook was to reorganise his own ministry : he examined into grievances, removed abuses and improved conditions for his staff. Henceforth he had an enthusiastic department working for him.

French taxation was based on a system which had been set up a hundred years ago and was overburdened with innumerable amendments and additions : he decided to replace it by a tax on incomes though he knew it would be bitterly opposed and take years of careful planning. In the meantime, to make life easier for people with low incomes, he reduced taxation on the necessities of life.

He was painfully aware of the historical reasons for hatreds between nations – the poisons and resentments generated by the barbarisms of war, and the desire for vengeance for past defeats – but he was convinced those hatreds were kept alive in the modern world by competition for world markets due to unbalanced and unlimited production resulting from technical advances; he wanted industry to be replanned, and controlled through the control of credit, first in Europe and then in other countries as well, so that Man would be able to enjoy the benefits of scientific discovery without suffering its disadvantages. As a preliminary step he secured the adherence of France to an international agreement on sugar : it was something new in commercial history. Each country surrendered a part of its sovereign right to do as it pleased, in order to allow an independent commission to fix prices and control marketing. The French producers opposed it – but they benefited in the end, and the people paid less for their sugar. He was a Free Trader at heart, an intense admirer of Gladstone, Cobden and Bright, but he held that modern techniques which led to countries dumping their surplus products onto other countries, with disastrous results, had made some form of control necessary.

He did not introduce his Income Tax Bill until 1907 when he was Finance Minister in the Clemenceau Ministry. After long discussion it was passed by the Chamber in 1909 but thrown out by the Senate : he therefore had to propose it again in the Chamber after it had been considered by various commissions, and the battle to get it incorporated in the laws of France continued year after year.

In his public life he was a model of integrity, moral courage and correct behaviour, but this could not quite be said of his private life.

During his parents' lifetime he had resisted all their efforts to get him safely married. He would have liked to please them, particularly his mother to whom he was devoted – she remained, after her death, a felt presence in his hours of trial – but he did not want to be tied to some little 'charming white goose who would have pestered him to take her to Mass . . . '

For his negative religious views they were partly to blame. They had made the mistake of giving him at first a liberal education and then providing a fanatical Catholic tutor who tried to convert him. When he was fifteen, his father sent him to a Jesuit College. Accustomed to speak his mind on all subjects, he found the rigid discipline exasperating. These experiences left him with a distrust of priests and a profound aversion to fanaticism of whatever kind. His mother was a devout Protestant, descendent of a Huguenot family many of whom had taken refuge in England and the Channel Islands from persecution and remained there. Brought up between two uncompromising faiths, he accepted neither. But his main reason for not following his parents' wishes was that he thought a wife and family would interfere with his career. He wanted to be free, at least until he had established himself.

Instead of marrying he formed a romantic and intimate friendship, about 1900, with a young married woman, Berthe Dupré: she was dark, intense and vivacious, a woman who attracted all eyes and had a host of friends. For several years he was perfectly satisfied. Then, in 1904, although he begged her not to, Berthe divorced. For him the charm of their friendship was no longer what it had been, and he could see he was being manoeuvred; and yet he felt some responsibility towards her as she had divorced on his account, though against his advice. He wanted to appear in his own eyes, and in the eyes of society, a gallant gentleman; and so, after hesitating for a long time, he married her in August 1906. It was, he said, a marriage of resignation.

Very soon he realised his mistake. Berthe as a wife was not the same as Berthe the elegant mistress. She made the most of her new position. She had the *salons* of the Ministry redecorated, and staged a series of lavish entertainments. She was a brilliant hostess, and another man might have thought these activities important for his career – but not Caillaux. He had gained his position through his own merit and by incessant work: unlike many of his colleagues he owed nothing to the influence of society hostesses. He thought it all a great bore and a waste of money. He found Berthe extravagant, a bad housekeeper and temperamental. Their earlier romantic way of life had been much more to his liking.

On a visit to his friend Barthou in 1904 he had met another charming young married woman, Henriette Clairtie. A year after his marriage to Berthe they met again, both lonely, both unhappy, and finding pleasure in each other's company. He fell desperately in love with Henriette, and she with him. He felt she was the one woman he had always been waiting for. She was very different from Berthe : she was fair, gentle, with rather a voluptuous figure, slender waist, large eyes and a Greek profile – a typical beauty of the period. She was cultured too, and familiar with the world of literature and the theatre, being married to a critic, Léo Clairtie, whose uncle was an Academician and administrator of the Comédie-Française. In 1909 she too divorced on account of Caillaux, and was given custody of her two daughters, one of whom died six months later. She lived rather quietly, as Caillaux did also, as far as official engagements permitted : he was rarely seen in the fashionable *salons* that were assiduously attended by his friends Poincaré and Barthou, but he went occasionally to the small *salon* of the Comtesse de Beausacq who had been a friend of his mother's, and where he met Pierre Loti and Prudhomme, and became friendly with Anatole France and the poetess Anna de Noailles.

His liaison with Henriette remained a secret until one unhappy day a servant brought him a note during lunch signed 'Riri'. He tried to laugh it off as a hoax but it aroused Berthe's suspicions : she soon discovered Riri's identity and there was a first-class row. He found his situation extremely difficult. The revelation that Berthe could behave like a fury seemed to threaten his career which had seemed so prosperous and so secure. He wrote Henriette a long letter saying they must behave with the utmost discretion because the elections were due in a few months and a scandal might cost him his seat. He told her a great deal about his unhappiness with Berthe and their incompatibility, and that he had seen his lawyer and hoped one day to regain his freedom, and that for nights he had scarcely slept.

This man whose daring ambition it was to bring peace to the world by re-organising the economy of Europe on co-operative instead of competitive lines, was painfully and profoundly divided within himself. For years he was torn between these two women. He could not at once shake off Berthe's fascination and his loyalty to their years of happiness together before they married, and now there was the conflict also between the demands of his personal life and his political ambitions.

It occurred to him that the letter to Henriette, if it fell into the wrong hands, could be used against him. He asked her to return it, addressed *Poste Restante* at Mamers. He collected it and locked it, with some of her letters, in his desk, intending to deposit them in his bank in the morning: but during the night Berthe forced his desk and took them. She refused to return them unless he would give up Henriette. Seeing no other way to save both their reputations, and his career, he agreed to her terms. The letters were solemnly burned in the presence of Caillaux's friend, Privat-Deschanel, and husband and wife, apparently reconciled, left for a holiday together. The curious thing was that Henriette agreed it would be better to part than face a scandal. She had been brought up strictly and educated in a convent: a typical *bourgeoise* of the period, she had always been taught that a scandal was a shame and a disgrace, and a daughter must never be allowed to know of her mother's frailty.

The holiday had barely started when Caillaux discovered Berthe had swindled and kept photographic copies of the letters. He immediately left her and went home alone.

In May 1910 he was re-elected, and he became for the third time Finance Minister. Now he could deal more firmly with his marital problems. To part from Berthe *en galant homme* cost him a very large sum of money – 210,000 francs besides an annual payment of 18,000 francs. The lawyers discussed the terms for more than a year: all his letters both to her and to Henriette were again solemnly burned, and this time Berthe signed a declaration before an attorney that she had kept no copies. The divorce went through on 9th March 1911. On 27th June he became Prime Minister. On 31st October he married Henriette. Poincaré was the first to sign the marriage register: the President of the Republic, Armand Fallières, gave a banquet in her honour, and she immediately became one of the leaders of Parisian society. Caillaux had at the same time solved his personal problems and reached the height of his career.

He had been in office for only a fortnight when there was a serious international crisis: Germany sent a gunboat, the *Panther*, to the small port of Agadir on the Atlantic coast of Morocco. According to the treaties she had no right to do this – it was a direct challenge to French interests. His Foreign Minister, de Selves, who was entirely in the hands of the Quai d'Orsay, the extremely nationalist French Foreign Office, proposed to take up the challenge by sending warships to Morocco : Caillaux vetoed the suggestion, convinced the purpose of the German move was to provoke France to an act of aggression – a view that was found to be correct when the private correspondence of the German Secretary of State for Foreign Affairs, Monsieur de Kiderlen-Waechter, was published. De Selves, however, in defiance of Caillaux's orders, telegraphed London, without informing him, asking whether Britain would send a warship to accompany a French warship to Morocco. As soon as Caillaux heard of this, he telegraphed London countermanding the request.

He was thus faced with a vital constitutional issue : whether he, as the elected representative of the people, was to make the important decisions, or whether the permanent officials, in this case the Quai d'Orsay, who had not been elected, were to be allowed a free hand. He had no doubt at all which course was the correct one : the business of a government was to govern. Not to do so would be to betray the people's trust.

Following complaints from the French Ambassador in Berlin, Jules Cambon, that the Quai d'Orsay were 'shooting him in the back' by sending him contradictory instructions and by making in-opportune press releases, he took personal control of the negotiations with Germany, discussing every important move with his Cabinet. He thus added to the list of his enemies another class, that of the permanent officials, whose influence in Paris was very great.

He handled the negotiations with masterly skill. For ten days he ignored the presence of the German warship at Agadir, then he instructed Cambon to ask the German Secretary of State for War the purpose of her visit. In the meantime he looked into the defences of the country and found them deficient in many ways. His War Minister, Messimy, reported that the Commander-in-Chief, General Merlin, though a brilliant strategist, did not enjoy the confidence of the other generals : it would be necessary to replace him. Caillaux favoured Gallieni : Messimy wanted Joffre. It was settled in favour of Joffre because Gallieni, whose active career had been in the colonies, thought he would not be popular with the metropolitan generals, and in any case he was due to retire in three years. He was appointed instead Military Governor of Paris.

Next Caillaux looked into the question of modern weapons and equipment : he found the army was almost entirely without heavy artillery whereas Germany was well provided. The principal reason was that many French generals considered that in case of war heavy artillery would slow up their advance : their minds were dominated by an almost mystic formula, 'Attack! Attack!' 'Give me 700,000 French breasts,' General Castelnau was in the habit of saying to any politician who would listen, 'and I will conquer Europe!'

Caillaux commented that this plan had not been successful at Crécy or at Agincourt. He ordered a 105mm Howitzer to be put out to tender and to be in production at the very latest by 1st January. There were Anglo-French staff talks in July and September at which it was assumed, as General Merlin had assumed also, that in the event of war Germany would immediately invade northern France through Belgium : Caillaux ordered the French armies to be concentrated to oppose this move and to defend their northern industrial districts, but on no account were they to cross the frontier into Belgium unless German troops had already done so. He had come to the conclusion, as Churchill did also at the same time, that France being the weaker would have to stand upon the defensive until allies came to her assistance, or until Germany by attacking had weakened herself until their respective forces were more equally balanced. But what allies? It was not likely that Britain, though in favour of the *Entente Cordiale*, would go to war about Morocco. He tried, through the ambassador, Sir Francis Bertie, with whom he was not on good terms, to get some public expression of support from Britain, and on 21st July Lloyd George, the Chancellor, made a speech at the Guildhall in London in which he came out very strongly, though non-committally, on the side of France. Germany at that time seemed by her warship-building programme to be challenging Britain's supremacy at sea, and Lloyd George stressed the point that Britain could not view with unconcern the prospect of a German naval base on the Atlantic coast of Morocco opposite Gibraltar.

This speech, Caillaux said, helped him, and it was a shock for the Germans but it did not change their attitude. They were quite prepared to take on Britain as well as France : 'No doubt the rival fleets will knock each other about,' Kiderlen wrote, 'but France will have to pay for the broken crockery.' The British Government were not prepared to give any firm undertaking for the support of France. There was a treaty of alliance with Russia but the very influential Imperial Ambassador, Isvolsky, informed Caillaux they were still trying to reorganise their unwieldy army after the defeat by Japan in 1906, and consequently they would be unable to intervene. France would be alone against Germany, the greatest military power in existence. To discourage fire-eaters and explain why he was negotiating, Caillaux asked Joffre at a meeting with the President of the Republic if, in the event of war, France would have a seventy per cent chance of success. Joffre said she would not.*

France, by international agreement, had political influence over but not military control of Morocco and was not allowed to make of it a French protectorate, because Germany as well as France had important commercial and financial interests there, and a share in the control and development of the railways; but French predominance had been steadily increasing: in May of the previous year, while Caillaux was Minister of Finance, it had culminated in a military expedition to occupy Fez, the capital. Being in London at the time, he had hurried back to Paris to stop it, but he was too late, and there had been nothing left for him to do but accept the *fait accompli.* The ministers who had authorised it said they had understood French lives were in danger. This expedition to Fez had provoked unfavourable reactions in Germany : 'You won't leave it again,' the Chancellor, Bethmann-Hollweg, remarked to the French Ambassador.

The purpose, therefore, of the defiant gesture of sending the *Panther* to Agadir was to demand a proper share of Morocco or some other French territory in exchange. Caillaux was in a position of extreme difficulty. He remarked to Messimy that if they failed in their efforts to make peace they would be stoned by the Socialists, and if they came to an agreement with Germany they would be hanged as traitors by the *Revanchards,* the Nationalists who were working for a war of revenge on Germany. Kiderlen demanded the whole of the French Congo in exchange for their interests in Morocco: Caillaux would not agree, and the state of tension continued for nearly the whole of July. De Selves made one more bid for independent action : he invited the naval and military chiefs to confer with him at the Quai d'Orsay : Caillaux forbade them to attend.

At last, on 25th July, came a little break in the clouds : a merchant, Fondère, who was an expert on African affairs, came to Caillaux and asked for instructions because the counsellor at the German Embassy, von der Lancken, had invited him to call. Because the counsellor was believed to be the Kaiser's personal representative, Caillaux told Fondère to go and see what he wanted, and if the negotiations were mentioned he was to say he had found Caillaux very pessimistic and indisposed to accept the German conditions, but that he sincerely

---

* It was a maxim of Napoleon's that one must have a seventy per cent chance of success before embarking on a campaign.

desired a broad and permanent settlement that would eliminate all cause of dissension between their two countries.

On the 26th Fondère came back and reported that von der Lancken had given him to understand Germany would be satisfied with half the French territory along the River Congo of which she had demanded the whole. Caillaux sent a trusted member of his staff, Pietri, to Berlin to give Jules Cambon personally this first intimation that the German attitude was weakening. Cambon received and acknowledged what he called, 'this precious information', on 31st July, just before his next meeting with Kiderlen.

Meanwhile de Selves brought Caillaux copies of two intercepted and decoded telegrams from the German Ambassador in Paris, the baron de Schoen, reporting the conversation with Fondère. In the text there was nothing at all objectionable except one line, 'Caillaux asks that these overtures be kept from Cambon for the present.' This was not true. Caillaux explained that so far from wishing to keep Cambon in ignorance, the information had been collected for him, and that Pietri was on his way to Berlin with it, or about to start. He had instructed Fondère not to be available if von der Lancken tried to carry on any negotiations with him, and he himself, for the same reason, was going to Biarritz for a few days holiday. It was true, of course, he had taken responsibility for the negotiations out of the hands of de Selves and the Quai d'Orsay – and for sufficient reasons – that is, so there would be a chance of peace instead of an inevitable war : but with Cambon he worked always in perfect accord.

Now the Germans had shown their hand, Caillaux spent two days working on counter-proposals – what Central African territories France would be prepared to give up in exchange for the Germans pulling out of Morocco. When these had been discussed and approved by the Cabinet he sent them directly to Cambon. The Quai d'Orsay, probably with the acquiescence of de Selves, tried to prejudice the negotiations by giving the press incorrect copies of Cambon's reports; and the holders of African concessions, who had been making scandalous profits out of them, financed a 'patriotic' campaign, in which the Nationalist papers joined, to impress upon the public it would be a shameful surrender if any French territory were ceded to Germany.

At a stormy meeting, Caillaux ordered Herbette, the Quai d'Orsay press officer, to stop feeling the newspapers with inflammatory material against him, 'Or I'll break you like that !' he exclaimed, breaking a pencil in half. For a short while the press showed more restraint.

During the weeks that followed, both Poincaré and Clemenceau noted a steady swing of public opinion against a peaceful solution and in Germany the militarists surrounding the Kaiser were intensifying their propaganda and increasing their influence; the Crown Prince at their head was demanding 'War, fresh and joyous!'

Caillaux stuck to his counter-proposals, unmoved by public opinion at home or pressure from Germany. Unsuspected by either side he was fighting with weapons of his own in another dimension. Nothing appeared on the surface except from time to time an international banker or financier called at his office. From the very beginning of the crisis he had instructed the French banks to restrict credit : the Germans had not taken this precaution. The long-drawn-out state of tension and uncertainty caused a recession in trade. In September many businesses failed, unable to meet their financial obligations: there was a rush to withdraw money from the savings banks : then Caillaux made a few quiet telephone calls with the result that vast amounts of international capital were suddenly withdrawn from the Berlin Exchange and there was a financial crisis.

Cambon wrote from Berlin :

I can hardly describe the impression produced here by the debacle of last week. I am sure it did a great deal to change the attitude of the German Government. Monsieur de Kiderlen perceived that when he talked of war he had declared one that he hadn't expected.

Germany hastily accepted Caillaux's terms, and the cruiser *Berlin,* which had relieved the *Panther* at Agadir, was withdrawn. On 10th November a treaty was signed between the two countries by which Morocco was secured to France, and Germany received in exchange about a quarter of the Central African territories she had at first demanded. The British Prime Minister, Mr Asquith, sent a message: 'Tell Mr Caillaux he comes back from Berlin like Lord Beaconsfield bearing on his flag, "Peace with honour !" ' but the ultra-nationalists on both sides were outraged. In Germany the Under-Secretary for the Colonies, de Lindequist, resigned as a protest. The Crown Prince told Lord Granville, 'Considering our situation in Europe and the superiority of our army, we have not obtained from France sufficient compensation for the immense sacrifice we made in abandoning Morocco to her.' Ex-Chancellor, Prince von Buelow, said, 'Like a damp squib the Agadir episode at first astonished the world, then made it laugh, and ended by making us ridiculous.' Others com-

plained that in exchange for Morocco Caillaux had given them
'Millions of tse-tse flies' – a remark which had some truth in it, for
the surrendered territories were infested with sleeping sickness. Only
250 Frenchmen resided in them, of whom fifty were merchants.

In spite of the abundant evidence that the Germans considered
Caillaux had got the better of them, the Nationalist campaign continued against him with unabated fury: he was accused of having
betrayed French interests; he was accused of having sold the French
Congo to the Kaiser who, in exchange, so it was said, had given
Henriette a crown of diamonds worth 750,000 francs as a wedding
present; he was accused of having made immense sums speculating
on the Berlin Stock Exchange. All this was pure calumny: he was
strictly correct in all his dealings and never speculated, or even
invested any money, while in office. The treaty was denounced as
having been negotiated 'under the guns of Agadir.' Clemenceau, who
throughout his career had condemned colonial expansion, did a
*volte-face* and protested against 'the surrender of part of our Congo'
as 'a shameful German victory.' He wrote in his memoirs, 'When I
tried to explain Monsieur Caillaux to myself I thought he looked upon
the country as done for, and was trying by every means to curry
favour with Germany. That was the most favourable interpretation.'[1]
Poincaré showed how he felt by commenting that the treaty would be
painfully resented in Lorraine.*

On 19th and 20th December, Caillaux had to justify his treaty
before the Chamber of Deputies: it was denounced violently by the
Nationalist speakers, notably by Pichon, one of Clemenceau's
lieutenants; and by the Catholic leader, de Mun, who deplored the
humiliating surrender to Germany by which France had lost the
magnificent plan of an empire extending from the Mediterranean to
the mouth of the Congo. Caillaux, taking over from de Selves who
spoke with some embarrassment and hesitation, took full responsibility
for the treaty and not only explained how he had saved the peace of
Europe and secured Morocco for France, but outlined a new policy
of international co-operation and the reorganisation of industry to
prevent future conflict. He appealed to France and Germany to accord
with each other in the name of civilisation.

The world-renowned Socialist orator, Jaurès, agreed that Caillaux's

---

* Poincaré was born in Lorraine, and the determination to free his homeland
played a large part in his future policy. He wrote: 'In my school years . . . I did
not see any purpose in life for my generation except to recover the lost provinces.'
Quoted in *Debout les Vivants* by V. Margueritte.

economic policy was 'a great door opened' and that capitalist solidarity, to be feared when manoeuvred for selfish interests, could become, at certain hours, a guarantee of peace under the common will and inspiration of the nations.[2] Being devoted to the cause of peace he approved of the treaty, but because he mistrusted Caillaux's methods of negotiating it he abstained, together with his party, the best organised of the Socialists, from voting for it. But there was never any doubt about the issue – refusal to ratify the treaty would imply war with Germany. Caillaux's authority in the lower house was tremendous and it was approved by 393 votes to 36.

It was from the committee appointed by the Senate to examine it that he expected more serious opposition because several of his most bitter antagonists were members.

Poincaré had advised him that if any question of secret negotiations came up he should say no one could question the means he had employed as Prime Minister to support French diplomacy. Before the Senatorial Committee he forgot this good advice : he justified his treaty with such good effect that he was carried away by his success and added, when it was not necessary to say more, 'I never mingled unofficial with official negotiations.'

This was strictly true, because he had never attempted to follow a personal policy as distinct from that of the government. All his efforts had been to assist the official negotiations by every means in his power, and none of his opponents dared say openly that the Prime Minister responsible to the nation had not the right to do this. They insinuated instead that something underhand and probably treacherous had been going on. But his statement that he had never mingled unofficial with official negotiations was open to malicious misinterpretations. Clemenceau pounced on it. 'I should like the Minister for Foreign Affairs to confirm that statement,' he said.

De Selves, who had been told about the Fondère information two days after Caillaux received it, had been showing the intercepted telegrams to the Nationalist leaders and 'crying on their waistcoats' as Caillaux expressed it. Now he could not say anything in reply to Clemenceau : he dared not withdraw the allegations he had made that Caillaux had been carrying on secret negotiations, and he dared not repeat them in his presence.[3]

Caillaux rose to answer for him, but the Tiger would not let de Selves escape from his claws : 'My question was not addressed to the Prime Minister but to the Minister for Foreign Affairs,' he insisted. Extremely embarrassed, de Selves muttered something about his desire to tell the truth being in conflict with the reserve imposed upon him by his office. This had the worst possible effect, making it look as if he knew something of which, out of loyalty to Caillaux, he could not speak.

When the session was over, Caillaux called both men into a private room and asked Clemenceau what it was he wished to say. This is Caillaux's account of what followed :[4]

> CLEMENCEAU : The unofficial negotiations . . .
>
> CAILLAUX : What? You call the information I collected through an intermediary 'negotiations'? What is there in that to criticise?
>
> CLEMENCEAU : This. I have been shown a document according to which you proposed to Germany a final settlement which seemed to imply the renunciation of Alsace-Lorraine . . .
>
> CAILLAUX : Not on your life! (*He replied so emphatically that Clemenceau seemed to doubt the truth of his information.*)
>
> CLEMENCEAU : What is most serious in the document I was shown was that you had asked that the Ambassador of France should not be informed of your negotiations.
>
> CAILLAUX : That is a lie, or a forgery.

Again Caillaux was right, because the correspondence shows that Cambon was informed. Clemenceau seemed satisfied, and said he had never doubted Caillaux's patriotism. When he had left, Caillaux gave de Selves a piece of his mind, with the result that he resigned.

The urgent problem now was to reconstitute his ministry. With the approval of President Fallières he arranged for Delcassé to transfer to Foreign Affairs, but he could not get anyone to replace him at the Navy Office. Then Clemenceau persuaded Fallières to withdraw his approval of Delcassé's transfer. Jaurès, who might have saved the situation, made no move to support the government. One leading politician after another refused to take office and face the storm of the outraged nationalism of Paris. Although on the question at issue Caillaux had just secured an enormous majority vote in the lower house, he had to resign – an event Churchill found 'hard to understand in view of his handling of the Agadir Crisis'.[5]

Tardieu's explanation was that 'These incidents had for their origin a campaign waged against the Government by the Department of the Ministry for Foreign Affairs.'[6] Under the British system Caillaux would have appealed to the country, and it can hardly be doubted that the electorate would have supported him so enthusiastically that the President would not have been able to avoid asking him to form a new government. Instead he sent for Poincaré, and a new era began in the history of France, and of Europe. The date of Caillaux's fall, 12th January 1912, took on greater and greater significance as it receded in time.

# CHAPTER TWO

# Crime Passionnel

When he surveyed the wreck of his ministry, Caillaux's greatest concern was for the fate of his treaty which had not yet been ratified by the Senate. He had hoped Poincaré as Prime Minister would continue the policy of international goodwill and conciliation, but when he called on him at the Elysée to hand over his files his reception was lukewarm and he began to have serious doubts: Poincaré expressed strong disapproval of his action in overriding de Selves and the Quai d'Orsay and taking upon himself the responsibility for the negotiations, but after a long discussion he agreed to submit the treaty to the Senate; he asked Caillaux, however, not to answer his critics or to speak again in its defence as this would not be in the national interest. Considering that Poincaré now carried the full burden of responsibility to the nation, Caillaux felt his only course was to agree, though it went sorely against the grain not to answer his critics. It was clear their divergent political interests had weakened their former friendship.

He saw Poincaré as a man living among his dossiers and working at them with remarkable intelligence and industry, but taking written reports too much at their face value because he lacked intuition and could not read between the lines. There was little spontaneous about him – his speeches were always carefully prepared and read out. He was an able barrister who had been disappointed in his ambition to become a *Bâtonnier*, or Leader of the Bar – an honour that went to Labori, the defender of Dreyfus[1] – and he had therefore devoted himself entirely to politics.

When the treaty came up for ratification he read out a speech formally supporting it, but he contrived at the same time to convey the impression that he was hostile to it, thus satisfying both sides. Clemenceau attacked it in a rousing patriotic speech which the Senate applauded – but they ratified the treaty by a large majority. Thus they set the seal of their approval on the actions and the policy of the leader they had discarded. Caillaux retired into private life and took Henriette for a belated honeymoon to Palestine and to Egypt where they met Kitchener and Rudyard Kipling, and travelled up the Nile to Khartoum.

When he returned to Paris, in May 1912, he sensed a change in the political climate : Poincaré had announced that his policy was one of 'National Pride', thus securing the support of the Centre and the Nationalists of the extreme Right who had been attacking Caillaux.[2] He was, at the same time, making concessions to pacify the Left. His foreign policy was directed towards a closer alliance with Imperial Russia. The newspapers were becoming increasingly Nationalist. His new Minister for War, Millerand, was staging a succession of spectacular military parades which were immensely popular : but in spite of all this there was a growing body of public opinion that war was an antiquated barbarism which must not be allowed to occur again.

In the summer of that year, 1912, Kiderlen expressed the conviction that 'peace had descended into the souls' of both the French and the German peoples, and that there was a general belief the Agadir Settlement had secured peace for many years to come. Mr Bonar Law said if war could be averted for a further ten or fifteen years it could be averted altogether. Now that the question of Morocco, which had bedevilled international relations in Europe for years, had been settled, the British and German Governments were becoming increasingly friendly. Lord Loreburn, while admitting the danger to peace of the militarist leaders surrounding the Kaiser, noted there was 'another and a very different Germany rapidly striding to power'.[3] In all countries the merchant classes, the whole business world and the artisans and farm workers wanted peace : the Socialists too, though differing widely among themselves on many issues, were universally on the side of peace : but the German Empire had been created by successful wars, the campaigns of Napoleon were still an inspiration in France and, as Renan said, 'The past is always a part of the present.'

No doubt the militarists both in France and Germany felt their influence waning and their time for decisive action short : General von Bernhardi, writing in 1911, deplored 'the aspirations for peace which seem to dominate our age and threaten to poison the soul of the German people.'[4] He subscribed to the doctrine that might is right and war a rejuvenating force.

Caillaux's naturally ally was the great tribune Jaurès : both were trying to curtail the privileges of the rich, and for both of them peace was a mission, a crusade. Being patriotic Frenchmen they took remarkably far-sighted measures for the defence of their country.

Patriotism in their eyes was not to be judged by zeal in waving flags or ordering military parades. A patriot was, in Caillaux's definition, a man who fearlessly did what was best for his country, and he believed that what was best for Europe was best for France also.

Jaurès was an original thinker having difficulty in adjusting his ideas to any party line, but trying to do so for the sake of the unity of the Socialist movement.[5] He could be seen any day in the Chamber of Deputies' Library reading classical authors in the original Greek or Latin, or strolling about the corridors talking excitedly surrounded by admirers, a broad sturdy figure with blond curly hair, a determined nose, fierce eyebrows and a beard. He usually wore a workman's blouse, jacket and boots, or an ill-fitting suit like a workman on holiday. He was a Socialist from love, not hatred, of his fellow men. He believed Karl Marx to have been profoundly mistaken in preaching hatred between classes and prophesying that the condition of the workers would become worse and worse until they were driven to Revolution. On the contrary, he said, their conditions were continually improving: they already had better houses, food and education, and when a democracy was ready for Socialism it could be effected by legal means. Neither was he the kind of man, being a profound lover of France, to accept Marx's dictum that the Latin races were destined to disappear.[6]

Strangely enough he was persuaded to support Poincaré instead of Caillaux with whom he had so much in common. The reason was that Poincaré promised him to submit to the Senate a measure which had already passed the Chamber of Deputies, altering the electoral law to bring in proportional representation by which the Socialists expected to benefit. When it came to the point, Poincaré did nothing of the kind. It was common knowledge the Senate were strongly opposed to the measure, and to submit it would have entailed inevitable defeat and consequent resignation, neither of which were in Poincaré's programme. Apparently no one except Jaurès expected he would. One can understand Briand's comment: 'God has given this wonderful man every gift except that of common sense.'

During the parliamentary vacation Poincaré paid an official visit to St Petersburg, stage-managed by Isvolsky. He went in a warship to avoid passing through Germany. He was brilliantly entertained, the crack Czarist troops were paraded before him and he came back convinced the Russian armies were superbly organised and equipped. The French Ambassador, Georges Louis, who had constantly reported their true state, was removed at Isvolsky's request and replaced by Delcassé whom Clemenceau described as 'a stupid Poincaré.'

Joseph Caillaux, Prime Minister.

Madame Henriette Caillaux, Society Hostess.

The seven-year term of office of President Fallières was due to expire in January of the following year, and therefore towards the end of 1912 the question of who would succeed him was agitating the political parties. The favoured candidate was Poincaré whose spectacular and widely reported visit to Russia had impressed the public. The leading newspapers were enthusiastic in his favour. Caillaux and Clemenceau campaigned against him, but his other friends, Briand and Barthou worked hard to rally supporters and succeeded in getting him elected by a narrow margin. Briand inherited the office of Prime Minister, submitted the bill for proportional representation to the Senate, was duly defeated and resigned.

President Poincaré's choice to succeed him was Barthou. The main preoccupation of his ministry was to introduce a measure recommended by the Supreme War Council to increase the term of compulsory military service from two years to three. Caillaux was its determined opponent. He objected to 200,000 young men spending an extra year square-bashing when they were urgently needed in industry. He considered the measure would not add a single soldier to their forces, that it was merely a gesture of defiance to Germany who had recently increased the size of her army and that its real purpose was to allow the High Command more time to inculcate into the troops the spirit of revenge for 1870 and the spirit of 'Attack! Attack!' He deplored that the material and technical resources of the country were to be employed for several years in building new barracks instead of in modernising their antiquated defences on their north and north-western frontiers.

Jaurès too was strongly opposed to the measure: he had brought out a book, *La Nouvelle Armée*, advocating the reduction of the time recruits spent in barracks to five months, the abandoning of their bright uniforms, and a university education for officers to prevent them becoming a class apart from the realities of civilian life: also he urged greater reliance on reserve regiments able to repel any attack but not constituting a threat to any other country. In spite of their combined efforts the measure was adopted on 19th July 1913 by 358 votes to 204.[7]

The Nationalist newspapers were jubilant and started campaigning against individual politicians who wanted peace, in order to eliminate them from public life. The daily *L'Action Française*, which advertised itself as 'the ancient monarchy with the claws of nationalism,' openly advocated violence, kept a gang of strong-arm boys, *les Camelots du Roi*, and boasted of their exploits. Caillaux wrote that the axiom of

Joseph de Maistre enshrined in its pages, 'To kill ideas you must kill men,' floated on the pestilential air of 1913–1914.

In August he went for a holiday, motoring in Brittany and the Sarthe. Henriette sitting beside him chided him for being silent and preoccupied and not even looking at the countryside through which they were passing : he was oppressed by his visions of the future while for most people the future was full of promise. 'They are leading the country into war,' he told her, 'and what a war ! . . .'

It so happened that about this time the eminent psychologist, Dr C. G. Jung of Zurich, had a fearful dream : Europe was spread out before him, and in many of the countries there were seas of blood and corpses in uncounted thousands, precisely in those countries, as it turned out, which were afterwards involved in the war. This dream weighed upon him so heavily that he almost doubted his own sanity. The atmosphere even seemed darker to him than it had been before.[8]

Caillaux had always been what he called 'a man of government' rather than of any particular party, though he was a staunch Republican. In October 1913 he was offered, and accepted, the leadership of the Radical-Socialists, which gave him 163 votes in the Chamber : they stood midway between extreme Nationalism on the Right and Communism on the Left, and were historically the direct descendants, according to Caillaux, of the *Tiers État*, the mass of the people who before the Revolution had had no privileges. They were in general well meaning and anxious for reform but were without a clearly defined programme. He began to hope he would be able to stave off the disasters he saw looming ahead.

On 2nd December the Government introduced a bill to authorise a loan of 1,400 million francs to pay for the cost of the Three Years Service Law, the subscribers to receive interest free of tax. Caillaux made a speech attacking its policy, maintaining the loan was unnecessary because defence was everyone's business and should have been allowed for on the regular budget instead of becoming a charge on the future. He maintained further that to allow tax-free interest would be to break the rule already established by the Chamber when they passed his Income Tax Bill. The Chamber supported him, and Barthou had to resign.

This defeat of the Government was looked upon as a defeat for Poincaré and a clear indication that at the forthcoming elections Caillaux would be returned to power. According to the rules, he should have become Prime Minister immediately, but Poincaré was unwilling to ask him to take office. Caillaux himself thought it might be better to wait until after the elections due in the following April particularly as Henriette was begging him not to form a government. He put forward another member of his party, Doumergue, for the office of Prime Minister. Poincaré objected, and asked three rival leaders in turn to form a government, none of whom was able to do so.

At last, when the Chamber was becoming restive because of his playing about with the constitution, he sent for Doumergue. Caillaux took his old office of Minister of Finance although Henriette prophesied it would bring them misfortune. Caillaux says, at the official ceremony of welcoming the new government, Poincaré addressed a few words to them, sour as vinegar, with teeth clenched, face contorted : 'For me his expression was charged with hostility . . .'

In December 1913 the Comte de Fleurieu, one of Caillaux's Nationalist opponents in the Sarthe, received a message from Briand that he would be powerfully supported at the election by very influential people – a violent press campaign was about to be launched to prevent Caillaux being re-elected. He did not know who these influential people were, besides Briand, but he thought, and he said it was generally believed, they included Poincaré and Barthou.

Almost immediately afterwards, *Le Figaro*, one of the leading daily newspapers, accused Caillaux of having kept his civilian employment after his return to power : it was a shot in the dark, and it misfired because unlike some other ministers he had not done so. A few days later *Le Figaro* accused him of appropriating public funds to finance his election campaign : this misfired also because it was entirely without foundation. The articles continued, appearing usually on the front page and signed by the Chief Editor, Calmette. One accusation followed another in rapid succession, each more vindictive than the last, and each dropped as soon as it was shown to be false. He was accused of having taken huge bribes from the inheritors of a millionaire, Prieu, who had died in Brazil – it was a sort of never-ending Jarndyce Case – he was accused of misusing his influence, of favouring a Jewish banker, Spitzer, of extorting 400,000 francs from the Discount Bank. In none of these accusations was there an atom of truth, but of course they were repeated in the foreign press, usually without Caillaux's regular denials. Then there were long and involved articles about the movements on the Stock Exchange during his various terms of office, interspersed with abusive terms – Swindler ! Crook ! France betrayed ! and so on, with occasionally a verifiable detail, a kind of journalism of which Calmette was a past master.

The general effect was to make the newspaper reading public think there must be something behind so many accusations and to suspect double-dealing behind everything they didn't understand. It seems extraordinary that he found time to answer this mass of calumny and carry the main weight of the government as well as that of his own ministry, and at the same time spend many long hours negotiating with the Senate to overcome their objections to the Income Tax Bill. Calmette seemed to be building up an affair as explosive as that of Captain Dreyfus which had ended only eight years ago after a long controversy and several trials which had aroused the bitterest emotions and split France into hostile factions. These emotions lay just beneath the surface, ready to break out again.

There followed a series of articles abusing Caillaux for his handling of the Agadir Crisis : he learned that *Le Figaro* had been given copies of the secret telegrams which had been decoded at that time : they were known as *Les Verts* because of the green paper upon which telegrams for the Quai d'Orsay were customarily written. He went to Poincaré and protested against their publication as this might lead to difficulties with Germany. Pioncaré agreed, and promised to speak to Barthou about them – both tacitly assumed he could control Calmette through Barthou. Publication was stopped at the last minute but the attacks continued through the latter part of January and the whole of February and into March.

On 10th March he was accused by *Le Figaro* of having interfered with the course of justice when he was Finance Minister eight years ago, in order to save 'his friend' Rochette who had been accused of swindling. This was more difficult to answer, particularly as he was visiting his constituency 200 miles from Paris when the article appeared, giving Calmette the opportunity to follow it up with the headline, 'Caillaux admits his guilt by not replying to the accusation'.

This was an interesting case in which the authorities had been as much to blame as Rochette himself : he was an able financier who, like some others, had been sailing rather close to the wind. He was enormously successful and had offices and businesses all over the country. Probably he would have been left alone, but he decided to acquire control of the newspaper *Le Petit Journal*, in which he was a considerable shareholder. As a preliminary step he brought out a circular criticising the management and pointing out that when the present director, Prevet, took over, six years ago, the shares had stood at £44 whereas now they had fallen to £12 while those of other newspapers had increased in value. Prevet, instead of bringing out a circular of his own justifying his management of the newspaper, appealed for help to Clemenceau who was Prime Minister at the time, and with whom he was on friendly terms.

The only way to prevent Rochette taking over *Le Petit Journal* at the next general meeting of the shareholders, which was about to be held, was to lodge a complaint against him and have him arrested – but no one had made any complaint. However, on 19th March 1908 a banker, Gaudrion, told Prevet he had found a man, Pichereau, who would, if paid £1,000, lodge a complaint. On the 20th, Clemenceau sent for the Chief of Police, Lepine, and told him to take action against Rochette. Lepine's office manager went at once to Prevet who introduced him to the other conspirators. At 2 p.m. on the 21st Pichereau signed a complaint against Rochette, stating himself to be the owner of shares to the value of £6,000 in two of his companies and that he had lost a great deal of money in consequence: it was a false declaration. He had neither owned any shares nor lost any money. On the 23rd Rochette was arrested.

Everybody knows that when a financier is arrested the shares in his companies fall in value, and everybody in business knows that if you have been told it is going to happen you can speculate on them falling and clean up: this is what the conspirators did, and they made £160,000 gambling for the fall of the shares while innumerable shareholders lost their money.

A Commission of Enquiry was appointed with Jaurès as President. He questioned Clemenceau who maintained it was quite a coincidence he had ordered Rochette's arrest precisely at the time the conspirators were expecting it. Jaurès and the Socialist Party did not accept this and continued to accuse him of having illegally ordered Rochette's arrest in order to keep Prevet in control of *Le Petit Journal*.

With all this Caillaux had had nothing at all to do except as a member of the Commission of Enquiry, where he seems to have been favourably impressed when Rochette was allowed to put his case: he showed that the complaint against him was faked, that 10,000 shareholders had petitioned the Chamber for his release, that thousands of his employees had been thrown out of work without warning – in one company alone 15,000 of them were clamouring for wages which could not be paid because the Government had sequestered the money – that all his companies, which had been declared bankrupt, were in fact perfectly sound financially with ample reserves. This was found to be correct. All creditors were paid in full although bankruptcy charges were £80,000.

Later, when Monis was Prime Minister, the affair was still dragging on. Rochette's lawyer, Maurice Bernard, who had handled Caillaux's divorce, requested him to ask Monis to have Rochette's trial postponed, firstly because he himself was overworked, and secondly because, given more time, the financial mess might be cleared up. Caillaux, thinking this might save the Exchequer myriads of francs, and thinking also of France's credit abroad, passed the request on to Monis. He was not a friend of Rochette's and in no way did he stand to gain personally. It made no difference to Rochette's fate: he was eventually found guilty but his sentence was quashed by the Supreme Court of Appeal because there had been irregularities in the trial.

Calmette based his accusation of Caillaux on what he called 'The Fabre Report', an extract of which he published : this was not a report to anybody, it was a note for his own files by Chief Prosecutor Fabre giving an account of his being told by Prime Minister Monis to postpone the Rochette trial. He considered this a slight to his authority. The 'report' had nothing to do with justice or morality; its theme was 'Never have I been so humiliated in my life'. (He was already under fire for having illegally ordered Rochette's arrest at Clemenceau's behest.) Instead of keeping this note in his files he had given a copy to Briand who treasured it for years and then passed it on to Barthou who also treasured it, waiting for a chance to use it with good effect.

Caillaux had nothing but contempt for Calmette. For him the campaign was an attempt by the minority Nationalist Party to rule the country by means of an unholy alliance with the newspapers. He had once fought a duel on a question of honour and he was tempted to send his seconds to Calmette, but duels were fought only between social equals and a minister could not challenge a journalist without making himself ridiculous and, in any case, a duel could not silence a newspaper. Besides, Calmette was, in his eyes, merely a lackey, a hack writer for more important people. Sometimes he thought the campaign must have its origin in Berlin, that it was the revenge of the Pan-Germans for the Agadir Settlement which had gone so much against them and disappointed their hopes : he knew there had been German financiers in the group which had gained a controlling interest in *Le Figaro* in 1902 and put Calmette in editorial control.

He was accustomed to being attacked and he bore the scurrilous abuse with patience and dignity, waiting for the real authors of the campaign to show themselves; but with Henriette it was different: these attacks on the husband she loved and intensely admired wounded her deeply. One day in the Chamber of Deputies when she went to hear him speak there were cries of 'To Berlin ! To Berlin !' as soon as he stood up, and there was a hostile demonstration in the gallery. Then at a dress show she heard one woman say to another, 'That is the wife of the swindler Caillaux', and they both looked her up and down as if to estimate the cost of the clothes she was wearing. In the drawing-rooms of her friends she heard insulting remarks about her husband : even in her own home she had no peace, for she knew her servants argued with each other about what they ought to be paid for serving so notorious a profiteer. Caillaux tried to console her with the North African proverb, 'The dogs bark; the caravan passes,' but it was in vain; she grew daily more worried and depressed. She couldn't sleep, she lost her appetite, she became ill. Frequently she came home in tears. Caillaux, not realising it was the poison of newspapers that was affecting her, sent her to consult a doctor.

Soon the dogs began to bite as well as bark. Caillaux was warned by Madame Estradère, who had worked for *Le Figaro*, that his love letters which Berthe had sworn she had destroyed and kept no copies, were being offered for sale to hostile journalists : his old friend Barthou told him Berthe had shown him copies of the letters and that she was very incensed against him. Then one of his colleagues, Painlevé, Minister for Education, who also had contacts with *Le Figaro*, said Calmette had bought the letters and would certainly use them.

On 10th March Calmette re-iterated his earlier accusations and boasted he had demonstrated that the object of all Caillaux's machinations had been to enrich himself. He continued, 'This is the decisive hour when I must not recoil from any proceedings however painful, however much frowned upon by our customs and tastes . . .'

What proceedings? Surely it could only mean he was about to publish the letters? This was soon confirmed. On 13th March accompanied by five columns of the usual abuse on the front page of *Le Figaro*, and under the headline, 'THE PROOF OF CAILLAUX'S SECRET MACHINATIONS' he published an extract of a private letter written to Berthe eleven years ago. It was in facsimile, and so that readers could compare the handwriting there was also a photograph which he had autographed :

In spite of every desire to do so, it was impossible to write to you yesterday. I had to endure two heavy sessions in the Chamber, one in the morning at nine o'clock which finished at midday, and the other at two from which I have just now come out, at eight o'clock.

I have, however, scored a splendid success : I have *crushed* the

Income Tax while appearing to defend it, I earned the acclaim of the
Centre and Right without too greatly disconcerting the Left . . .
                                                    Ton Jo.

If he had said in the letter what he had actually done – defeated a
premature attempt to introduce the Income Tax – there would have
been nothing wrong with the letter, but it had not been necessary to
specify this at the time it was written, as Berthe knew what he was
talking about. Divorced from its context and maliciously exploited it
looked as if he had been betraying the cause of equitable taxation for
which he had fought during the whole of his public life, whereas he
had simply been boasting of his cleverness to his mistress.

Calmette continued :

The proof, the indubitable proof, terrible, shameful, unhealthy, I give
it with profound regret, I confess, alas ! and I affirm it on my honour.
It is the first time in my thirty years of journalism that I publish a
private letter, an intimate letter against the wishes of its recipient, its
author or its owner : it affronts my dignity and I accuse myself before
those whom my act will cause to suffer.

But how could I keep hidden any longer, for the triumph of this
campaign of national salubrity the evidence destined to open everyone's eyes? Do not forget I am fighting against a man who suppresses
the laws themselves when his interest demands it. I must therefore
consider myself obliged, for the deliverance of my country, to disinter
from everywhere the corrupted truth : this truth I gather wherever it
can be found, wherever I can in this horrible excavation of things
villainous; but it is to purify, to ennoble, to put it to the service of the
most noble of causes, and I raise it to the height of a flame at the top
of the flagstaff ! I shall be judged later . . . He is unmasked. This
public evil is denounced. Whatever happens, Monsieur Caillaux's
mysterious intrigues, exposed to the plain light of day, are thwarted;
they cannot withstand this powerful disinfectant : the truth !

My task is accomplished. Go ! Clear out !

On Monday 16th March Calmette announced in *Le Figaro* that next
there would be a COMIC INTERLUDE. He added, 'Monsieur Caillaux has
a mania for underlining in his *imprudent correspondence* the precise
word which most cruelly illustrates the foolishness of his letter and
sums up its significance.' It was a clear announcement of his intention
to go on publishing the private letters, and this time, no doubt, it would
be those he had written to Henriette – Calmette had alluded to a
sentence in one of them in which Caillaux had made fun of his electors,

so it was evident he had the letters. Caillaux recalled some of the endearing and embarrassing things he had written to Henriette while she was still married to Clairtie : when they were published, the fact that they had had a liaision would become known to everybody.

The day had started badly. *Le Figaro,* as usual, was lying on Henriette's breakfast tray. She took it to Caillaux's dressing-room, her face haggard, her features distorted with grief, and said, 'Aren't you going to do anything? Are you going to let these wretches defile our home?' She screwed up the newspaper, threw it down and went out, banging the door. He hadn't realised till then the depth of her distress. He told her he would go at once to President Poincaré who was the one man who could prevent any more of their intimate letters appearing.

He found Poincaré imperturbably polite, but with a manner 'as dry as pumice-stone'. This time he showed no inclination to restrain Calmette who, he said, was too gallant a gentleman to publish private letters (ignoring the fact he had just published one). He suggested sending the lawyer Maurice Bernard, who was a friend both of Poincaré's and Calmette's, to the *Figaro* offices to discuss the matter – a suggestion Caillaux considered perfectly futile in view of the urgent need to prevent a letter appearing in the next issue. 'If he does publish them, I shall kill him!' he said angrily : a few minutes later he was at a Cabinet .meeting explaining the financial measures he intended to bring before the Chamber.

At midday Henriette came for him. On their way home in the car she told him she had had a talk with Monsieur Monier, President of the Seine Court of Assizes, who had told her it was useless to take out an injunction against Calmette, that any attempt at legal redress would only make matters worse : it was doubtful if they would win, and for weeks the newspapers would revel in the publicity. 'The law is powerless,' he had told her. 'You must defend yourself.'

She asked Caillaux, 'Are you going to defend me?'

He replied, 'If Calmette publishes our letters, I'll smash his face in!'

Lunch was a miserable affair. Caillaux complained of the cooking and hurried back to the Chamber of Deputies. Henriette, who hadn't been able to eat anything, felt unwell, lay down and slept for half an hour. When she awoke she was possessed by the thought that Caillaux would find no way out of their dilemma except to kill Calmette. She went about her daily routine, but the thought would not leave her. She sent Caillaux's dress clothes to the Ministry so that he could go direct to a dinner at the Italian Embassy, excusing herself on the

grounds of illness. She discussed with the Protocol, Monsieur de Fon-
quières, by telephone an important dinner she was giving at the
Finance Ministry on the 13th. In ten days time she was to be presented
to the King and Queen of England: they too would have read *Le
Figaro*. How would she feel with the whole world laughing at the
'Comic Interlude' of her intimate life? She changed into an afternoon
gown for a tea at the Ritz, and she ordered the car because she had an
appointment with the dentist.

Then she went to an employment agency to engage a new cook, but
her mind was working on two levels, for it was there the idea came to
her that she would go to the *Figaro* offices and have a showdown with
Calmette, threaten him, perhaps fire a shot, even wound him – anything to prevent the letters from being plastered over the front page of
*Le Figaro* tomorrow. She went home to the rue Alphonse de Neuville
and wrote a note which she handed to her daughter's English governess to give Caillaux :

> My beloved husband . . . France and the Republic have need of you.
> I shall carry out the task! If you should receive this letter it will mean
> I have obtained, or tried to obtain, justice. Forgive me, but my patience
> is at an end. I love you and I embrace you with all my heart.
>
> Your Henriette.

Without quite abandoning the idea of keeping her appointment at the
Ritz, she went to the gunsmith's Gastinne-Renette, where she was
known because she and her husband had bought sporting guns there.
She bought an automatic pistol, tried it out in the range beneath the
shop, loaded it again and put it in her muff. She told her chauffeur to
remove the cockade from his cap and drive her to the *Figaro* offices,
rue Drouot twenty-six.

Calmette was out. She refused to give her name, and was shown
into the waiting-room. The minutes ticked slowly by. The offending
number of *Le Figaro* was lying on the table in front of her . . . 'now
there will be a comic interlude . . .' Through the open door she heard
voices from the editorial room. People came and went. On the wall
above her head was a framed portrait of the King of Greece, recently
assassinated. Facing her there was a clock. The hands moved slowly
from five o'clock to five past . . . quarter past, twenty past . . . the wait
seemed endless. She sat motionless, her hands in her muff. Six o'clock.
Still Calmette had not returned.

Caillaux after leaving the Chamber of Deputies went to the Finance
Ministry to sign his letters. He was probably the most powerful man

in France. The telephone rang, and in a moment he knew he was ruined : Henriette had shot and gravely wounded Calmette. He turned ashen pale, but all he said was, 'Where is she?' then ordered a taxi.

Henriette had been taken to the police station in the rue Faubourg Montmartre. It was a tough neighbourhood. An immense unruly mob had gathered. Caillaux was recognised getting out of his taxi : there were shouts of 'Death to Caillaux!' 'Assassin!' He pushed past the gendarme at the entrance who had orders to admit no one, and told him off for not saluting the Finance Minister. He was allowed a few words with Henriette.

'What have you done?' he asked her furiously.

'I only meant to frighten him,' she said, 'I hope I haven't killed him.'

His heart melted. Picking up the Inspector's telephone, he got through to the Prime Minister and resigned from the Cabinet – he said he wished to devote himself entirely to his wife's defence.

After being interrogated for an hour and a half, Henriette was taken out by a side exit which led through a grocer's shop to a narrow side street. Caillaux sent for his taxi to come round, and left by the same exit. A menacing crowd followed it. He had just time to jump in and drive away before they caught up with him.

Henriette was taken, also in a taxi, with three plain clothes detectives, to the women's prison of St Lazare, built in the twelfth century as a leper hospital : it was dark, insanitary, cold, damp and overrun with rats. Here the 1,200 inmates lived in gloom and silence except for the grating in the locks of the cells of the huge mediaeval keys. At night a few sputtering gas lamps in the long brown-painted corridors only accentuated the darkness. It was ruled by nuns who never spoke an unnecessary word. Henriette was put into the largest cell, No 12, for special prisoners. The walls were painted black. She lost her name, almost her identity, and became 'No 12'. Another prisoner slept in the same cell to keep her under constant observation; she was a sullen woman, serving a sentence for murdering her husband with a penknife. There was a view, through the barred and wire-netted windows, of the old courtyard in which, during the Revolution, those condemned by the tribunals had been herded into the tumbrils to be taken to the guillotine. Two candles were allowed, stuck with their own wax onto the wooden table.

Special editions of the evening papers came out while Paris was at dinner. Poincaré was informed of the shooting just before leaving for the Italian Embassy where he was the guest of honour : he had expected Henriette to be sitting next to him. At nine o'clock they were told Calmette was recovering. Shortly after midnight they were told he was dead.

Poincaré had just returned to the Elysée Palace when Barthou was announced. Asked why he had come at such an hour, Barthou replied:

I have come to confess to you. It is I who conducted the *Figaro* campaign, it is I who dictated all the articles against Caillaux. I am the cause of the drama. I am punishing myself. I am handing in my resignation as a Deputy. I am retiring to my own country, to Oloron . . .

Instead of taking him to task for the evil he had done, and approving his contrition, Poincaré argued him out of it. *Il le remonta*, he set him up again:[9] he set him up to such good purpose that next morning in the Chamber he took an active part in a political manoeuvre that might have cost Henriette her life: a Royalist Deputy, Delahaye, tabled a motion implying that the purpose of her attack on Calmette had been to prevent the 'Fabre Report' from being published. Apparently none of the Deputies, except Briand and Barthou, had seen it although many newspapers had copies. Fabre himself had denied it had ever existed. 'Does it exist?' Jaurès asked. Whereupon Barthou, with a dramatic flourish, drew the original document from his pocket and read it aloud. It is not surprising Fabre had tried to disown it: it was an expression of his resentment and self-pity, or 'mental agony' as he put it, at being told to postpone the trial when he was already in trouble about Rochette's illegal arrrest. When interviewed he complained bitterly that Barthou had no right to this private document and that his use of it was a shameful abuse of his confidence.

Like Delahaye, Barthou insisted Henriette had shot Calmette to prevent this report from coming out: it seemed a ridiculous claim, for *Le Figaro* had already published all that mattered of it, but if he could get credence for his story it would insure Henriette's conviction, for it would have been a calculated, premeditated crime, and it would have completed Caillaux's ruin.

The Radical-Socialists, dismayed by the sudden fall of their leader, made no effective reply: only Ceccaldi, Deputy for the Aisne, spoke warmly in his defence. Barthou was able to press his advantage and carry a motion for the original Commission of Enquiry into the Rochette Case under Jaurès to be reconstituted.

By these proceedings and by the mystery and secrecy surrounding it, the Fabre Report was blown up into something of enormous importance and provided headlines for many weeks, though in Caillaux's opinion there wasn't enough in it *pour fouetter un chat*, to whip a cat. He took no part in these discussions in the Chamber but stayed at home in the mornings, and in the afternoons visited Henriette whenever possible. There were indignant protests and articles in the newspapers saying he had sent her a lorry load of furniture and comforts for her cell – all of them untrue. She was allowed, with other prisoners, to have her meals brought in, but only the simplest fare. Her only 'comfort' was a threadbare rug laid over the broken tiles of the floor.

No one seemed to feel that Calmette was in any way to blame. Raphael, Paris Correspondent for the *Daily Express*, wrote that the campaign was 'necessary' because Caillaux had attacked the privileges of the rich. The Comte de Fleurieu said the publication of Caillaux's private letters was 'necessary' because it was difficult to find anything to attack in his public life.

In France, anyone accused of a serious crime is liable to be tried first by an Examining Magistrate who carries out detailed interrogations of the accused and the witnesses. If he considers him guilty he passes the case on to the Assizes to be heard by a jury. As anyone can go to the Examining Magistrate and tell his story, the proceedings usually take a very long time. In a case as sensational as that of Henriette Caillaux, the depositions that have been made during the day are handed to the newspapers in the evening, and there is no restraint on the use that is made of them. *Le Figaro* and the Nationalist papers did everything in their power to prejudice the case against Henriette, seizing upon every circumstance, however trivial, to inflame the public against her. When Caillaux, the principal witness, made his deposition, the Examining Magistrate treated him with scant courtesy, almost as a criminal. The *Daily Express* Correspondent wrote :

France boasts of its liberty. Whenever a sensational case occurs and public feelings are stirred, that liberty is allowed to degenerate into licence, and to disagree with the reactionary Press is to ask for abuse. Everybody who says a word of pity for Madame Caillaux in France nowadays is accused of trying to make the course of justice deviate. The examining magistrate whose duty it is to try and find the truth out and report on it is insulted if he dares to be impartial. Everybody who dares to suggest that the very bitterness of the Caillaux campaign was largely responsible for its deplorable climax is held up to obloquy as an enemy of France.

The Commission of Enquiry into the Rochette Case, when it reported on 1st April, made no direct charges, and Jaurès, against the feelings of the majority, censured Clemenceau and Briand (who had been Minister of Justice under Clemenceau) for putting up a fake plaintiff to have Rochette arrested with no benefit to the state, and described the intervention of Monis and Caillaux as a deplorable abuse of influence. This result was not as injurious as Barthou had evidently intended it to be.

When he resigned from the Cabinet, Caillaux had let it be known that he intended to retire altogether from public life. There was an immediate reaction from the Sarthe : a deputation from his constituency bearing a petition with 9,000 signatures implored him to stand again at the election to be held on the 26th April. This expression of confidence renewed his courage. He decided to go on fighting.

The peasants of the Sarthe had nothing but contempt for the vendettas, calumnies, hatreds and press campaigns of the big city : they dismissed them all with a shrug as 'Histoires de Paris.' They wanted peace, they wanted the rich to be taxed, they wanted the three years military service reduced to two – they wanted Caillaux. Wherever his long grey car appeared it was loaded with flowers. The woodcutters' wives of the Forest of Perseigne subscribed their halfpennies to buy a large bouquet for him to take to Henriette. The district was deluged with abusive anti-Caillaux propaganda pamphlets, posters and newspapers, a new candidate was put up to split the Republican vote – it made no difference. He was re-elected with a comfortable majority. His defeated Royalist opponent, d'Aillières, issued a poster thanking his supporters for having had the courage not to approve of crime or of the collusion of a minister with a crook. Caillaux challenged him to a duel. They met with their seconds on the outskirts of Paris. D'Aillières missed, Caillaux fired into the air and honour was satisfied. 'He's not as good a shot as his wife,' was the comment on the boulevards.

The elections showed a tremendous swing in favour of the Radicals, and Caillaux would have been Prime Minister if Henriette had not been in the prison of St Lazare awaiting trial for murder. The electorate, voting for the first time since the Agadir Crisis, had expressed their approval of Caillaux's policy as opposed to militant Nationalism.

Caillaux determined now to force the resignation of President Poincaré whose presence in the Elysée Palace he considered a threat to the peace of Europe. Jaurès, whom Caillaux called 'the conscience of democracy', agreed with this view. Their obvious policy was to form an alliance. Caillaux had frequently attempted this in the past, but

Jaurès had always considered himself bound by a decision of the
Amsterdam International Congress of 1904 that Socialists must not
accept office. Their admiration was mutual, their differences theo-
retical. Jaurès was inclined to suspect all financiers; Caillaux had
little interest in doctrinaire politics or belief in Jaurès's conception of
an ideal state in which all men would be made healthy by work and
the era of violence would be abolished. On the immediately practical
issues they were in complete agreement : on the necessity of getting the
Income Tax Bill through the Senate, on the policy of lowering the
prices of the necessities of life and, dominating everything else, the
necessity to take urgent measures to prevent the Balkan War spreading
to the rest of Europe.

What the two statesmen feared most was the influence of the
Russian Ambassador, Isvolsky, over Poincaré : he too was an embodiment of hatred and the longing for revenge, but directed against
Austria rather than Germany.[10] During the presidential election campaign he had supplied a large sum of money from the Russian Imperial Government with which half a dozen Radical and Socialist
newspapers had been bribed not to oppose Poincaré, and some reactionary newspapers stimulated to support him; the payments were
allocated by the Minister of Finance, Klotz, in the Poincaré Government. Isvolsky had reported with evident satisfaction the success of his
machinations, explaining to his government that in France it always
depended upon the President to determine the composition of the
Cabinet and to choose a Minister for Foreign Affairs entirely reliable
from his point of view : 'we are therefore, for the period of his seven
year term of office, perfectly safe from the appearance of such persons
as Caillaux . . . at the head of the French Government or of the diplomatic administration.'

Of course the bribing of the French newspapers by Isvolsky was
done surreptitiously, but Poincaré's public pronouncements, and the
replacing of Georges Louis as French Ambassador in St Petersburg by
the militant Delcassé, seemed to indicate he intended to give military
support to Russia in her possible intervention in the Balkans, or an
attempt to gain possession of the Dardanelles, whereas the official
treaty between the two countries provided for their mutual assistance
only if one of them were attacked.

A meeting between Caillaux and Jaurès was reported by a mutual
friend, Paix-Séailles, as follows :

One day in June they had a long conversation on one of the settees which line the corridors of the Chamber. Monsieur Caillaux said, 'We must, as soon as possible, form a great Ministry of the Left with a programme in Foreign Affairs which will seek for the basis of a broad conciliation of Europe.' That was also Jaurès's opinion. 'But,' Caillaux added, 'the thing is only possible if the Socialist Party give their whole-hearted support, collaborating not only in parliament but in the government . . . I don't see that it is possible for me to take the responsibility of office at this moment unless you come into the Cabinet as Minister for Foreign Affairs.' Jaurès agreed in principle, but raised a formal objection, quoting the decisions of the Congress of Amsterdam. In the end, however, he granted that in view of the imminence and the gravity of the danger threatening them, he would be justified in setting aside the doctrinaire decisions of the Congress.[11]

The way was clear, therefore, for a Caillaux–Jaurès Ministry. Its establishment would give new heart to those working for peace in all countries and immediately lessen the tension in Europe. Jaurès made only one condition – Henriette must first be acquitted. At that moment the peace of the world seemed to hang upon the issue of the trial. He told Conrad Haussmann at the interparliamentary conference at Bâle;

> Caillaux is the most capable man we have in France. He is not only capable, he has sure judgement, determination and character. That is the reason he is so violently opposed. If his wife is condemned in the trial which is about to open, that will be an obstacle to his return to politics . . . The Paris juries are frequently Nationalist, and you cannot imagine how passionate our Nationalists are . . . It is Caillaux, precisely Caillaux, who can give us a firm and clear policy.[12]

And he told Ramsay MacDonald, whom he met in Copenhagen about this time, that coalitions might be necessary in defence of liberty, and a time must come when Socialists would have to make themselves responsible for the government of countries which, though not yet Socialist, were nevertheless moving in that direction.[13]

In June of that year, 1914, there happened to be in Paris a deputation from the Hungarian Independence Party, headed by a remarkable statesman, Count Károlyi* whose liberal views led him to oppose the

* Count Károlyi became the first Prime Minister of liberated Hungary after the collapse of the Austrian Empire in 1918.

Caillaux canvasses in the Sarthe while Henriette is in prison.

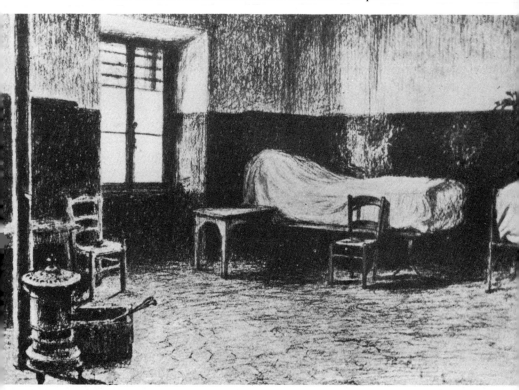

Cell No. 12 in the St. Lazre.

Gaston Calmette, Editor of *Le Figaro*.

Calmette's office after his assassination. Blood-stained shirt on the chair.

pro-German party in power. His mission was to avert, if possible, the intervention of Austria in the Balkans which might lead to a war in which Hungary would be forced to fight against her own interests and beliefs. He wanted a foreign policy for Hungary independent from that of Austria, and to detach her from the alliance with Germany. He wanted to enter into friendly relations with France and her allies. With these ends in view he had conferred with Poincaré, and several times with Caillaux for whom he had the greatest admiration, and of whom he reported :

> He showed the clearest possible comprehension of my plans, and saw at once their anti-German points. He watched the interests of France with passion, with sparkling intelligence and with a happy felicity of ideas.[14]

On learning of the accusations of treachery levelled against Caillaux, he brought him certain top-secret documents which had been given to him as leader of the opposition by a disgruntled agent of the German-dominated Hungarian Government, Leopold Lipscher. They proved it was Calmette and *Le Figaro* who had sold their country.

On 28th June the Archduke Ferdinand of Austria was assassinated at Sarajevo.

Three weeks later, on 20th July, the trial of Henriette Caillaux opened in the largest criminal court in Paris.

# CHAPTER THREE

# The Trial of the Century

On Sunday 19th July Henriette was transferred to the Conciergerie prison where she passed the night in a cell close to that once occupied by the unhappy Queen Marie Antoinette. Next morning, after Caillaux had paid her a brief visit, she was brought by underground ways to the Court of the Assizes in the Palais de Justice. Hundreds of security police patrolled the streets. Within the building, barriers had been set up in the entrance hall, the Vestibule de Harley, to control the crowds. As soon as the doors were opened there was a rush to secure the best places: the centre seats were supposed to be reserved for the witnesses and the press, but barristers in their robes, having the right to attend, overflowed into them from their own benches. When Caillaux arrived the aisles were full of people pushing and arguing, but he was immediately spirited to his seat by the Corsican bodyguard provided by his friend Ceccaldi, Deputy for the Aisne: a necessary precaution in view of the threatening attitude of the *Camelots du Roi*. Unmoved by the general excitement, a guide was conducting a party of English and Swedish tourists along the galleries, pointing out the beauties of the architecture.

> This is the Assize Court of the Seine as staged today for the strange drama of the trial of Madame Henriette Rainouard Caillaux ...
>
> All the barristers in France seemed to be there, and among them were the charming gowned forms of at least a dozen women lawyers, leaning a friendly arm on their male colleagues of the Bar, and craning eagerly forward for a good view.
>
> During the buzz and hum, famous figures appeared and crossed the scene of this moving picture. Here was Monsieur Barthou, ex-Premier, whose ministry was overthrown by Monsieur Caillaux ... His *pince-nez* glittered on his white, fat face, fringed with a short beard, crisp and turning grey.
>
> Here are other witnesses, those whose names have been tossed to and fro for the last month – Madame Gueydan, the first wife of Monsieur Caillaux, to whom was written the fateful letter that set the seal on

Gaston Calmette's doom. There was Monsieur Caillaux, bold-eyed, defiant, and extraordinarily unmoved, with shining bald head, immaculately groomed in morning coat of fashionable cut, a glossy silk hat in his hand.

There was nothing tragic in his figure, nothing in all his appearance to show anything of the tumult that must have been in his mind as he – the most powerful politician in France– surveyed the crowd that came to see his wife tried for the murder she had committed in his interest.

The *Daily Express*, 21st July 1914.

The courtroom was a long rectangle with green walls above a surround of beautiful oak panelling : two massive chandeliers hung from the high gilded ceiling, and from somewhere overhead came the soft drumming of ventilators specially installed, so it was said, out of consideration for Madame Caillaux. One half of the room was reserved for the judges, the jury and the dock : it was separated from the other half by an oak barrier with a gate in the middle.

The Counsel for the Defence was Maître Labori who had defended Dreyfus and Zola : he came in with a cheerful flourish of his black gown, trimmed with ermine to indicate his rank as *bâtonnier*, a broad sturdy figure with smiling blue eyes: he shook hands with several friends and then sat down among his assistants immediately below the dock. He took off his small black hat, disclosing thick grey hair set in a fringe across his forehead. On the same level, on the other side of the central opening in the barrier, sat Maître Chenu, representing the *partie civile** which meant, in this case, Calmette's two orphaned sons: he was a very clever barrister who had traditionally defended extreme Nationalists when they were accused of crimes against the Republic. He too held the rank of *bâtonnier*.

The audience were still not settled in their places when an usher announced, *La Cour, Messieurs!* and the Court entered in their red robes and tall brimless hats trimmed with ermine. Monsieur Albanel, the presiding judge, or President of the Court, elderly and highly respected, had a pointed beard and *pince-nez* gold-rimmed glasses: he took his place at the judges' bench which was on a raised platform overlooking the well of the courtroom. A more sinister figure, Maître Herbeaux, the Public Prosecutor, wearing similar red robes and tall hat, sat at a desk on a level with the judges' bench : he had smiling features and a fierce moustache. He rested his chin in his hands and contemplated the empty dock.

*In France the relatives of the victim are allowed to intervene in the trial with a view to securing the conviction of the accused and to claim damages.

As there was still some confusion in the audience, the ushers called again and again, *Assis! Assis!* for them to be seated. A small door of polished oak immediately opposite the jury box opened, and Henriette entered, attended by three guards in uniform.

According to *Le Matin*, it was :

A studied entrance, perhaps, but displaying great self-possession and knowledge of the world. How appropriate her modest black costume slightly relieved by a mauve *corsage* ! Two black wings rose above her smooth satin toque, an airy nothing. With eyes lowered, her face pale under her blonde hair, she looked indeed a damsel in distress.

*Le Matin*, 21st July 1914

She took off her long black gloves, tapped the rail in front of her for a moment, conscious all eyes were upon her, leaned forward and spoke to Labori who stood up and turned towards her. Then she opened her handbag, took out some papers and arranged them in front of her.

Meanwhile in another room the jury had been selected. Most of them were small traders or craftsmen – engraver, hatter, constructor, distiller etc., and two of independent means and an architect. They filed solemnly into the jury box. The questions for them to decide were two : did Henriette intend to kill Calmette, and was her act premeditated? According to the Criminal Code she could have been condemned to death, but no one expected this. For murder without premeditation the minimum sentence was five years in prison. Several British and American press correspondents were sitting at the back of the court. One of them wrote :

Her eyes were downcast at first, as though she feared the shock of all that multitude staring at her. Everything else in court seemed to fade from my vision before this humble woman in black, for when she first came in she brought with her a bearing of meekness and humility in the downward curve of her neck and the pose of her arms.

I have never seen a prisoner more tastefully dressed. She wore a simple gown of black ninon, and her throat showed white through the V-shaped opening . . . Her slender arms were sheathed in long black kid gloves, and these arms became as expressive as Yvette Guilbert's when she pressed her hands to her head or crossed them before her dress or opened them wide in a Frenchwoman's shrug.

Something of the beauty of the girl still remained with her in her fair hair, the chiselled outline of her profile and the melody of her voice . . .

As she faced the judge and lifted her head at last to look round the court, I marked the extraordinary dignity and calm in her handsome face. Not once did her lips falter or her eyes flinch. She seemed in a kind of exaltation and gave the impression of one who feels all the superiority of her safe position.

So she stood while the recorder read the act of accusation, the long indictment . . . all the jury had read it in the papers the day before. So strange are the methods of French justice.

For twenty minutes the recorder rattled on with his reading while the fans whirred and Madame Caillaux's eyes roved the court in search of someone.

She found her quest at last. I saw her smile, and there was gladness and hopeful encouragement in her smile at her husband, the masterful politician, as he stood at the door, never taking his eyes from the black figure of his wife . . .

The *Daily Express*, 21st July 1914

The act of accusation ended :

Whatever her emotional state may have been, the facility with which she arrived at her determination to commit the crime, the logical steps by which she prepared for it and the sang-froid she showed in executing it, must be admitted. In consequence, Gene-vieve, Josephine, Henriette Rainouard, wife of Caillaux, is accused: Of having, on the 16th March 1914 in Paris, committed a deliber-ate homicide on the person of Gaston Calmette, and this homicide was committed with premeditation as provided for in articles 295, 296 and 302 of the Criminal Code.

The President of the Court added,

ALBANEL : And so, *Madame*, you are accused of having of your own free will committed an act of homicide on the person of Gaston Calmette, and with premeditation. You are going to hear the charges against you. Kindly be seated.

The usher then called the names of the witnesses. Each in turn answered, 'Present' and left the courtroom, Caillaux among them. Henriette was asked to give particulars of her age, which was thirty-seven, her identity and previous marriage . . .

ALBANEL : At the preliminary enquiry you gave further particulars about yourself. Would you kindly repeat them for the benefit of the jury? Tell them everything which seems to you appropriate.

This was the real drama of the trial. From this moment her personality dominated the day. I have never seen anything like the strength and mastery of this woman, after many months of imprisonment, telling at last in open court the whole of the circumstances that led up to the murder. . . . Every sentence held its dramatic effect. She flinched at nothing. She let the judge and the jury into the intimate secrets of her past. She analysed her motives, and tried to make judge and jury see her state of mind.

With her long slender hands on the ledge of the dock, she spoke at first in a faint, halting, tremulous voice, as though she were not assured of her strength. But gradually courage came to her . . .

The *Daily Express*, 21st July 1914

She said that like all young women of her time and station she had never been to school or left her parents until she married. Her husband was Monsieur Clairtie, a man of letters. Their characters were incompatible. There were dissensions in their home from the very beginning. Several times she was on the point of leaving him, but she had a daughter, and then another, and for their sake she waited. At last, in 1908, when there were new dissensions, she asked for a divorce, and obtained it. She was given the custody of her daughters. Unhappily she lost one of them a few months later . . . she was seven. (Henriette's voice faltered, but she quickly recovered her self-possession.) She described how, in 1911, she married Monsieur Joseph Caillaux, and with him she found all the happiness in life that she could wish for – if they had not been pursued by calumny. He returned a hundredfold the affection she cherished for him and for her remaining daughter, the joy of their household. He had a great career, and they both had independent means :

HENRIETTE : And I should like to say at once this is not the illicit fortune attributed to us by our detractors, but the fortune we received, each of us, from our parents and which has not increased from the day we received it. My counsel has proof of this, and will submit it to you, if you wish.

We were no sooner married than calumny broke into our lives . . .

She twisted a little black-bordered handkerchief in her hand and dabbed it on her eyes for a moment as she came to the terrible campaign against her husband's political position which had poisoned her life.

'Everywhere we were slandered – in the drawing-room, in the Chamber, in the shops – everywhere,' she said, glancing defiantly round the court. 'One of the most abominable slanders was that my husband had sold the French Congo to Germany for a large sum of money and that a coronet worth £30,000 had been given to me by the German Emperor.'

She drew a tragic picture of her life as the wife of the hated minister. She heard insulting remarks in the tribune where she sat as the minister's wife. 'At my dressmaker's I was pointed out to customers as the wife of that beast Caillaux.' She pressed her hands to her eyes in agony. 'Ah!' she cried, 'If I lived another hundred years, I should still have those words burned into my heart . . .'

Over and over again she told the court of the anguish she suffered for her husband's sake . . .

It began to get astonishingly like a tragic play. Madame Caillaux's long arms rose and fell as she revealed her past in words that a dramatist might have envied, yet never once was she hysterical. 'My house became a perpetual nightmare,' she said with a little gesture of despair. She clasped her fingers together, and her face was drawn with pain. 'This *Figaro* campaign was implacable,' she exclaimed. 'Every day! Every day! I could hardly sleep. I was tortured with fear. I feared my husband would be murdered. I heard that in the drawing-rooms and the clubs it was common to hear regrets that no one had the pluck to rid the country of "this fellow Caillaux".'

The *Daily Express*, 21st July 1914

HENRIETTE : On 13th March, Calmette announced he would stop at nothing to bring my husband down. Then the *'Ton Jo'* letter appeared, and I had every reason to believe mine would follow. My suffering was intense . . . I lost my head, and . . . there it is . . .
ALBANEL : Until 13th March the campaign seems to have had a political character. You think it was personal . . . Kindly explain to the jury why you think so.
HENRIETTE : Surely, *Monsieur le Président*, no one who has read the 138 articles in *Le Figaro* could possibly maintain they were political! . . . In all of them Calmette accused my husband of using dishonourable means to serve his political ambitions . . . There were, of course, political articles as well in which Calmette was entitled to express his views. I am not counting those.

She read out extracts from the *Figaro* article giving examples of Calmette's false accusations:

HENRIETTE : (reading):

Caillaux deducted from the taxpayers five or six millions under the childish pretext of returning them to the Prieu inheritors. He gave them 20% . . .

The 80%, it was alleged, he kept for himself. For this affair the directors of *Le Figaro* tried to buy false witnesses – this can be proved. But that didn't worry Calmette in the slightest. He simply took up a new affair . . . Will you permit me, *Monsieur le Président*, to read a few more extracts?

ALBANEL: Continue, *Madame*. The gentlemen of the jury must know all your defence; consequently you have the right so say whatever you think would assist you.

HENRIETTE: In one article Calmette called my husband, 'The plutocrat demagogue of the Algerian Land Bank' – but, sirs, he has never been part of the Algerian Land Bank. And the article continues: 'of the milliard contributed by or for his friends, at least a quarter is irremediably lost. In six months a milliard of francs has been taken from our towns and country districts by this man abusing his official position to augment his personal fortune.' It would be impossible to accuse anyone more directly of being a traitor to his country, and a thief. And listen to this: (reading)

> I hope the crime will soon be taken to the tribune of the Assembly so that the official malefactor may receive public chastisement . . . All is summed up in a single word, 'Infamy', and by a single word, 'Caillaux'.

Could any unprejudiced mind maintain that that is not personal? In spite of all his efforts it became evident to Calmette at last that his articles were having no effect on the Chamber of Deputies where my husband's perfect integrity is known to everyone, so he had to go further. On 10th March he wrote in *Le Figaro*:

> This is the decisive moment when one must not hesitate to use any methods, however unpalatable to a man who bears no personal animosity but who must act in the interests of his country . . .

Three days later, on the 13th, the first of three letters appeared . . .

The President asked her to explain about these three letters, how they came to be written, what they contained and how they came to leave private custody. She hesitated, and said to do so she would have to involve her husband's first wife, Madame Gueydan, because the whole affair revolved around her, but she would do so as discreetly as possible.

ALBANEL : You don't have to say more than you wish to.

HENRIETTE : Well, when my husband discovered she had taken these letters she told him she didn't intend to use them to get a divorce but to dishonour me. She intended to take them to my father so that he would disinherit me, and to my former husband so that he would reclaim the custody of my daughter, a girl of fifteen years old who would read the letters also. Monsieur Caillaux's fears for me were so great that he told me we should have to give each other up . . .

As Madame Caillaux spoke . . . her face flushed, her eyes flashed. Sometimes they were fixed intently on the jury, sometimes she glanced questioningly round the courtroom. In her long monologue there were moments of intense emotion when her voice broke and she sobbed . . .

*Le Matin*, 21st July 1914

HENRIETTE : I received a letter from his secretary at the beginning of November saying I had nothing more to fear as the letters had been burned, and Madame Gueydan had given her word of honour she had kept no copies or photographs; and that he had left for Egypt with her because they were reconciled. . . . I returned broken-hearted to Paris. Monsieur Caillaux had indeed done everything to protect me. The letters had been burned before witnesses, it was a condition of their reconciliation. I don't need to tell you of my grief, of what a winter I passed through : then suddenly things changed for the better.

She told of Caillaux's divorce, and of how once again Berthe had agreed to destroy all the correspondence between them, including the *Ton Jo* letter which had been written ten years ago. She assured the jury there had been a sincere and complete breaking off of the relationship between Caillaux and herself : her name had not even been mentioned in the divorce proceedings, so if Madame Gueydan divorced it was because she wanted a divorce.

For an hour or so Henriette was questioned about the letters. She said they were tender and courteous : they described the three years of his marriage to Berthe and his hopes of being one day free again, but he had scruples of conscience about breaking up a marriage though it had brought him little happiness. But what could make them useful to *Le Figaro* was that he gave reasons of local politics for not divorcing until after the next election, reasons intermingled with intimate personal considerations.

The President asked when did she learn that the letters had not in fact been destroyed. She replied it was just after her marriage to Caillaux, or a few days before: they learned from several different sources that Madame Gueydan had offered them to Monsieur Vervoort of the *Gil Blas* and to Monsieur Bailly, director of *L'Intransigeant*, both of whom had refused to publish them. For two and a half years they were offered around, but she had to say for the honour of the press that not even the most insignificant journal would use them. Then they heard through the Princess Estradère that Calmette was negotiating for them, but until the *Ton Jo* letter appeared they did not believe he would publish them. Then Monsieur Ceccaldi, and Monsieur Dubarry, director of the *Journée Républicaine*, informed them Calmette was about to publish the other intimate letters: they were able to identify them because of the notepaper on which they had been written.

On 16th March Calmette had announced there would be a Comic Interlude and spoke of a minister's indiscreet letters with many words underlined – which Monsieur Caillaux had done in these letters. For three years the perpetual menace of their publication had been hanging over them: now they heard from all sides they were going to appear on 17th March. She was entirely convinced of this, and deeply disturbed, thinking of the responsibility she had in the matter.

The President asked her about an attempt she had made to have the publication stopped by legal means. She said she had consulted a lawyer, Maître Thorel, to see if a writ could be served. She was advised by a friend, Monsieur Morand, that because of Monsieur Caillaux's position as a minister, Calmette would deny the competence of the civil tribunal, and this would lead to a trial at the assizes which would be playing into the hands of the newspapers who would make so much capital out of it. On the morning of 16th March, Maître Monier advised her that for a man holding a public position there was no protection against defamation by the press. 'One has to defend oneself,' he had told her.

HENRIETTE: He was far from suspecting the effect his words had on me. He didn't know the torture I had endured for the past three months. His words discouraged me completely. I had to resign myself to the fact that nothing could be done. I was plunged into the depths of despair, but I didn't immediately realise that a fearful chasm had opened before me, that there was nothing I could do, nothing, nothing at all, to prevent the publication I so greatly feared.

She had gone to the Finance Ministry to tell her husband what Monier had said, and he had commented, 'Well, if there's nothing we can do I'll smash Calmette's face in.'

HENRIETTE : My husband has been much criticised for saying this instead of advising me to be resigned, but he was only doing his duty. It even cheered me up a little. It made me feel my husband was my natural support. If he had said, 'There's nothing to be done. You must face it,' I should have considered him a coward. If he had not found some way to defend me, I should have despised him. On our way home he repeated, 'I'll smash his face in!' 'My God!' I said, 'When? Now?' 'No,' he replied, 'In my own time.'

You can imagine how that horrible thought pursued me, how I suffered all that day. There was no getting away from it. My husband whom I knew to be so good, so honest, was going to kill a man, and he was going to do it for my sake. But it wouldn't have saved us from dishonour. I wanted to kill myself, but that wouldn't have solved anything : it would have been said, no doubt, that I had proof of my husband's dishonour and didn't want to survive it. I would gladly have given my life that day if in exchange the campaign had ceased and the letters not been published.

ALBANEL : Your conversation with Monsieur Caillaux ended when you arrived at your home. During lunch there was no serious conversation because of the servants coming and going. Monsieur Caillaux left for the Senate, I think about two o'clock. Before he left, however, you told him you felt ill, and even said you wouldn't go to the Italian Embassy that evening . . .

HENRIETTE : Yes, *Monsieur*. At that moment I was desperate. I felt I hadn't the courage to go and keep up appearances at a great dinner. I was already ill. I was on a strict diet. I ate nothing at lunch, I felt so unwell with the conflicting thoughts in my mind . . . I felt I was in a situation from which there was no escape . . . I had been told the letter was to appear next day. Fear that my husband would kill, be arrested, all the consequences . . . The idea of making a supreme attempt myself came to me.

I can see today that the state I was in prevented me from seeing what might happen ... My reason, my common sense, deserted me. I said to myself, 'I'll go there, I'll try to do something. Somehow I'll stop the letter being printed.' It was like that the thought came to me, to act myself. I was mad, of course I was, I know – mad!

But at the same time I knew we had people coming to dinner next day and I needed a new cook, so I went out. I went at three o'clock to the employment agency. While I was there the idea of a tragic confrontation with Calmette was not in my mind, for I engaged a cook for the following day and gave him full information about the kitchen, and about expenses. Then I said to myself, 'Shall I go to the *Figaro* offices?' and I said to myself, 'If I don't obtain satisfaction, the attempt will be ridiculous ... they'll laugh at me ...' It was then the idea came to me to cause a scandal.

I should explain I was accustomed to carrying a small pistol. We got the habit, my sister and I, from my father, to have one among our toilet articles as a precaution when we were travelling. I don't know, but it seemed to me ... you may smile at this, that a voice was saying to me, 'Take a pistol.' I had lost mine years ago, and I always meant to get another ... The election campaign was about to begin, and I should be travelling much alone, and so the idea of going to buy a revolver to take with me to *Le Figaro* came to me.

I went to Gastinne-Renette's, telling myself that if Monsieur Calmette did not give me satisfaction I would make a scandal, I would read the riot act at the newspaper office, and after that it would be very difficult for them to publish the letters. But if I had foreseen the dreadful result ...

ALBANEL : When you left the employment agency you went to Gastinne-Renette's and asked an employee, Monsieur Fromentin, who will be heard, to give you a revolver because you were going to travel by car alone. He offered you a Smith & Wesson, and you suggested trying it.

HENRIETTE : Yes, *Monsieur.*

ALBANEL : You went to the lower ground floor, and there you found another employee.

HENRIETTE : Yes, *Monsieur.*

ALBANEL : And they let you try the revolver. This one wasn't very handy for a woman, and you hurt your thumb.

HENRIETTE : Yes, they noticed the blood.

ALBANEL : And they said to you, 'You had better take a Browning, it is easier to handle, though perhaps more dangerous.' So they brought you a Browning. Would you please explain to the jury what happened next?

HENRIETTE : First, this weapon – you can't use it if you don't know about it. It's not like the others . . . They said, 'We'll show you how to use it' . . . They did so, and I fired one magazine.

ALBANEL : Then you went upstairs and told them to charge it to Monsieur Caillaux?

HENRIETTE : Yes, we have an account there. They got me a small case for it. If I had only wanted it for that evening, I wouldn't have required a case for it.

ALBANEL : You loaded it yourself?

HENRIETTE : Yes, they said it was the rule of the house.

ALBANEL : . . . and then, after a visit to the bank to collect some papers, you returned home at about four o'clock?

HENRIETTE : Between four and five. I still didn't know whether I should go to *Le Figaro* or to an afternoon tea to which I had been invited, for with this in mind I changed my gown and put on one more elegant. If at that time I had intended to go to *Le Figaro* I wouldn't have changed my dress for that. When I came downstairs I still didn't know which I would go to, but drawn by a will that substituted itself for my own, I wrote my husband's note and then left for the *Figaro* offices.

(*Albanel read out the note she had left with the governess.*)

ALBANEL : The Prosecution maintain that this letter, together with the purchase of the revolver, establish premeditation. Kindly give the gentlemen of the jury as complete an explanation as you can regarding the terms of this note.

HENRIETTE : When I wrote it, I think I still did not know what I should do. I attached little importance to it because I was still far from deciding to go to *Le Figaro* to cause a scandal, but it was like this : I said to myself if I cause a scandal it will delay my return home, and so I wrote it . . . If, as certain people have said, I had coldly determined to go to *Le Figaro* to kill, I wouldn't have been so stupid as to leave something that could have been used against me.

When I said in the note, 'to do justice', I did not mean I intended to kill Monsieur Calmette; I meant only to teach him a lesson, cause a scandal, stop the horrible publication . . . not to kill. *Grand Dieu!* I was well aware that to kill him would have reacted against my husband.

And then I said, 'If they give you this letter,' – so there was a doubt. You can see well I was not decided. When I gave the letter to my daughter's governess before going out, I definitely said, 'if by chance Monsieur Caillaux comes in before me, give him this letter. If not, return it to me.' If at that moment I had had the intention to kill I would not have said this because I should have known very well when I should come back.

ALBANEL : So that is your explanation. You got to *Le Figaro* at a quarter past five. You waited nearly an hour before seeing Monsieur Calmette. Please tell the jury what happened during that hour.

HENRIETTE : I was in the waiting-room There were quite a few people coming in, waiting, discussing things while I was there. Because there was a door partly open I overheard the lads in the office talking about the *Figaro* campaign. I heard the conversation of the people who were there. They said that next day an important article would appear . . . I wanted to leave . . .

ALBANEL : . . . you said at the enquiry that when the office boy came to fetch you, you heard a voice say, 'Let Madame Caillaux come in,' and that another voice repeated your name. That was what you said?

HENRIETTE : Yes, *Monsieur le Président*.

ALBANEL : Explain this to the jury.

HENRIETTE : Someone came to ask my name. I gave him my visiting card in an envelope. I heard, 'Let Madame Caillaux come in !' so I rose from the armchair. It gave me a shock to hear my name because I knew I had come very imprudently, hoping no one would hear of my visit, hoping no one would know I had come. It upset me when I realised all these people knew now who I was and that I had come to the building whence every day new attacks were formulated and directed against my husband. It gave me such a shock that I rose to my feet. The office boy found me standing when he came to fetch me.

ALBANEL : He brought you to Monsieur Calmette's office?

HENRIETTE : Yes.

ALBANEL : Kindly tell the jury what you did then, for you are the only witness, Monsieur Calmette not having been able to testify before his death. Tell me everything that happened.

HENRIETTE : . . .

ALBANEL : At the enquiry you said you felt at that moment an overpowering and unreasoning fear at finding yourself alone in the presence of that man, your enemy, in an office rendered still more mysterious by its obscurity. After exchanging the usual conventional words you said to him, 'No doubt you were expecting my visit?' to which he replied, 'No, I wasn't really. Won't you take a seat?' With your left hand you released the safety-catch of your pistol which you had taken from its case on entering, or before entering, Monsieur Calmette's office, and then the shots fired by themselves. Is that correct?

(*She nodded.*)

ALBANEL : You added, 'Calmette went round his desk, stooping to take cover behind it. And you said, 'I thought he hadn't been touched.' Have you anything to amend in what you said?

HENRIETTE : No, *Monsieur le Président*.

ALBANEL : You said later, at the enquiry, that Monsieur Calmette's office was in half light . . .

HENRIETTE : I'm sure the room was lighted only by lamps standing on the desk, and that the room was half in darkness.

ALBANEL : It seems to other witnesses that the last two shots were fired after a slight interval. Sirat, the office boy who rushed in at the sound of the firing, holds that you fired at least one shot in his presence. Do you recall this detail?

HENRIETTE : I don't believe it. When I fired the first shot I had only one thought at the moment – to aim low, at the floor, to cause a scandal, as I have explained. But the shots went off by themselves . . . I saw Monsieur Calmette retreat, bend down. I thought he had not been touched, and that's all. It all happened in a second.

ALBANEL : . . . you haven't any further information to give us? Anything that could help us to establish the facts?

HENRIETTE : Only to express my infinite regret . . . I have passed my whole life without having any desire to kill . . . How could anyone possibly imagine that I wished to cause his death? Apart from the question of conscience, which is a terrible one for me, there is the question of logic. Apart from these abominable calumnies and the menace of the letters being published, which has pursued me for the past three months, I have everything in life, so why should I have wished to kill? To kill a man – that is a frightening thing, shameful . . . would I have renounced everything for this? My husband's love, my daughter's affection, my pleasant life, everything in fact, to go and kill? I wanted to cause a scandal. I had no idea a horrible fate was about to descend upon me. I over-estimated my strength, I am well aware. I thought I had the fortitude to go through with my plan to demand an explanation, an undertaking. I lost my head when I found myself in front of the man who had done us so much harm, who for three months had poisoned my life. It was through trying to ward off a catastrophe I committed this act, irreparable for the unhappy victim, irreparable for my husband also, and most certainly irreparable for me and for my peace of mind, and also for my daughter. I would have let them publish anything they pleased if I had known this would happen . . .

ALBANEL : You have nothing to add? Please tell the gentlemen of the jury what led you to commit this act. You told us just now, but could you make known all the circumstances which might be advantageous for your defence?

HENRIETTE : *Monsieur le Président*, if you will allow me, I'll tell you of the effect *Le Figaro* had on me, and also why I was so much afraid . . . The articles becoming more and more violent and vindictive, their words, so cunningly phrased, pierced my heart every day like daggers. As they were circulated throughout the country, public opinion was stirred up, so that the appearance of the Finance Minister on the theatre screens was greeted with whistles. In a music hall there was a scene, greeted with much applause, showing my husband in South American costume strangling *La République*.

She detailed the insults she had received in the shops, the *salons*, in the Chamber of Deputies, then

I need not tell you that such an existence, continued for three months, affected my health. I couldn't sleep, I frequently started up during the night, my temples throbbing, wondering what would happen to my husband next day : I was afraid he would be assassinated . . . I had heard a police inspector telling him a plot had been discovered and they were keeping him under police protection; and it was being said, 'Will no one rid us of Caillaux?' I was in constant fear. I used to search for him as the Assembly was coming out . . . I can assure you that for a wife who loves her husband, who knows he is an honest man, and loyal – because, sharing his life I knew him to be a man of the greatest integrity and the most honourable of men; for a woman who hears her husband accused every day of new horrors, who sees the accusations becoming every day more serious, it is an intolerable situation.

Henriette in the dock.

Henriette testifies.

Ah! I tell you that for three months I endured a Calvary I wouldn't wish upon my worst enemy. I suffered from seeing my husband's good name trailed in the mud, yes, I suffered, no one can know how much, you cannot know.

ALBANEL : You may be seated, *Madame*.

HENRIETTE : But may I add just one word? I want to make it clear why I feared so greatly the publication of these letters. I feared first of all for my husband, for his position. I feared also for myself; I feared also for my daughter. I feared for myself because to publish these letters, or part of them, would be to expose all my intimacy, my dearest secret, the most hidden. It would be to make my honour as a woman naked. I have always been taught that the honour of a woman was to live a life in broad daylight without liaisons, without adventures. I was brought up by parents already old . . . My poor father, whom I lost last year, always told me, 'A woman who has had a lover is a woman without honour.' Certainly if he had known I had had a liaison with Monsieur Caillaux he would have turned me out of the house . . .

Oh, I am well aware, I have often been reproached for it, that I belong to the *bourgeoisie* – it is true, and I'm not ashamed of it. And when the letters were filched from Monsieur Caillaux we preferred, both of us, the bitter grief of parting to the exposure of the letters : we preferred to renounce our happiness rather than see our intimacy exposed.

And I feared also because of my husband, because other people wanted above all to humiliate him, to make him ridiculous, to jeer at him by publishing two letters to two different women signed *Ton Jo* . . . It was above all to make a Minister of the Republic ridiculous, the head of the Radical Party. They wished to humiliate the Republicans through him. (*Sounds of protest from the audience.*) Of course they did! To jeer at them, to make them ridiculous!

But above all I feared for my daughter. She is nineteen, of marriageable age. She too would be affected, naturally, by their publication. Poor child! I shouldn't have to be ashamed before her, but I already saw in her little face . . . I couldn't hide *Le Figaro* from her, there would always be kind friends to tell her all about it . . . She had always looked upon her mother as a model, and I have brought her up as I was brought up myself, with the same principles, ideas and scruples – and then, to satisfy the hatred and vengeance of the journalists I am obliged to be ashamed before her – No, there are things that should not be asked of a mother. It is too much.

ALBANEL : Have you anything more to add, *Madame*?

HENRIETTE : I wish to add profound regrets from the bottom of my heart for the great misfortune I have caused. I declare here that I would have preferred to allow them to publish anything at all rather than to have been the cause of what has happened.

It was a remarkable performance and ranks with the most eloquent pleading ever heard in a court... 'I never thought that Calmette should be punished by death for his attack against us. By killing him I have brought irreparable misfortune not only on myself but on my daughter and on those I most care for.'

She could keep back the tears no longer. They streamed down her cheeks. All the splendid pride and dignity of her manner had gone. Between her sobs, in agonised sentences one heard the cries of regret and remorse.

The *Daily Express*, 21st July 1914

ALBANEL : You have nothing more to add? Kindly be seated.

She sat down, dabbed her face with a handkerchief, and looked anxiously at the jury.

Maître Dumas now made formal application to the Court to receive Monsieur Prestat as guardian of Calmette's two orphan children, the *partie civile*, to condemn Madame Caillaux to the punishment ordained by the law and to award the benefit of its conclusions to the *partie civile*. This was granted by the President, and the first witnesses were heard: they were the *gendarmes* who had been called to the scene of the crime. They said they had been unable to carry out an investigation because the *Figaro* staff had prevented them from entering Calmette's office: after repeated requests the revolver had been handed out to them. They testified that Henriette had been calm, but not arrogant, and she had anxiously expressed the hope that she had not killed Calmette.

The last witness to be heard that day was Maître Monier who confirmed he had advised Henriette there was no legal redress for an eminent statesman against calumnies in the press. He too testified Henriette had been calm. He said he was the most astounded man in Paris when he heard of the tragedy.

Sharing the front pages with the Caillaux trial there were headlines and leading articles about President Poincaré's state visit to

Russia describing receptions by the Czar and the Czarina, military reviews, banquets, toasts and mutual expressions of solidarity between the two nations. The extensive anti-war strikes triggered off by the visit and the numerous casualties resulting from clashes between the workers and the military were less prominently featured.

Before leaving for St Petersburg, Poincaré had made a deposition under oath at the Elysée Palace, swearing to tell the truth, the whole truth and nothing but the truth. This was read out in court by the Advocate General. In it Poincaré described how Caillaux had come to him on the morning of 16th March and told him he feared Calmette would publish his private letters and that it would be very painful for him and Madame Caillaux :

I replied that I considered Calmette to be a gentleman and absolutely incapable of publishing letters that could compromise Madame Caillaux, but I tried in vain to convince him of this ... At one moment he got up and said, 'If Calmette publishes the letters, I'll kill him !'

# CHAPTER FOUR

# Enter Caillaux

From one point of view the case was clear: Calmette had conducted the most prolonged and one of the dirtiest campaigns in the history of the press, and had finally been shot down by a woman he had driven to distraction: but for the defence to insist on this was, in the eyes of his friends and of the public, to add insult to injury, a desecration of the dead. He had many friends because *Le Figaro* was a very important newspaper, particularly for the artistic and literary life of the capital, and he was, by all accounts, a man of great charm and always ready to be helpful: he had tried, though unsuccessfully, to find a publisher for Proust's *Swann's Way* which was dedicated to him. In his social life there was none of the vindictiveness that was evident in his anti-Caillaux press campaign. In his relations with women he was not above reproach: if he had lived one day longer his divorce from the daughter of Prestat, Director of *Le Figaro*, would have become absolute: she found herself unexpectedly the inheritor of a much larger share of his very large fortune than she had anticipated.

Calmette had a habit of carrying about with him important letters and documents he intended to publish, but the intimate letters were not found on him. It transpired that some of the papers taken from his pockets had been burned by Prestat, his father-in-law, who had now taken over editorial responsibility. When questioned, Prestat asserted that the papers he had burnt were not the intimate letters but only copies of the Fabre Report, which was common property, and the *Ton Jo* letter which had already been published. He did not consider them to be of the slightest importance. He had burned them, he said, because they had been the cause of Calmette's death. It was not a convincing story: he had no right to tamper with the evidence, and the impression remains that he burned Calmette's copies of the intimate letters which he had evidently been about to publish. According to the evidence of another member of the staff, Emile Berr, who took the papers from Calmette's portfolio, they were nicked by Henriette's bullets.

68

Members of the *Figaro* staff bore witness to the affection they felt for Calmette, and they looked upon Henriette's rash deed as cold, deliberate and unprovoked murder. They all agreed she had been perfectly calm and they angrily contradicted her assertion that she had heard Caillaux being discussed in an office near the waiting-room; his name was not mentioned, they said, and the article about him announced by Calmette was not being set up: neither was her name called out when he was ready to see her.

Henriette insisted they had mentioned the article, and she gave details of their conversation.

Maître Labori said Madame Caillaux was a most reliable witness: all her statements about where she had been and what she had done had been checked and found to be correct. That she heard these things was certain. If in fact they were not spoken, they were none the less real to her, a kind of hallucination. The same applied to her impression that Calmette's office was in semi-obscurity.

The opposing counsel, Maître Chenu, commented that when the time came for these things to be discussed he would have the unhappiness not to be in agreement with Maître Labori on several points concerning Madame Caillaux's sincerity.

The first important witness on the second day of the trial was the well-known critic and author, Paul Bourget, who was with Calmette when Henriette was announced. They were about to leave together when her card was brought in. Calmette hesitated, showed him the card: he read it and asked, 'You're not going to receive her? What can she have to say to you?' 'I cannot refuse to receive a lady,' he replied, and turned back. Bourget waited for him on the landing. A few minutes later he heard the detonations, so close together that he couldn't count them.

By a curious co-incidence, Bourget had recently published a novel, *Le Démon de Midi*, which had a plot turning on the publication of intimate letters leading to a fatal shooting incident. Maître Labori asked him if he agreed with the words spoken by one of his characters, which were (he read from the book):

A letter belongs legitimately to someone, the writer, the addressee, I don't know which, to one of these. Monsieur Savignan has not given them to you, neither has the person to whom they were addressed. Therefore they must have been stolen. By using them, you are making yourself the accomplice in a theft . . .

and further, Labori said, the publication of intimate letters is called in this book, 'a hideous and cowardly action, an irreparable degradation.'

Bourget thanked him for the publicity, and replied that an author could not be held responsible for the views expressed by his characters; but that Calmette had held the same opinion about the publishing of private letters, and only what he conceived to be a higher duty had impelled him to do so : 'My dignity suffered by it,' he wrote; and if this man was so greatly troubled because he had published a phrase, purely political, from one private letter, it proved he would have shrunk with horror from the thought of publishing the rest.

The chief spokesman for the *Figaro* staff was the journalist Latzarus. He testified he had seen Henriette enter Calmette's office, but there had been nothing about her to arouse his suspicion. As soon as the door closed he heard the detonations, and with other members of the staff he had rushed into the office : one of his colleagues was holding Henriette by the arm. She said, 'Let go,' but he did not. She repeated in a haughty and indignant voice, 'Let go! I am a lady. I am Madame Caillaux. My car is waiting below to take me with the gendarmes to the police station.' Having left Calmette in the care of one of the staff who had qualified as a doctor of medicine (but not practised), he came, he said, face to face with the murderess :

LATZARUS : I had never lost anyone I loved, but now I passed one of the most unhappy moments of my life. We looked at Madame Caillaux with horror and a kind of stupor . . . She said, 'Because there is no longer any justice in France . . .' One of us told her, 'Hold your tongue, *Madame*, after what you have done . . .' She seemed rather irritated, and said, 'I'm not talking to you.' Then three *gendarmes* appeared and they made a thousand difficulties about taking her in charge : they wanted the revolver, they wanted I don't know what. And besides they kept at a respectful distance and didn't dare to address her. We had pushed her into the secretary's office. She remained there staring at us without the slightest embarrassment, without any fear and, it seemed, without any regret. At last we got hold of a *gendarme* and told him, 'You can't inflict on us any longer the sight of this woman who has killed Calmette . . .' They took her away after about twenty minutes, and I saw Calmette being carried down on a stretcher, his face was the colour of ashes, and he said, as if in a dream, 'My friends, my house, I have only done my duty.' I didn't see him again.

Latzarus, continuing his deposition, said :

Now, gentlemen of the jury, I wish to supply you with information about the papers in Calmette's possession. In the latter half of January I happened to speak with him for quite a long while alone about the campaign he was conducting. He told me of representations made to him by certain important financiers to stop the campaign when he was trying to establish the pressure exercised by Monsieur Caillaux on the loan societies, and then, taking from his portfolio two hand-written documents, he made me read them : they were two documents of extraordinary importance, it seems to me, from a political point of view. I think that every good Frenchman who has read them would realise the infamy and the treason of the man implicated in them. He said he would not publish them because their publication would be a danger to the country. This man, who is accused of having neglected nothing to blacken Monsieur Caillaux's reputation, of having been ready to descend to the basest manoeuvres, if he had wished to brand him he would only have had to publish these two documents. That is all I have to say.*

Maître Labori remarked that as for the moment they couldn't discuss what Monsieur Latzarus had said, he requested him to remain in the courtroom. He hoped Monsieur Caillaux would be called that day, and it would certainly be necessary for these two gentlemen to confront each other.

Caillaux was the next witness. Before calling him, the President read aloud articles 501 and 505 of the Criminal Code dealing with disturbances in court, and Maître Chenu, in order to prepare the ground for his line of attack, read to the jury, with the President's permission, the *Ton Jo* letter and the Fabre Report.

ALBANEL : Call Joseph Caillaux.

He marched in, impeccably dressed as usual, in morning coat, striped trousers and white waistcoat, his monocle swinging from a black cord.

---

* When Barthou was forced to resign as Prime Minister he made copies of secret documents which, though not in fact discreditable to Caillaux when properly understood in their context, would be useful to the Nationalist press to stir up public opinion against him, and at the same time create bad feeling between France and Germany. He gave copies of these documents to Calmette and two other newspaper editors with instructions not to use them until he gave them the word to go ahead.

He went straight up to the dock, gallantly kissed his wife's hand and took his place at the bar of the court.

ALBANEL : You are the husband of the accused. I shall not ask you to take the oath. You will be heard by virtue of my discretionary powers. Make your deposition.

It was the entrance of a duellist. He was erect. He looked straight in front of him, his jaws contracted.

*Le Matin*

For a moment he stood there, square-shouldered and upright in a combative way, as though he knew he was going to fight. Then he began to speak in a curious high-pitched voice, something like the voice of Mr Winston Churchill, but without the lisp.

The *Daily Express*, 22nd July 1914

CAILLAUX : Gentlemen of the jury, with your permission I shall begin by telling you the story of my private life from the time of my first marriage to the sorrowful event which brings me to the bar of the court. My first marriage was in August 1906. I married Madame Gueydan, divorced wife of Monsieur Jules Duprè. Misunderstandings soon arose between us, and increased. The causes and origins of these misunderstandings I set down in an intimate letter, in September 1909, to Madame Rainouard, a very close friend, a letter of sixteen pages which contained an account of my entire life. It was written under the letter-heading of the Chamber of Deputies, which I habitually used. Next day, while presiding at my local District Council, I wrote her a second letter, of two or three pages, under the letter-heading of the Prefecture of the Sarthe. I ask the jury to note this particularly. The detail is important. It was the first and only time in my life, except for hurried insignificant notes, I have written a personal letter on this paper.

Afterwards I reflected that Madame Rainouard – she was alone at Dinard – might lose the letters, or perhaps have them stolen from her. I asked her to return them . . . I was wrong not to have burned them as soon as I received them. I locked them in a drawer. Next day they had disappeared.

He spoke with amazing fluency. It seemed to me as if I were no longer in a court of law, where the wife of this man was on trial for murder, but rather in the Chamber of Deputies . . . He spoke with the freedom of one who is used to addressing vast audiences with perfect confidence and assurance and a wonderful choice of words.

The *Daily Express*, 22nd July 1914

CAILLAUX : My wife, Madame Gueydan, who at that time was Madame Caillaux, had arrived at Mamers a few days before. I immediately offered her a divorce on whatever terms she pleased, or a reconciliation, stipulating only that the stolen letters should be returned . . . they were burnt on 15th October 1909, on the understanding that no copies or photographic-copies had been kept. I determined that the reconciliation would be loyal and complete. I put everything else out of my mind . . . but some months later I had to sue for divorce. I had no alternative. It became absolute on 9th March 1912.

On 25th March there was a settlement between my wife and myself in which it was stipulated that all the correspondence between us should be destroyed in the presence of our lawyers.

In November 1911, he said, soon after his marriage to Madame Rainouard, he was informed that a journalist, Monsieur Vervoort, had been offered three of the intimate letters, one of which was addressed from the Prefecture of the Sarthe : Monsieur Vervoort could not have invented this, and he was able to repeat certain familiar phrases Caillaux had used. Both this journalist and the director of the paper he represented refused the offer of these letters, and Caillaux had thought at the time that not a single journalist in France would so dishonour his profession as to publish them.

Of his marriage to Henriette he said :

Never could I have experienced happiness more complete and more absolute than I have found in our union. My wife has been, and still is, not only the most affectionate, the most tender partner, but the most informed and keenest intellectual companion you could possibly imagine. We have lived, and shall continue to live, in the closest intimacy of heart and mind. There was, however, between us, not any kind of discord but some divergence of opinion on some subjects, certain differences in our characters which it is important you should understand. Although she shares my political views, which are known to everybody, she finds me too ardent in pursuing them – a fault, or a quality, just as you please, in my temperament.

She endeavours to restrain me, and I have frequently been thankful that I have listened to her advice.

When on 2nd December the Barthou Government fell – I had some share in that event – I found my wife in tears. 'Whatever you do,' she begged, 'don't accept office in the new government. The Income Tax bill has made dangerous enemies for you. Listen to me, please, it will bring us misfortune.'

She was so distressed that I promised her I wouldn't accept the responsibility of forming a new government; but when my friend, Monsieur Doumergue, appealed to my loyalty to the Radical Party and said he would not form a government unless I would accept office in it, I explained to her that because of the responsibility I had undertaken before Parliament by overthrowing the former government on a financial question, it was encumbent on me to join the new government.

Being a dutiful wife, she withdrew her opposition – but I can still hear her saying, 'Calumny has had its effect. There is a strong feeling against you in certain classes of society. You'll see, it will bring us misfortune.' I didn't suspect that the words of my poor wife were prophetic. I was sure of a majority in the Chamber. I would only have press campaigns against me, and for them I had always professed, though not always felt, indifference.

He explained that from the beginning of his career, when he had defeated one of the Royalist leaders at the polls, he had been the object of Nationalist attacks, and these were intensified when he introduced the Income Tax Bill; but he had adopted as his motto the words of the Republican leader, Waldeck-Rousseau, 'It is only necessary to be right, and that is sufficient.' His wife did not agree. She thought he was wrong not to fight these attacks: 'To discredit a man,' she said, 'they fasten legends onto him.' But he had ignored them to such an extent that he allowed only his Chief Private Secretary to mention them in his presence.

I should like for a moment to describe to the gentlemen of the jury what life is like for a Minister of Finance who has at the same time to defend his budget before the Chamber and the Income Tax Bill before the Senate. If he truly wishes to be a minister and to survey every department of his ministry besides attending debates in the Chamber and in the Senate, he has not a minute to spare.

The articles attacking me disturbed and troubled me, but I concentrated on my ideas and followed them. I marched straight forward. The interdiction on my staff not to speak to me about the campaign extended also to my wife. She withdrew into herself. There were serious consequences.

When the *Ton Jo* letter appeared – I had been warned on the previous day but, as I said to my wife, I could not believe that a journalist, the director of newspaper, would be so forgetful of the dignity of his profession as to publish a private letter. I was stupefied when I saw it in *Le Figaro* of 13th March. It has been said it was the political passages only – what? Are there political passages in a private letter? . . . and who has the right to detach a phrase? . . . that is more serious than to publish it in its entirety : then at least one could see it was written in a style of amorous boasting, 'Dandyism Balzacien' as Jaurès called it . . . It was an intrusion into the intimacy of private life. My wife was greatly troubled by it . . . From that moment we imagined it being followed by the publication of the other letters, and warnings to that effect simply rained upon us.

He detailed the names of friends and newspaper editors who had convinced them the intimate letters were in Calmette's hands – they had been seen and identified by the letter headings.

On the morning of 16th March – I knew she had slept badly. It was in my dressing-room when she burst in with *Le Figaro* in her hand – she had, unfortunately, the habit of reading it every morning. She said, 'Look at the article, "Comic Interlude", look at *Ton Jo*, your intimate name . . . Tomorrow it will be mine. Tomorrow one of my letters and your endearments to me will be plastered over the front page. Everything, our closest secrets, our most intimate life, how we met, how we have loved, will be spread out before the public to ruin you. It can't go on like this!' and she threw the newspaper onto a chair and went out.

On the front page of *Le Figaro*, he said, there was an announcement that the *Ton Jo* letter would be followed by a comic interlude, and that there would be a special message for the electors of the Sarthe – a clear indication that Calmette was about to publish the longer of the intimate letters in which Caillaux had made fun of some of his constituents and their boorish ways at an agricultural show – it was a matter of some importance because once again the time of an election was approaching.

He described how Henriette had come to the Ministry that morning and told him the President of the Seine Assizes had assured her there was no legal action they could take to stop Calmette:

She was shaking, and she asked me, 'What are you going to do?' I sensed she was feeling alone and unprotected. I said to her, 'Just leave it to me. I'll go and smash Calmette's face in.' Yes, that's what I said: 'Between you and any man who attacks you, there is your husband, your natural protector . . . They will touch you only over my dead body.' I could see my words brought her great relief. She felt safe.

In the car on the way home she again became anxious, and said, 'But is it now, today, you are going to do what you said?' I replied rather shortly, 'No. In my own time. I said you had a defender. Here I am. Stop worrying. Now it is between men.'

We got home at around one, or a quarter past. Lunch was late and badly prepared. I kept looking at my watch – I had to be at the Senate at 2.30. We had no chance to discuss anything. She said, 'Do you mind if I don't go to the Italian Embassy this evening? I'm too tired.' She had hardly eaten, she was distressed, she looked very unwell . . . 'You'll send my evening clothes to the Ministry by my valet?' 'Certainly.'

I left for the Senate, taking with me the impression of my wife looking so low that I sent one of my best friends, Ceccaldi – one of those whose worth one discovers in time of trouble – I said to him, 'I'm worried about my wife . . . I'm so occupied, please go and see how she is. I left her in such a state of despair I'm afraid of what she might do.'

I got to the Senate and took my place at the tribune. The battle there worked powerfully on my spirits and relieved the state of tension I was in. It was six in the evening when the session ended.

He went to sign his letters at the Ministry of Finance where he was informed of Henriette's attack on Calmette.

Gentlemen, to understand my wife's state of mind at that moment, one has to remember the heavy Calvary she had endured for months. If one is a man and in the midst of the political strife, one gives blows and one receives them, and one is absorbed in work –

and I can claim, and both friends and adversaries will admit, I have produced a considerable amount of work. One has all one's thought concentrated on the battle. One does not see at one's side a poor being who suffers, who feels every day her suffering increase.

That is something of which I accuse myself before the jury – that I have not been attentive enough to my hearth and home, that I did not realise the ravages the press campaign was causing there. If I had foreseen it I could have acted – but I didn't. I could not have, any more than I could have foreseen the effect on my wife of what I said to her that morning . . . I recognise that the phrase which had calmed her for the moment had come back later into her mind and may have decided her to do what she did, because of the extreme love she has for me. I excuse her : I accuse myself. There are things which it is humanly impossible to foresee and to guard against but, I repeat, the wrong I did her was that for months I did not notice how the press campaign was preying on her mind. I repeat, one is a man, one fights. One is accustomed to profess indifference, at least I am . . . but there is also a poor human being who suffers, who dissimulates her grief. One asks, 'What is the matter with you?' She replies she is unwell – she transforms moral suffering into physical suffering. One fails to understand. The fire smoulders under the cinders, and then one day, the flames flare up. That is what happened.

At this point Caillaux seemed to be overcome with fatigue and emotion. He asked to be allowed to rest for ten minutes. This was granted, and there was a short intermission. Then he continued his deposition :

I thank the gentlemen of the jury for according me a rest for ten minutes. I'll try not to occupy their attention for too long, but I'm sure they will understand I am under the imperious necessity to enlighten them about the campaign . . . in which attempts have been made to injure me politically by casting reflections on my honour and integrity, and at the same time injuring my wife's honour because our home life was attacked.

How did the campaign begin? I've known many campaigns, but never of such persistence and violence as this one, which ignored, disdained, replies and denials. What was its motive? At the risk of appearing to introduce a political issue, it must be said that it was to stop the introduction of the income tax.

I believed, and I do believe, and profoundly, that a reform of our system of taxation is necessary . . . that it needs to be renovated by the introduction of democratic forms already being used in all great modern countries . . . If the classes favoured by fortune had understood their true interests, we should be in a better situation now; but I came up against the most obstinate resistance. Any method, however disreputable, was good enough to bring down the man who envisaged this reform. This resistance – I'll tell you exactly what I feel – comes less from those whose fortunes, like my own, are stable, than from those who have made rapid fortunes and who do not wish it to be investigated how great those fortunes are, or how they were acquired. The campaign began with the Prieu Affair . . .

He dealt with Calmette's accusations in *Le Figaro* one by one and demonstrated that there was not in any of them a particle of truth. Then :

Gentleman of the jury, you may be astonished to hear me go into all this, but it is a question of my honour and of my wife's honour . . . We belong to the *bourgeoisie*. We haven't thirteen millions, but we defend our honour and our integrity, and we intend to do so here in spite of all the mud which has been thrown at us and which, for a moment, blinded and confused my wife.

It has been suggested Madame Caillaux acted to prevent the publication of the Fabre Report.

In March 1911 I advised the Prime Minister, Monsieur Monis, that Maître Bernard had come to me and asked for a postponement of the Rochette trial for reasons of illness and also of expediency . . . I heard on all sides that this would prevent a publication which would damage French credit. We were at that moment on the eve of the Expedition to Fez, and formidable financial difficulties were looming on the horizon. As Minister for Finance I was responsible for the maintainance of public credit which I might have to call upon at any time. I didn't know what the morrow would bring. My elementary duty was to speak to the Prime Minister, as I did, and to tell him I made the request not for personal reasons but as an act of government.

It was indeed an act of government . . . There are responsibilities which sometimes members of the government have to accept, if they have the same conception of their duties as I have. That was all. I explained this to the Prime Minister, and I said no more about it. I heard only months later that the trial had been postponed.

Of what am I accused? It has been said in certain newspapers that there was a swindle, that there had been financial operations as a result of the postponement. A Parliamentary Commission of Enquiry was appointed before which I appeared : it completely set aside any suggestion of underhand dealing because the postponement didn't affect the course of justice . . . It said only that there had been an abuse, a deplorable abuse of personal influence. I do not accept this. It was, I repeat, an act of government . . . It is not my way to shrink from my responsibilities, and I say that if a similar case presented itself today . . . I should act again as I did then.

I have often spoken to my wife about the Fabre Report and explained to her my share in it. She concluded it was a political dispute which didn't concern her . . . As for the suggestion that fear of its publication by *Le Figaro* might have been her motive for acting as she did – it could not have been so, and there are many reasons why. We had known since 14th March that Monsieur Barthou had the original, and Monsieur de Mesnil told us on the same day that it was about to be published by one of the evening papers.

I have also to answer Monsieur Latzarus who has raised the question of the Franco-German negotiations. *Monsieur le Président*, I must in all fairness be allowed to reply . . .

ALBANEL : Although the diplomatic notes have been vaguely touched on, I don't think it is necessary to go into that question.

LABORI : Monsieur Latzarus says he has seen documents which, if published, would dishonour Monsieur Caillaux. The question cannot be allowed to remain there.

CAILLAUX : You may rest assured that I, who was head of the government during those troubled times, could not possibly say anything that could injure my own country. Let those who raised the question take the responsibility for doing so.

He sketched in a few words the history of the Agadir Crisis, difficult of solution and dangerous because of France and Germany's conflicting interests – unlike the present crisis which directly concerned neither of them. As Prime Minister, responsible to the public both for the interior and the exterior policy of the country, he believed that he must not fail to use all the channels of information available to support his diplomacy. He had succeeded in securing Morocco for France, and he had succeeded in the further aim which he had pursued since the beginning of his public life – he had preserved peace. Peace with dignity and pride for his country, of course, but the kind of peace a democracy demands. It was only natural, he said, that he should be opposed by the Nationalist parties and by those who could not see the importance of North Africa for France;[1] and there should be conflict of ideas : but he protested with all his strength against the methods his opponents used – accusing him of he didn't know what vile projects and ulterior motives : it was against this he raised his voice :

I don't know what documents they referred to just now. I have seen veiled allusions to them frequently in the press, and I know certain diplomatic documents have been acquired by *Le Figaro* with a view to publishing them . . . Have I ever feared these revelations? Gentlemen, when one has had the honour to govern the country, one has to have the courage not only to defend oneself : one has to have, in certain circumstances, the courage to remain silent. I have often imposed upon myself the trial of the young Spartan who let a fox devour his entrails rather than speak. Sometimes France needs a man who can submit in silence to the devouring jaws of calumny . . . and pass over an outrage without replying.

But allow me to say, the measure is full and overflowing. If they have documents, let them produce them! They will force me to bring here the correspondence I had with our ambassador during this difficult time, and I shall prove without the slightest difficulty that I remained in permanent, in uninterrupted contact with him, and that he thanked me for the information I was able to gather from the channel of information to which I had recourse . . .

I am determined to defend myself. I shall bring forward all the proofs necessary rather than allow my honour, and indirectly my wife's honour, to be outraged . . .

You, gentlemen of the jury, who are good Republicans . . .

There was immediately a protest from the Nationalists in the audience who saw in these words an attempt to influence the jury through an appeal to their political views. A journalist reported :

A disturbance? Caillaux drew himself up, turned and faced the audience with such an air of defiance that the muttered protests swelled into a roar of anger. In a moment he changed his attitude, picked up the thread of his interrupted discourse, and was again in control . . . The public listened attentively to his arguments, appreciated his sincerity, recognised the points he made.

They found it difficult to accept his personal apology, or his apology

Callaux in court.

Berthe Gueydan, figure of destiny.

for his politics while Prime Minister, but they sympathised with the warm and ingenious defence by a husband of a wife accused of a crime.

When he reproached himself with real emotion for having allowed his interest to be engaged by the political conflict so that he didn't pay sufficient attention to his home, and when he admitted his angry words had increased the effect of the campaign on a being more fragile, more nervous, than himself, they were moved by the common humanity of his emotions.

But this *mea culpa* was only a short interlude. Monsieur Caillaux's style is the offensive. He only abandoned it for a moment to breathe, then he was rushing on again; and this time it was the victim he was attacking.

*L'Illustration* 25th July 1914

CAILLAUX : So far I have spoken impersonally, but now I am obliged to speak about the director of *Le Figaro* himself. I shall do so not only with the necessary restraint but, please believe me, with the most profound emotion, because in spite of the harm he has tried to do to me, in spite of the torrents of mud in which he has attempted to bury me, if I could give him back his life on condition that he should continue to pour mud over me, I should do so immediately. And I come to speak of him now because I cannot do otherwise, because it is a question of defending my honour.

What qualifications had he to reproach me with bringing about an accord between France and Germany? At the end of 1911 *Le Figaro* constantly supported this policy . . . Why this sudden change of attitude? It is a story that must be told.

When, in 1901, Monsieur Calmette wished to take over the management of *Le Figaro* he did not have the necessary capital to command a majority at a shareholders' meeting. . . .

He described how a group of financiers had been formed to acquire a controlling interest in *Le Figaro* and to appoint Calmette its director : these financiers were headed by Monsieur Bayer, representative of the Bank of Dresden.

Caillaux left this statement to sink into the minds of the audience and draw what conclusions they pleased, and turned to the question of *Le Figaro*'s dealings with the Austro-Hungarian Imperial Government. He said there had been protests recently in the parliament at Budapest by the opposition leaders about the tone of the articles in *Le Figaro* of Paris which their government had sponsored. He explained the situation there :

In Hungary there are two parties : that of the Government which favours the Central Powers, and then there is the Independent Party which seeks an alliance with France . . . Which side ought the French newspapers to support? Obviously the Independent Party which favours France. On which side has *Le Figaro* been, unexpectedly, since last August? On the side of the Hungarian Government which favours Germany.

The articles that had appeared in *Le Figaro,* Caillaux alleged, had been written in the press office of the Hungarian Government, and *Le Figaro* had been paid to print them.

Finally Caillaux protested against *Le Figaro*'s accusations that he had amassed a great fortune, that he had abused his authority to enrich himself. He stated he had inherited from his parents one million two hundred thousand francs, and through all his years of office, this amount had not increased. His accounts were open to inspection. Calmette however, his accuser, had started without resources and had amassed a fortune of thirteen million francs. It was very unwise of him, therefore, to attack anyone on that score; and why had he not considered that beside the politician whose honour and integrity he had attempted to besmirch there was a poor woman who loved him and who suffered more from day to day, particularly when he switched his attacks to the private life of his enemy and shamelessly published a private letter. This poor woman saw what must inevitably follow – that he would continue to publish the private letters.

He concluded his speech with an appeal to the press not to involve women in their campaigns, to let their quarrels be between men.

Monsieur Caillaux is an indomitable fighter, exceptional and prodigious ! We have seen him put up a great fight in the Chamber, and he did the same this week in court. The spectacle should have been seen – it had its moments of grandeur. He glided quickly through the public benches and entered the well of the court as if it was an arena, head held high, face flushed, short moustache, commanding eye. He spoke – and suddenly we were surprised because his voice was sweet, gentle, with inflexions that caress, and so youthful that it seemed at times almost childlike. Soon the tone changed, became hard, piercing, whistling, stormy, as it expressed indignation, rage, threats. This fighting figure has nothing of the calm of the woman he is defending and who listened to him from the dock with emotion, admiration – and with love.

*L'Illustration* 25th July 1914

The second session evoked mysterious documents recalling the suspicions, the passions, the violence, of the Zola Affair . . .

But it showed us also a man made greater by misfortune, a man who faced all the accusations, all the insults piled up against him and shook them off so roughly that they seemed to recoil upon his adversaries. The audience, largely hostile, could not restrain their involuntary homage . . .

*Le Matin*, 24th July 1914

Albanel asked the jury and Maître Chenu if they had any questions to put to the witness. Chenu replied, 'None at all.'

LABORI : *Monsieur le Président*, it is indispensable that Monsieur Latzarus be confronted by Monsieur Caillaux.

ALBANEL : Certainly, but on condition that it is a question only of things that can properly be discussed here.

LABORI : We are in the hall of justice. Each must say everything for which he can undertake the responsibility and which may lead to the establishment of the truth. It is necessary, therefore, that Monsieur Latzarus either affirms or withdraws his statement with regard to certain documents . . . Monsieur Caillaux, as his wife's defender, claims this right independently. If Monsieur Latzarus withdraws his statement, the incident is closed.

ALBANEL : Monsieur Latzarus, please approach. What have you to say?

LATZARUS : I find myself in a strange situation. Monsier Caillaux seems to demand that I give particulars of these documents . . . but he seemed to indicate also that it might entail a certain peril for the country, so what is my situation? . . . Monsieur Caillaux said, 'One must complete an accusation,' but when I instanced these documents, was I accusing him? I instanced a document illustrating the morals of a man whose wife is an assassin. I said, 'He (Calmette) had terrible documents in his hands, but he was able to keep them to himself, he was able to control his indignation.' I don't think Monsieur Caillaux can reproach me for that tribute which I owed to the man I loved and whom he has had assassinated.

ALBANEL : Withdraw those words!

CAILLAUX : I cannot tolerate that!

ALBANEL : Your expression has outrun your thoughts.

CAILLAUX : My answer will be short. When one accuses one must complete the accusation. First point. Secondly, permit me to say I do not reproach you for paying any affectionate tribute you please.

But I state this : I defy anyone at all to produce an authentic document which casts the least slur, not only on my patriotism but, allow me to add, on the farsightedness of the policy I carried out at that time. I want this question settled once and for all! (*Murmurs of protest mingled with applause.*)

Maître Chenu here intervened with the suggestion that as these documents had been handed to the President of the Republic it would not be proper to enquire further what had happened to them. He said that personally he did not have these documents, he had neither the right nor the means to use them; therefore they were outside the discussion. He asked only that Monsieur Caillaux should not use them either.

CAILLAUX : Ah! that would suit you very well!

LABORI : Gentlemen, it is impossible to leave an incident like this hanging over the debate unresolved . . . I shall not accept – and I say this most emphatically – any equivocation or uncertainty . . .

CAILLAUX : I agree.

LABORI : . . . that leaves a doubt, or a shadow of a doubt on this incident. The *partie civile* has not said, and Monsieur Latzarus has not said . . . that the documents can in no way compromise Monsieur Caillaux's honour or patriotism. This situation cannot continue. . . . It was not without surprise I learned that the documents had been dispersed that Monsieur Calmette had upon him at the moment he was the victim of the drama with which we are unhappily concerned today. Some were given to Monsieur Prestat, some to the experts and a third lot, scraps of paper . . .

CAILLAUX : Forgeries.

LABORI : . . . were taken to the President of the Republic who had the right to accept them or refuse them. He accepted them, thus conferring on them, I imagine, a kind of authenticity . . . and I know he passed them on to the Foreign Office. Today they are in the hands of the government. I say, therefore, and I insist, that the government must make an official and public declaration to settle the matter.

The Public Prosecutor said in his opinion the question was settled by the declaration of 15th March 1912 made by Monsieur Poincaré's government, to the effect that everyone concerned in the late crisis had loyally carried out his duty, though with various methods . . . Was not this a sufficient reply to Monsieur Latzarus?

LABORI : . . . the government, by accepting these documents found on the body of the victim . . . accepted a responsibility. They could have been sent to the examining magistrate because, after all, this Court, the magistrates and lawyers employed on this case, can respect a secret and preserve it as well as Monsieur Latzarus and Monsieur Calmette . . . In this situation no further equivocation can be permitted. I therefore ask the Public Prosecutor if he is authorised by the government to declare that they contain nothing which can in any way cast a stain upon Monsieur Caillaux's honour or patriotism. If he has not authority to make this declaration, I ask him to obtain it, and we shall continue the debate tomorrow.

CAILLAUX : I make the same request.

PROSECUTOR : I am absolutely authorised to make the declaration I have just quoted from the official journal . . . (*Cries of protest.*)

The scene was becoming stormy. Maître Labori continued to demand that the government produce the documents, his great voice thundering above the cries of rage or approval from the audience who had divided into factions.

Yes, Monsieur Caillaux is an indomitable fighter, and even when he has retired to his place among the witnesses one feels he is still fighting : his expressive face leaning towards the well of the court follows the depositions of the witnesses and convulsively mimes his approval or denial. Sometimes he stiffens up, waiting for a call or a sign from the President, waiting to leap up . . .

*L'Illustration*, 25 July 1914

LABORI : It is a declaration from the present government, which you represent, that I require.

PROSECUTOR : But I'm not in a position to make a declaration about documents which I have not seen.

LABORI : Very well . . . I demand the seizure of these documents. Why are they not before the Court? I shall not plead under these conditions. I do not see why I, Counsel for the Defence, should be a party to any equivocation which may be acceptable in parliament but not in a court of justice so long as I am at the bar !

The Public Prosecutor objected that as the examining magistrate did not see fit to seize the documents they had no judicial character or value.

The President brought the session to a close amid scenes of extraordinary emotion.

*Le Matin*

On the way out, Caillaux and his little group of friends were hemmed in by hostile and admiring crowds, booing and hooting, or shouting *vivats*! With great difficulty they descended the monumental steps to the Place Dauphine but could get no further until the *gendarmes*, after several unsuccessful attempts, succeeded in clearing a passage for them, and they drove off in a taxi.

TRIAL ENTHRALLS FRANCE. The Caillaux murder case has attained almost first place among the world's great criminal trials. Starting quietly . . . it has grown in interest hourly, until now it completely dominates the thought of France. The visit of President Poincaré to Russia and the possibility of an Austro-Servian War being only minor matters to fill the left over space in the newspapers . . .

The present trial . . . is to the few American journalists permitted in the courtroom a drama greater than has ever been played on any stage Woven about the central fact is the tangled skein of political and personal passions, hatred, jealousy and greed . . . Such a revelation of secrets of the strongest men and the most brilliant women of a mighty republic has seldom been made.

*The New York Times*, 26th July 1914

# CHAPTER FIVE

# A Figure of Destiny

On the following morning as soon as the Court had entered and were seated, the Public Prosecutor announced he had been authorised by the government to make this statement :

The papers which were handed to the President of the Republic were only pretended copies of documents which do not exist and which have never existed. They cannot, therefore, in any way be quoted to cast a stain on Monsieur Caillaux's honour or patriotism.[1]

LABORI : *Monsieur le Président,* as far as I am concerned, I consider the incident closed.

CHENU : The incident is closed indeed. It is closed to the satisfaction of Monsieur Caillaux, not to mine. I cannot in fact consider yesterday's incident but as a diversion, a clever manoeuvre, superbly carried out by Monsieur Caillaux, assisted by Maître Labori's superb eloquence and violent declamations, but – it was only a diversion.

It has pleased Monsieur Caillaux to come here and graft a political trial onto a trial of common law, and he has appointed for his judges the jury of the Seine Assizes. They are not here to judge a political trial but solely to judge Madame Caillaux for the crime of assassination ...

We are faced with the paradoxical situation that Monsieur Caillaux is going to leave this court with a certificate of national loyalty because of documents that no one here knows anything about, except himself. Much good may it do him !

Yesterday he spoke about a one-sided document – he has obtained one. He is content, and so am I, because I wish at last to come back to the grave affair that brings us here today : that is to say, yes or no, did Madame Caillaux assassinate Gaston Calmette?

Maître Labori pointed out that it was Maître Chenu's and the Prosecutor's own witness who had introduced the political issue of the diplomatic documents:

LABORI: As far as I am concerned, I am pleading a single case, that of Madame Caillaux who has done me the honour of entrusting it to me. But it was not possible for me to plead under the weight of I don't know what suspicions, allegations and secret documents against which one is defenceless; suspicions which, through her husband, could have prejudiced Madame Caillaux's defence.

The next witness was Monsieur Prestat, Director of *Le Figaro,* who spoke as follows:

PRESTAT: I have asked permission to explain in a few words the various matters referred to by Monsieur Caillaux in his deposition yesterday: matters which are extremely grave for the journal to which I belong, and of which I have had the honour of being President for the past thirty years. The suggestion is that *Le Figaro* has been sold to the Germans. I wish to give you the facts about this, to demolish these attacks and to show you the insanity of this accusation.

I didn't expect, I must say, to have to give these explanations here, but yesterday such outrageous attacks were levelled against *Le Figaro* and against Monsieur Calmette's memory that I could not let them pass without an energetic protest.

LABORI: I'm sorry, Monsieur Prestat, to have to ask to make an observation on a point of order. Actually Monsieur Prestat's declaration follows Monsieur Caillaux's deposition, and I'm sure I'll encounter no opposition from the *partie civile* if I express the wish that you would ascertain if he is present and, if necessary, at the bar.

PRESTAT: I should not have permitted myself to address the Court . . . without making sure Monsieur Caillaux was present.

LABORI: But perhaps he ought to be at the bar.

CAILLAUX: That is my wish also.

The President asked Caillaux to come to the bar. He did so with alacrity.

PRESTAT : As I was saying, for thirty years I have been with *Le Figaro*, and for the whole of that time, how careful we have been of the interests of our beloved country! How jealous in our patriotism! And now we are supposed to be dictated to by foreigners! Two incidents have been brought forward to justify these imputations. I shall reply to them briefly.

I'll take first the Bank of Dresden – it's a very old affair. Monsieur Caillaux himself said so. It dates from 1901. I lived through it, and although I am neither a politician nor a minister I have none the less the heart and sentiments of a good Frenchman. I suffered enough at the time from the calumnies, spread so thoughtlessly by another newspaper, to have all the details still present clearly in my mind. Yes, Monsieur Bayer – not the Bank of Dresden – note it well, gentlemen – was a shareholder in *Le Figaro*. He was the representative in Paris of the Bank of Dresden and also of a London bank, the General Mining Corporation.

He wasn't a German, but an Austrian, which doesn't make much difference. In reality he had become altogether a Parisian. I don't really know, but he may have been applying for French nationality at the time of his death. He had bought shares in *Le Figaro* for himself and for some of his friends – and I defy you to prove that it was on behalf of the Bank of Dresden! He was counting on a rapid increase in their value as the paper was in the full tide of prosperity. The shares stood at 1,200 francs. Then came the Dreyfus Affair: the shares quickly fell to 500 francs, or even lower. Whereupon Monsieur Bayer, who didn't like losing money on the stock exchange, was extremely irritated. He joined with other shareholders ... and formed a syndicate to protect their interests. It was this group, and this group alone, who brought about the change in the management of *Le Figaro*. I can give you the names of these shareholders, and you will see they are the best of Frenchmen and the most ardent Nationalists.

Monsieur Bayer had in this affair only a limited number of shares without importance to the general result – about 800, if my memory is correct – and that really doesn't represent a large enough interest to be called, 'selling *Le Figaro* to the Germans ... ' The Bank of Dresden addressed this letter to *Le Matin* :

We learn that you published in your issue of the 18th inst., an article indicating that the Bank of Dresden was interested in *Le Figaro*. We declare categorically that the news is false, that we have never had any interest at all in this journal, nor have we at any time owned shares in *Le Figaro*. We request you to withdraw the statement you have published.

(Signed for the Directors of the Bank of Dresden, Gottman, Steiger.)

A few days later Monsieur Bayer was relieved of his duties as their representative : they did not wish to be involved in the disputes of the *Figaro* shareholders. . . .

*Le Figaro* remains, therefore, essentially a French journal, through those who are at its head, its direction and chief editor, by the élite of its staff, by its shareholders – and if there is the least doubt about this I am ready to submit to the Court a list of the shareholders at our last general meeting . . .

I come to the Lipscher contract. This contract has never existed except as a project, and we never began seriously to carry it out. This gentleman, Lipscher, presented himself in July 1913 to the Director of Publicity for *Le Figaro* and asked him to undertake an illustrated supplement of the Hungarian spas : it was to come out during the winter. He asked for a correspondent's card, which was given to him. He sent letters from Budapest which appeared in *Le Figaro*. This surprised his colleagues there who enlightened us as to the true worth of this individual . . . immediately, on 23rd October, Monsieur Glaser, our Director of Publicity, broke off all connection with him. 'We have decided,' he wrote, 'not to continue with the project for publicising the Hungarian spas about which you came to see us, and about which we have corresponded.' And we asked for the return of his correspondent's card. A project for an agreement for publicising the spas which *Le Figaro* refused to complete : that is the Lipscher Affair ! That is what Monsieur Caillaux called 'the *Figaro*'s pro-Germany policy' ! . . . Monsieur Caillaux said yesterday he would stop at nothing to defend himself. To defend against him the memory of Calmette, heroic and loyal, we too shall stop at nothing !

I have finished, gentlemen . . . but in this tragic trial where all efforts seem to be directed towards favouring the accused, wife of a powerful politician, forgetting the victim, it was necessary to correct the errors, unintentional no doubt, but which nevertheless are the most painful attacks on the memory of the man who has died assassinated, carrying out what he conceived to be his duty; painful because they cast a reflection on what was most dear to him – his absolute independence and his love for his country.*

Caillaux, monocle swinging, had already turned to reply when Chenu, seeing that Prestat was going to be in trouble, leapt to his feet and addressed a rousing speech to the gallery, threatening Caillaux with eternal shame for speaking against Calmette...

CHENU : I can well understand Monsieur Prestat's moving and noble sentiments, but perhaps he will permit his counsel to say that he took a great deal of trouble over it, and in my opinion it would have been sufficient to indicate to Monsieur Caillaux that we know of no enterprise more contemptible than to come to a public audience to profane the tomb his wife has opened... (*Acclamation and applause.*)
CAILLAUX : Gentlemen of the jury, I shall reply with as much restraint and moderation as I showed yesterday, and which will be the best way to answer these attacks for which, I imagine, Maître Chenu does not accept personal responsibility... (*Applause.*)
CHENU : I take the responsibility for every word I utter. You threaten me? You are wrong! You don't know the man you are addressing! (*Applause.*)
ALBANEL : If these disturbances continue, I shall clear the court.
CHENU : Instead of calling the public to order, call the witness to order! (*Applause.*)
ALBANEL : It is the lawyers who are applauding! I shall call the police!
MAITRE HENRI ROBERT (*President of the Barristers' Association*): It is the civilians. I can see them from here... I beg you to consider the incident closed and continue with the examination of the witnesses.

When order had been restored, Caillaux, who was standing so erect that he was almost leaning backwards, began again. He asked what was the origin of this acrimonious debate? It was because his

---

* It was not generally known at the time that the directors of *Le Figaro*, with those of other leading newspapers, were receiving a large monthly stipend from Isvolsky, by arrangement with Poincaré, in exchange for supporting Russian Imperial policy and reassuring the holders of Russian securities.²

honour had been incessantly attacked. He had been accused of every
fault, of every crime, and he was entitled to answer his accusers:

CAILLAUX: I raised two questions, and insisted upon them. The
question of 1901 – a little old now, Monsieur Prestat, I agree –
and the Hungarian question, much more recent. We shall see
what *Le Figaro*'s denials are worth. May I refer to my notes,
*Monsieur le Président?*
ALBANEL: Yes. Monsieur Prestat also consulted his notes.

Caillaux proceeded to demonstrate the falseness of Prestat's statements one by one: even the declaration by the Bank of Dresden that
it held no shares in *Le Figaro* he proved to be untrue by reading two
letters from Monsieur Bayer detailing the shares he had bought on
their behalf and the interest he had credited to their account. He
followed this with an extract from the *Berliner Tageblatt*, deploring
the Bank of Dresden's attempt to influence the French public by the
purchase of *Le Figaro*. Turning to the Hungarian question, he said,

CAILLAUX: If I have properly understood the arguments of the
honourable Monsieur Prestat, *Le Figaro* sought nothing but the
publicity for the Hungarian spas which had been proposed to
them; but allow me to point out that in the Hungarian Parliament two letters were quoted, one from Monsieur Gaston Calmette to Monsieur Lipscher, and one from Monsieur Glaser to
Monsieur Lipscher. Both are so clear they completely refute
Monsieur Prestat's interpretation, particularly the first letter. Here
it is, from Monsieur Glaser . . . I ask the gentlemen of the jury for
permission to read it, and I ask them to listen attentively:

Monsieur, – In reply to your letter I hasten to inform you that
we accept your offer of collaboration. You will find enclosed the
letter from the Director of *Le Figaro* accrediting you. Concerning
the contracts . . . it is understood they are to be concluded on the
basis of 30,000 francs a year, and apart from this a supplementary
payment of 10,000 francs is to be allocated to *Le Figaro* to pay for
the cost of materials, paper, etc., for a supplement similar to the
one we devoted to Vichy . . .

The letters showed perfectly clearly that there were two projects –
one by which *Le Figaro* was to bring out a supplement advertising
the Hungarian spas; the other, for 30,000 francs a year, was for

other services. Caillaux asked if the letters were authentic.

PRESTAT : Nothing was paid.

CAILLAUX : But are the letters authentic?

PRESTAT : ...

CAILLAUX : I have the right to ask.

SELIGMAN : No! You have no right to put questions to the grand-father of Calmette's children!

ALBANEL : Don't envenom the debate.

CAILLAUX : ... I ask if the letters are authentic. I get no reply. I therefore take it they are authentic.

SELIGMAN : Not at all. I do not permit you to question Monsieur Prestat!

LABORI : I intervene only because Maître Seligman obliges me to ... Certainly Monsieur Caillaux has the right to ask Monsieur Prestat a question. Had he not done so, I should have requested permission to ask the question myself.

CHENU : With all my strength I support Monsieur Prestat's refusal to reply or to prolong the discussion which seems to be outside our main subject, but which could find a place in our final pleas. That is my reason for requesting Monsieur Prestat to remain silent, and from that silence no conclusion must be drawn against him.

Caillaux seemed satisfied with the complete discomfiture of Monsieur Prestat, and did not on this occasion press his accusation further against Calmette. The Court concerned itself for the remainder of the day with minor witnesses, and the interest gradually built up toward the question of the intimate letters.

Madame Estradère, who had been an employee of *Le Figaro* and at the same time a friend of Henriette's, testified that Calmette, disappointed in people who had promised him documents on Caillaux but had not produced them, hearing that a letter existed which should have been destroyed, went to see a mutual friend and told her he would give Madame Gueydan whatever she pleased, even 30,000 francs, for that letter – but she refused this offer.

ESTRADERE : Then Monsieur Calmette, wishing to make a spectacular climax to his attack on the Income Tax ... asked me to arrange for him to meet Madame Gueydan at my home. It is true he had a thousand and one ways to meet Madame Gueydan, but they had all come to nothing, so he turned to me. I was very upset that I had to refuse, because we were close friends ...

One piece of evidence was particularly shocking: a director of the Discount Bank testified that he received a visit late one evening from a representative of Calmette, who told him he must support the accusations against Caillaux or he would himself be attacked. Upon his contemptuous refusal he was denounced in the next issue of *Le Figaro* as 'Caillaux's accomplice'.

> Down low and immediately in front of the President, usually sitting in a huddled position, is the lawyer Charles Maurice Chenu, representing the family of the dead Calmette. His face is pale, and he never smiles, except to allow an occasional faint flicker to cross his face when one of his quiet thrusts goes home.
>
> *The New York Times*, 26th July 1914

On the morning of the fourth day of the trial, Monsieur Vervoort, editor of the *Paris-Journal*, deposed that when he was a journalist on the staff of *Gil Blas* in 1911, he had come into his editor's office and said laughingly, 'Do you want an article on the loves of the Prime Minister?' The editor, Monsieur Mortier, had asked if he was trying to be funny.

> VERVOORT: 'Well,' I said, 'I know there are certain letters which Monsieur Caillaux has written and which, I believe, would compromise him.' 'We can't take advantage of that,' Mortier said, 'On the contrary we must warn him.'
> He sent me to Monsieur Caillaux's Principal Private Secretary to whom I explained I had become friendly with Mademoiselle Marie Gueydan, Madame Gueydan's sister – an artist and a charming woman, good and intelligent, but she was on the side of her sister who was pursuing Monsieur Caillaux's second wife with real hatred . . .

Marie Gueydan, he said, had tried to persuade him to write articles about this, but he had refused. Then, in November 1911, she told him he ought to go and see her sister who had something of great importance to tell him, and some letters to show him.

Because he considered it his business as a journalist to know everything, he went to the Hotel Astoria and was shown into Berthe's bedroom where the two sisters told him the most intimate details of Caillaux's private life. Berthe took some papers from her trunk which she said were typewritten copies she had made of some of his intimate letters: she begged him to make an appointment for her to show them to Monsieur Mortier. He answered that if she wanted to impress the director she would have to show him the originals, whereupon she produced them : one was written on the notepaper of the Senate and the other on that of the Prefecture of the Sarthe. She offered these to Vervoort, but he wouldn't take them, and he advised her to give up trying to get them published. She said if she couldn't find a publisher she would have them printed and distributed as a brochure.

Pierre Mortier, director of the *Gil Blas*, confirmed what Vervoort had told him. He added he had come to know Monsieur and Madame Caillaux well after the latter's resignation as Prime Minister, and he could bear witness to the affection they had for each other, and their mutual confidence : he said he had never seen a happier household, that is, until the press campaign started which every day distressed Madame Caillaux and wrung her with anguish. It had needed a campaign like that to wreck their perfect happiness and drive her distracted to the point of assassination – this woman of whom all who approached her could testify to her gentleness, her tranquillity, her goodness of heart. He had observed her acute anxiety and mounting despair. Speaking on behalf of the Press Syndicate, of which he was the youngest president, he said he knew nothing more ignoble than the campaign of daily calumny, and nothing more contemptible than to use private letters for political ends, without even respecting the familiar name used by a woman in corresponding with one she loves.

According to another witness, Monsieur Abel Bonnard, who had been negotiating with Berthe for the letters on behalf of Calmette, she had refused to sell them to *Le Figaro* or to consent to their publication. There followed depositions from Monsieur Painlevé, Minister for Education, and various other newspaper editors and journalists who had been told Calmette would publish the letters, and who had passed the information on to Caillaux. Then Berthe's name was called.

She came in with slow majestic steps that had something fateful in them. She is a tall woman, taller than Madame Caillaux, with none of her plumpness. Her body has a natural way of assuming graceful poses, and her head is poised superbly on a slender throat.

Beneath a toque of blue velvet with nodding blue feathers, like a Viking's helmet on her black hair, her face looked like the face of a Medusa in its cold anger. The woman in the dock appeared by contrast fragile and weak beside the suggestions of power that Madame Gueydan gave.

The *Daily Express*, 24th July 1914

The atmosphere underwent a subtle transformation as soon as she appeared at the bar of the court. She gave her age as forty-five, but she was astonishingly well preserved. Her voice was low and musical. She was the very picture of the deserted wife whose life has been ruined by an adventuress. She seemed to represent all the faithful wronged women of the universe, bearing her hard fate with patience and humility.

Here they were, facing each other, one dark and sombre, bearing the grief and humiliation of the past, the other, pale and blonde, bearing the grief and humiliation of the present. It was the fate of these two women to love the same man, the first giving up her home for him and earlier marriage, the second committing murder in his defence.

We look at the man responsible for these misfortunes : he watches with attention and seems anxious about what the past will say to the present.

*L'Illustration*, 1st August 1914

ALBANEL : Madame Gueydan, kindly make your deposition. I see you have brought papers with you. You may not read them.

BERTHE : I ask permission to consult some notes.

ALBANEL : It is against the law.

BERTHE : Then it is impossible for me to make my deposition.

ALBANEL : You have already made one to the examining magistrate.

BERTHE : I said nothing to the examining magistrate.

ALBANEL : I'll ask you some questions about what you said then.

BERTHE : That will be difficult as you know nothing about the affair ... Didn't you allow Monsieur Caillaux to use notes? I have clippings from newspapers. I can't do without them. You must understand my situation is desperate, almost impossible. I see before me a mountain of lies and I must dispose of them one by one. I am alone. I have no husband to protect me. I am accused of things I have not done, and no lawyer will undertake my defence. ... I have only my poor voice. In my present state of emotion, it could betray me.

Madame Gueydan was at the bar of the court. She was wrung by an emotion which, for the whole of the first part of her evidence caused her voice to reach us only as a feeble murmur, a woman with a beautiful tired face, and hollow eyes which looked as if they could shed no more tears.

Maître Labori
defends Henriette.

Maître Chenu
accuses Caillaux.

The Presiding Judge, Monsieur Albanel.

Caillaux at bay.

She came to protest against the imputation that she was primarily responsible for the crime. She swore that never had these letters, the intimate letters of her hated rival and of this man whom she insulted but whom she had so greatly loved, passed from her hands to the hands of his enemies.

*Le Matin*, 24th July 1914

Maître Chenu asked if the law would really be violated if she glanced at her notes.

LABORI : I am full of respect for Madame Gueydan's situation, but for me she is a witness, and nothing but a witness.
BERTHE : You are quite sure of that, Maître Labori?
LABORI : For me, *Madame*, that is what you are – but if you become an accuser . . . you will find me on the side of the defence against you.
BERTHE : If you have spoken with Monsieur Caillaux about me, he must have told you I have some spirit.

Labori insisted she must make a spontaneous deposition as the law required. The President made another attempt to persuade her to do so, then Labori asked him to put it on record that the witness refused to make a spontaneous deposition . . .

LABORI : It is perfectly simple. *Madame* deposed several times before the examining magistrate with sangfroid and authority . . .
BERTHE : You weren't there. You know nothing.
LABORI : . . . with sangfroid and authority of which the records bear witness.
BERTHE : What do you mean by that?
LABORI : *Madame*, please. I don't wish to engage in an argument with you, at least not for the present. The respect I owe you, provisionally at least, forbids it. Madame Gueydan made a deposition before the examining magistrate. She has been brought here by the Prosecution to depose orally as the law requires. If she refuses, . . . I shall object to her evidence.
BERTHE : I was distressed to see in the Act of Accusation that calumnies had been collected from the gutter to throw at my head, and they know nothing about me. I was astonished that all the pity seemed to be for the intruder who insinuated herself into my

home, and that there was not a word of sympathy for the good and faithful wife who was the victim of this intrusion and who has never done anything, or said any of the things, of which you do not know the baseness. That is my reply.

The public were tremendously impressed by this unusual witness. If her capacity to love equalled her capacity to hate, she must have been a remarkable lover, one of those heroines of passionate drama that the modern theatre has not been able to portray in her tragic simplicity. We find them only in the ancient Greek tragedies.

*L'Illustration*, 1st August 1914

LABORI : Permit me to remind Madame Gueydan that she has sworn to depose without hatred. But for the moment we are discussing a matter of form. *Madame* has her deposition before her. It is not possible that I should permit her to read it.

ALBANEL : The law forbids it.

BERTHE : It has been said that if Maître Labori's client has committed a crime it is because photographic copies of letters were being circulated; and that these should not have existed because of an agreement between myself and the man who was my husband. Well, that is false.

ALBANEL : Well, let us speak of these photographs. The jury must be informed on this point.

LABORI : Though Madame Gueydan has been asked not to read from her notes, I cannot be sure that she . . .

ALBANEL : *Madame*, please hand your notes to the usher.

BERTHE : I brought papers because I saw Monsieur Caillaux used some . . . you must understand my situation, *Monsieur le Président*, I put myself under your protection.

ALBANEL : All the witnesses who are under oath make their deposition verbally.

BERTHE : I am not like all the other witnesses.

It was explained to her that Monsieur Caillaux was not on oath, neither was Monsieur Prestat, therefore they were allowed papers.

LABORI : Can the law make itself respected ? . . .

CHENU : It is with the greatest diffidence that I intervene. I see before me a lone woman at the bar of the court, the subject of comments and remonstrances . . .

ALBANEL : None whatsoever.

LABORI: If you are referring to me, my dear *bâtonnier*, I do not accept your statement.

Chenu then advised Berthe to answer the President's questions and promised they would all help her if her deposition was a little confused.

She gave the papers to the usher.

BERTHE: What do you wish me to say?

ALBANEL: Your divorce from Monsieur Caillaux was in 1905 I think?

BERTHE: No, in 1911.

ALBANEL: Let us go back a little. In 1909 there was dissension with your husband?

BERTHE: No, *Monsieur*. You are completely mistaken.

ALBANEL: Can you tell me what happened at Mamers?

BERTHE: We were the happiest couple, and the most united, that one could possibly imagine.

ALBANEL: Reply to my question.

CHENU: *Monsieur le Président*, you insisted upon a spontaneous deposition.

ALBANEL: Speak then. Pray do.

BERTHE: I don't know what you are asking me.

ALBANEL: I said, in 1909 there were certain dissensions between you and Monsieur Caillaux?

BERTHE: None whatsoever. We were the happiest couple and the most united that you could possibly see. We had for each other the most beautiful love, and the most pure.

ALBANEL: And you parted in these circumstances?

BERTHE: No. I'll have more to say about that!

ALBANEL: Say all you have to say. You have a right to do so, and you have taken the oath to say everything.

BERTHE: You asked me if there was dissension, and I said 'No'.

ALBANEL: There was some dissension because, at a certain moment, there was a reconciliation. That is what I want to say.

BERTHE: No, there was never what you call a 'reconciliation'. I told you, *Monsieur le Président*, you know nothing about it . . .

ALBANEL: Now these letters, which have been discussed here; we shall have to know how they fell into your hands, how they were destroyed and how it is you have kept photographic copies?

Instead of answering directly, Berthe talked at length about a different letter, that of 14th June 1908, which had been brought to Caillaux one day while they were at lunch and which was the first that aroused her suspicions.

ALBANEL : Tell us now about the letters written by Monsieur Caillaux to Madame Rainouard.

BERTHE : The one I was talking about was written by Madame Rainouard to Monsieur Caillaux.

ALBANEL : In a letter found in Madame Rainouard's safe deposit box, Monsieur Caillaux says that in September 1909 he saw you come in one day at Mamers in a bit of a temper, and that there was rather a violent scene . . .

BERTHE : No, no.

ALBANEL : . . . and it was during the night after that scene the letters disappeared. Can you tell us about this?

BERTHE : I have just told you about the letter of 14th June. I have just told you we were a perfectly happy couple, and so close to each other that I didn't suspect for a moment my husband had a mistress.

A free woman stood in the court, the first wife, dark haired, with the pallor of the southerner, her eyes burning with long-harboured hatred for the other woman who is loved by the man who once loved her. There was no doubt of her hatred. It was living and hissing and relentless in every word of her evidence.

'I did not know that my husband ever had a mistress,' she said once, and that word 'mistress' darted out like the forked tongue of a snake in two envenomed syllables, while she looked at that other, the fair-haired, white-faced woman in the dock who shot a man for her husband's sake . . .

                                        The *Daily Express*, 24th July 1914

BERTHE : It wasn't until 14th July of the following year – I remember the date – that I forced him to explain . . . I felt an atmosphere of deceit around me, of corruption. I asked him that day if he was deceiving me. He made a half confession, gave me the name of some woman or other, saying it really meant nothing to him. And I must say he was deeply moved that day. He threw himself on his knees before me and asked my forgiveness, and said things I can't repeat to you. He said he was unworthy of me, that I placed him too high, that he could not breathe there : he was so humble that it was I who consoled him – and next day he saw that person again. And that person understood that her prey might after all escape her, so she put her hand more firmly upon him, and from that moment, really, she had my husband . . .

I only had my suspicions, I knew no more than I have told you; that is, what Monsieur Caillaux said to me on that evening of 14th July – it was beautiful, it was really beautiful. I thought I saw into the depth of his heart. But he was not speaking the truth, even in his tears.

It was the beginning of September when I got back to Paris. Next morning . . . I received an anonymous letter in which I was informed that a blonde divorcee wished to take my place, that I didn't know what was going on secretly, and that I should look out . . .

That afternoon Monsieur Caillaux returned. He hadn't seen me for five weeks . . . Very soon afterwards – and I'm sorry to tell you all this – he came to my bedside and said, 'I came here during the night to kill you, but I didn't. Next time I shall.'

I made no reply. I said nothing at all, but I saw it would be a good thing to put a safe distance between us for a few days to let him recover. I went to an hotel at Versailles and sent him a telegram to let him know where I was . . . I was sure, knowing he loved me as I loved him, he would come an hour later and bring me home. He didn't come. I telephoned and found he was in the Sarthe – he had driven through Versailles without stopping . . . I felt things were becoming serious, and I returned to Paris.

Just at this time there was a family funeral – the uncle of his nephew – so I felt sure he would come back for it, but he did not, and you will see why, you will see appear on the scene the lawyer, Maître Thorel, whom I have called 'the lawyer of the conspirators'. You will see him advising my husband not to see his wife, and trying to take her in a trap. I went to the funeral, sure to meet him there, but he had been advised to avoid me . . . I assure you he would have found a gentle wife who loved him.

Well, he didn't come. I wrote to him that things couldn't go on like this, that I couldn't go on like this without my husband, and that I was going to join him in the Sarthe. He replied, yes, of course, and that he would await me there.

So, on 20th September I arrived at Mamers. Am I making myself clear, *Monsieur le Président*? I'm not sure.

ALBANEL : Go on, *Madame*. You have no need of your notes.

You are making a very complete deposition. Take your time.

BERTHE : On 20th September I arrived at Mamers – now we've reached the point that interests you, haven't we? After dinner we had a long talk. I found him changed, much changed. He said things that were hurtful, vindictive. I asked him if this change in his behaviour towards me was on account of the person we have mentioned. He said, 'Yes, it is true.' I told him I knew certain things about her, and that perhaps he would do well to beware of her. He seemed very impressed, as if that corresponded to his own deepest thoughts, and you will see that in fact he was afraid. We talked until very late, and in the morning he left for le Mans where he had to attend a council meeting.

I was alone for the whole day, and thinking of all the atrocious things he had said to me, I went into his study ... I felt overwhelmed by misfortune. Something was going on. There was an oppressive atmosphere. I was surrounded by lies.

I don't know why, but I thought of the drawer where he had put his letters ... I took the key of the bookcase, I tried it in the lock of the drawer, and it opened as if by magic.

In the drawer I found two of Madame Rainouard's letters ... I took one ... There was no longer any uncertainty, the disaster was greater than I could have believed. It wasn't until two hours had passed that I decided to take the other.

I expected that Monsieur Caillaux, being very quick tempered, would commit some act of violence. I felt my life was in danger. I didn't care. When he came back, he didn't notice anything. Next day, and for the following days, he went again to le Mans, and he put a large packet of letters into the drawer.

After dinner he went to bed very early – and I went up to my room also; but then I thought, perhaps I didn't yet know the full extent of the disaster, that there might be more to be learned.

I went down to the study, again took the key from the bookcase and opened the drawer.

I took the packet of letters up to my room : what I learned was so horrible for me, I couldn't read them through to the end.

Next morning when he came into my room I said at once, 'I've taken the letters.' I expected him to kill me, but – it was astonishing – he sat down on my *chaise-longue*. He didn't move. 'Where are they?' he asked, 'You will give them back to me.' 'No, I've already sent them away. I've posted them.'

For once he didn't feel he was the stronger. He thought of a stratagem, and said nothing. I mean he said only, 'You must give them back to me.' I replied, 'You speak of divorcing after the elections. The whole conspiracy against me is unmasked. Why wait for the elections? We shall divorce immediately.'

Then he threw himself at my feet, he knelt and begged me not to divorce. He said I was the one he loved, that he no longer loved that person and that I must return the letters. Again and again he said, 'Pass the sponge over it, wipe it out,' but I told him I should have to think about it. I was too deeply troubled by what I had just read to reply at once.

At that time there was illness in my family. I returned to Paris, not knowing what to do.

I saw so much bad faith in his letters, so much deceit and infamous plotting, that I no longer had any confidence, no longer believed him when he said he would break with that person, and when he came to Paris two days later . . .

LABORI : Do you think you could ask Madame Gueydan to be good enough to speak a little louder?

ALBANEL : It is essential, *Madame.*

BERTHE : I am giving it all the force of which I am capable. The story is so painful for me, you understand. I came back to Paris . . .then Monsieur Caillaux came back from the Sarthe – and I should like to emphasize to you, *Monsieur le Président,* that when you use the word 'reconciliation' it is not appropriate : you should have said, 'supplication'. Monsieur Caillaux implored me on his knees, but it wasn't a question of reconciliation. The whole story has been falsified, and I beg the gentlemen of the jury to recognise this.

We went back to the Sarthe. I had not yet made up my mind. Monsieur Caillaux said, 'Give me back the letters,' and I replied 'When you have given me proof that you are leading a worthy life,' because I knew he was still seeing his correspondent, and that in spite of what he had told me, he had not yet written the letter breaking off all relations with her. I knew she had fastened onto him again. Perhaps he had written it, I don't really know . . .

Monsieur Caillaux was to leave on 6th November for Egypt. Exactly a week before that, when he asked me to give him the letters, I replied, 'It is agreed. I'll give them back. You have my promise.'

From that moment he was very attentive to me and, I don't

know if I should say this, everything bad about the accused that could be said was said to me by Monsieur Caillaux at that time. I can be more precise and give you the details and you'll be able to see that I couldn't have invented them. In his heart he was delighted by the incident of the letters which gave him the opportunity to break with that person.

I told him, 'You'll have the letters on the evening of your departure, 5th November, and we shall destroy them.'

And that is what happened. In the morning I said, 'I will give you the letters, but if you change one day, if you start again, I shall have given you the letters and you will deny what was in them' – because I must say that in the letters Monsieur Caillaux said he didn't have a fault to reproach me with, and you can understand how precious that was from a man who wished for a divorce, for the betrayed wife to read this phrase written by her husband, that he hadn't a fault to reproach her with!

I said, 'When I've burned the letters there will be nothing left of what you said in them: shall we have a witness to this act? Choose a witness from among your friends or mine, as you wish.' Naturally he chose one of his . . .

In the evening after dinner we were awaiting his arrival, and I said, 'I'm going to destroy the letters, but I ask you for one thing: I should like you to listen to what you wrote about me, and what was written to you about me.' I began to read, and he said, 'That's enough, enough.' The reading seemed to pain him, and when I had finished he threw himself into my arms, asking himself how he could have written such things.

I said to him, 'Why don't you write down now what you have just said to me? You might forget . . .'

My small desk was there . . . so he sat down and wrote me a letter which I can give you, *Monsieur le Président.* Will you allow me to read it?

ALBANEL : After your deposition you may read it.

CHENU : One could have it now.

ALBANEL : By virtue of my discretionary powers, I shall read it. (*The letter was handed up to him, and he began to read:*)

Paris, 5th November 1909 – My dear Berthe, I thank you profoundly for your act of high generosity . . .

(*Numerous voices called, 'Louder! Louder!'*)

# entering

ALBANEL : Perhaps Monsieur the Advocate General would like to read it?

ADVOCATE GENERAL :

Paris, 5th November, 1909. – My dear Berthe, I thank you profoundly for your act of high generosity which you have just performed in burning before me today, 5th November, the letters which Madame X sent and which I wrote.

These letters, injurious to you, left no doubt of the relations between Madame X and myself, nor the project for divorce after a certain date that we secretly conceived and planned. I promise you that all my efforts will be directed to make even the memory vanish of these cruel events which I made you pass through. I swear that far from thinking of divorce in future I shall apply myself to protect you, which is, besides, my duty.

But if, against all expectation – because I am acting in complete loyalty and with the desire to make you happy – I go back on the engagements I am undertaking, it will be my duty to declare and recognise on my honour that you would be within your rights to quote against me, in support of whatever demand it may suit you to formulate, the adultery of which I have been guilty in conditions particularly painful for you.

Believe once more, my dear Berthe, in my profound thanks, and rely upon my continuing and unalterable tenderness.

[Signed] Caillaux

P.S. This letter was given to Madame Caillaux in the presence of Monsieur Privat-Deschanel who can bear witness to it.

LABORI : *Monsieur le Président*, I have a question about that letter that has a certain bearing on the subject. Do you think, if Madame Gueydan agrees, I should ask it now or keep it till later?

ALBANEL : I think, as we're going on to a different subject, you'd better ask it now.

LABORI : Did not Madame Gueydan, on 25th March 1911 . . .

BERTHE : You're going to make a big mistake, Maître Labori . . .

LABORI : Allow me to make it, then . . . Did not Madame Gueydan, on 25th March 1911, at the time of her divorce, which was concluded by a settlement, sign an agreement in these terms: 'Article 4 . . . to burn at this moment, as soon as the divorce is concluded, all the correspondence between husband and wife in their possession'?

BERTHE : Maître Labori anticipates my story. I haven't yet come to the point where they strangled me in forty-eight hours. They prepared the papers and made me sign them without reading them. And besides, Maître Labori, can you maintain that it would cover that letter, which is rather a sort of receipt?

LABORI : As Madame Gueydan does me the honour to address herself to me, I say it is most definitely a letter exchanged between the husband and wife and part of a correspondence. A letter which, for me, apart from all the moving considerations that *Madame*'s grief forbids me to touch upon, should have been destroyed. I don't think it has much bearing on the trial, but all the same I am astonished that it is in Madame Gueydan's possession.

ALBANEL : You understand, Madame Gueydan, according to Maître Labori, this letter should have been burned with the others.

BERTHE : Yes, *Monsieur le Président*, but I shall reply, and I shall tell of all the machinations that were woven around me to overwhelm me. You shall see what a guilty husband does to attempt to prove it was the wife who was to blame. I shall put my finger on everything that was done to me. At the time of the divorce Monsieur Caillaux asked me to give my word of honour, orally or in writing, to return the correspondence. I refused to give my word of honour, and I did not wish for his, knowing what it was worth. (*Stir in the audience.*)

Besides, I said I did not wish Monsieur Caillaux to have letters of mine – he had two or three – and it was I who had all the letters, so it was simply nonsensical, the article they introduced there . . . I have given many things, particularly something that Monsieur Caillaux wanted more than anything.

ALBANEL : Have you much more to say? It's time for the intermission.

BERTHE : Allow me to add one thing. It is that never has there been an agreement between Monsieur Caillaux and myself. I brought that Article 4 to show you : that is all there is between us. You can see that it's not serious. I repeat I have never concluded an agreement with Monsieur Caillaux, no more for the letter about the Income Tax than for the intimate letters. It concerns our personal correspondence, doesn't it?

LABORI : If Madame Gueydan will permit me a word? . . . There were evidently a number of incidents. It would perhaps be advisable to deal with them separately.

CHENU : Don't confuse the dates. I think Madame Gueydan's story got up to 1909. Is it right to discuss now what happened two years later?

LABORI : I asked Madame Gueydan how it came about that the letter was still in her hands. I read out an article, the existence of which she does not dispute. But she adds there was no agreement.

BERTHE : I'm speaking of the correspondence.

LABORI : There was an agreement which guaranteed Madame Gueydan an annual income of 18,000 francs which Monsieur Caillaux has paid regularly.

BERTHE : Pardon, Maître Labori, you are stating facts of which you are ignorant.

LABORI : Madame Gueydan will explain?

BERTHE : Pardon me, Maître Labori, it is Monsieur Caillaux who will explain.

LABORI : If Monsieur Caillaux has not paid the allowance, regularly, Madame Gueydan will tell him?

BERTHE : That is nobody else's business, Maître Labori.

LABORI : I say I have here an agreement of four pages in which definite conditions are laid down, not only the financial conditions that will guarantee Madame Gueydan an income of 18,000 francs a year, besides a capital sum which she has received, but also certain moral conditions which are laid down in Article 4. Well, that is called a divorce settlement.

BERTHE : Well, what is your question, *Monsieur le bâtonnier*?

LABORI : I'm simply replying to Madame Gueydan following upon a question which I put regularly.

ALBANEL : The question is to find out if the letter which has just been read should have been burnt.

LABORI : No, the question is to establish if what I have here is truly an agreement, and I ask Madame Gueydan if she is aware of its existence?

BERTHE : I reply, *Monsieur le Président*, that I should have preferred to arrive at this date in its chronological order, and to tell you in what manner I was divorced; and you will find there the Rochette Affair and other matters of great interest.

At this point there was an intermission.

ALBANEL : *Madame*, please continue your deposition.

BERTHE : Gentlemen of the jury, I have realised there is great confusion about the word 'settlement'. Perhaps you imagine that when, purely out of generosity and kindness of heart I consented to destroy the letters known as the intimate letters, there was an agreement between my husband and myself : there was absolutely no reason for the destruction of the letters except the supplication of Monsieur Caillaux, and there was only the letter you have heard read. I'm sure that can't be called a settlement. Is it really a settlement, *Monsieur le Président*?

ALBANEL : It is not for me to answer your question.

BERTHE : Excuse me, it was the Public Prosecutor, I think, who introduced the word. They are trying through this word to give me some responsibility for the crime. Well, I'm here to tell the truth and to clarify these obscure discussions. They are trying to make people believe that these letters were circulated. They try to represent me as disloyal, hoping my alleged disloyalty will serve as a basis for the extenuating circumstances they want to establish. Therefore I must defend my honour . . . No. There was no kind of settlement, I repeat. There was only generosity on my part, and you will see how I was requited . . . I must say as loudly as I can that all the accused has said is untrue, completely untrue, and also what Monsieur Caillaux has said about this. (*She turned to the President.*) You said there had been a reconciliation between myself and my husband, and everyone believed it. Everyone believed the word 'settlement'. Well, those words must be obliterated.

She pulled out a packet of letters and explained it was correspondence between Caillaux and herself.

BERTHE : You are not going to read this?

ALBANEL : No, not now. We must study it first, and then read it.

BERTHE : It seems to me it would be clearer now.

ALBANEL : It will be equally clear later. It is correspondence you have taken?

BERTHE : Oh, no!

ALBANEL : You said so, from the drawer.

BERTHE : Taken! You saddle me with a word like that!

ALBANEL : Then where did the letters come from?

BERTHE : Don't forget I was the wife, and as mistress of the household I was entitled to them.

ALBANEL : Go on.

BERTHE : But you don't help me to go on.

ALBANEL : You submit a packet of letters. Where do they come from?

BERTHE : Perhaps you are going to say I stole them! Well . . . I no longer know where I am, I'm so continually interrupted. Under these conditions it's impossible to say anything.

ALBANEL : You were talking about submitting the letters. Would you repeat for the gentlemen of the jury what you were saying about them, to avoid confusion?

BERTHE : I have spoken, gentlemen of the jury, of the time preceding the knowledge I had of my husband's adultery. I have said, and I wish to repeat it, that it was the most beautiful marriage it could possibly be, that we loved each other tenderly, that we had for each other the most noble love. That is what I said, and what I repeat... For another year I lived side by side with him without in the least suspecting the plot that was developing around me in the shadows.

I have said that during that evening, of 14th July 1909, which was so moving, Monsieur Caillaux said things to me that were so beautiful about his love for me, about the *estime* he had for me, he promised that evening to save himself from the danger he felt threatening him – but we could not go away because he was a minister at the time. We stayed where we were, and the next day he again saw the person in question. And the person in question once more seized upon her prey... (*Murmurs from the audience.*)

I have told you how Monsieur Caillaux begged me to give him back the letters, promising he had given up his mistress and that he had come back entirely to me... You have heard read Monsieur Caillaux's letter in which he thanks me for my act of great generosity. So now I'm sure there is no longer in anybody's mind the idea that there was an agreement about these letters.

Gentlemen of the jury, I should like you to ask me questions if I have not been sufficiently clear. There was no agreement about the letters. Monsieur Caillaux was a guilty husband, he asked me for the letters and I gave them to him without making any conditions, with nothing, and he wrote to me what you have heard – that he gave me his word of honour never to divorce. That is clear enough. We are not going to talk any longer about an agreement, are we?

... the liaison, in spite of what they have told you, was not interrupted, as I can prove. You do not know, perhaps, gentlemen of the jury, that Monsieur Caillaux fled from the conjugal home? ... he went away on 29th June 1910...

Madame Gueydan spoke for a long time in a voice that was hesitant, shaken, quietly at first but which was gradually raised to cry out, to shriek out pitiless things. One senses this woman will not forgive, cannot forgive, that her open wound will never heal.

*L'Illustration*, 1st August 1914

Every day in *Le Matin* I read: 'Monsieur Caillaux is instituting divorce proceedings against his wife.' Everyone thought he must have something to reproach me with. During a whole year, nearly, I read that. Monsieur Caillaux, powerful as he is, for he is powerful, Monsieur Caillaux, would never have been able to get a divorce from me – but I was a lone woman without defence, like a bird taken in a net . . .

One fine day in 1911, when I was exhausted, my lawyer said to me to come and see him: I didn't know why. It was 9th March 1911. He said to me, 'We must make an end of it. *Il faut en finir.* There must be a divorce, you must agree to a divorce,' and he showed me the articles of the divorce settlement already drawn up. I was at the end of my strength, you see, but strength and courage, I assure you, were still needed for the months and years I have passed under the calumnies and machinations of which you cannot conceive the baseness . . .

I freed myself from all these people. That is what gave me strength to go on living. I tried to carry my head high, and that is why I am still alive after all the trials I have endured.

The President brought her back to the question of the intimate letters. She said it was her sister, Mademoiselle Marie Gueydan, who had had them photographed and who brought them to her: they had not been in anyone else's hands except for the lawyers. When Caillaux left her she had shown them to some of her friends, and she believed it was her right to do so: 'at that time,' she said, 'Monsieur Caillaux was spreading all sorts of calumnies about me. These letters were my justification.'

ALBANEL: Besides these friends of whom you are speaking, Monsieur Vervoort, who was confronted with you at the enquiry, maintained that towards the end of the year 1911, on a date which he could not establish exactly but was about the end of September or the beginning of October . . .

BERTHE: Allow me to interrupt you in my turn . . .

ALBANEL: Let me finish the question.

BERTHE: You are mistaken.

ALBANEL : If you don't know my question, you can't reply to it.

BERTHE : I divine it.

ALBANEL : Monsieur Vervoort maintained that Mademoiselle Gueydan who, eighteen months previously had spoken to him of all
your troubles, asked him to go to the Hotel Astoria where you were
then living, and that you had a discussion with him during which
you spoke to him of these photographs, or of these intimate letters,
and that you showed them to him. He spoke of typewritten copies.
Can you tell us about this?

BERTHE : I have no more to say than I said at the enquiry.

ALBANEL : The jury don't know what you said.

BERTHE : I said that is all a lie. Monsieur Vervoort – and this is
the truth – was confounded before the examining magistrate. I
said it was an imposture what he said there, and I repeat it here.
Monsieur Vervoort came to ask me for the letters to use against
Monsieur Caillaux. I told him to leave. He went immediately to
the Ministry of the Interior, to my husband, and told him it was I
who offered them to him. That is the truth, *Monsieur le Président*.

ALBANEL : After Monsieur Vervoort's visit you were solicited by
others . . . You received a visit from Monsieur Bonnard who asked
you, on behalf of Monsieur Calmette, the authorisation to publish
the *Ton Jo* letter?

BERTHE : Yes, *Monsieur le Président*.

ALBANEL : Well, tell us about that interview . . .

BERTHE : It is very simple. Monsieur Bonnard wished to have my
authorisation for a certain publication. I scarcely allowed him to
finish, and I told him I did not wish to hear anything at all about
what it might contain. I believe I made myself very clear.

Asked how she could explain that the photographic negative of the
*Ton Jo* letter could have fallen into Calmette's hands, she replied
that she did not explain it.

ALBANEL : To sum up, you have never at any time given the
negatives of these letters to anyone at all?

BERTHE : I swear it.

ALBANEL : Maître Chenu, have you any questions?

CHENU : Yes *Monsieur le Président*. I should like to ask Madame
Gueydan a question . . . What is in these three letters of which
everyone has been talking for four months, and for four days, and
of which everyone is ignorant?

BERTHE : There's absolutely nothing in them to interest the public.
Nothing at all.
CHENU : Second question. Madame Gueydan, interrogated just
now, said 'These letters remained in my strong box until today.'
Where are they now?
BERTHE : They are here. (*She lifted her handbag.*)
ALBANEL : When the examining magistrate asked you to submit
these letters you replied, 'I refuse categorically.'
BERTHE : Precisely.
CHENU : Third question. Has Madame Gueydan changed her
mind? Will she give these letters to the President which she refused
to give to the examining magistrate?
BERTHE : . . .
ALBANEL : Answer, Madame – if you feel obliged to answer?
BERTHE : I prefer not to submit them . . . because I don't want to
take the responsibility . . . There is a woman here for whom it could
be a question of the death sentence : well, I don't wish, by submitting the letters . . . you will understand me.

What was Madame Gueydan going to do? Pursue her vengeance
to the end? She hesitated. She considered. She remained silent.
Then, with a supreme impulse of generosity : 'It is to you, Maître
Labori, I entrust them.'
    At this unexpected development, emotion constricted the throats
of the most insensitive listeners . . .

                                          *Le Matin*, 24th July 1914

The scene had very obviously been carefully planned by Chenu.
The last thing Labori wanted was to have to read out Caillaux
and Henriette's love letters before a critical and predominantly
hostile audience : they were bound to have the effect of an anti-
climax as 'all-Paris' had been speculating about them for weeks.
However, he was fairly landed with them. He thanked Berthe with
exaggerated courtesy :

LABORI : No one, *Madame*, since I began my career as a barrister,
  has done me so great an honour. I respectfully accept – if you
  still wish to give them to me.

It was agreed that he would take the letters, study them in consultation with Chenu and make a statement about them next day.

Maître Labori.                Berthe Gueydan.

Henriette in distress.
Studies in court, after the contemporary artist Forain.

Berthe surrendered the letters and was told to return to her place among the witnesses.

The vast debates . . . had become more harassing at each session – now they were all gall and hatred. The accused in her box seemed distant, she had almost ceased to exist. No one thought of her now, and her crime was scarcely mentioned, but around the crime wounded pride and disillusion struck with poisoned daggers before hesitant magistrates – they too were affected by the prevailing atmosphere . . .

*L'Illustration*, 1st August 1914

Monsieur Joseph Caillaux, his head in his hands, his body shaken by convulsive sobs, had listened to her implacable voice. Then he clenched his teeth, lifted his head determinedly, and directed at his adversary a glance in which burnt a fierce flame. It was as if before his eyes he saw once more the days long past – with her too he had been happy! With her, like all men, he had believed in the eternity of happiness . . .

*Le Matin*, 24th July 1914

ALBANEL : Monsieur Caillaux, please come forward. You have asked to be heard . . .

CAILLAUX : I have indeed asked to be heard – not that I intend to hark back sorrowfully to the chapters of my private life of which the pages are now closed, but because I cannot allow matters to rest as they have been presented to you by Madame Gueydan, particularly as they concern someone who is very close to me.

Maître Labori has just praised, quite rightly, the gesture she has made in returning the letters, and I wish my first words to be an expression of thanks to her. In this courtroom the fog of misunderstanding has surrounded them : with this simple gesture she has dispelled it. She has spoken of calumnies. There has been no calumny on our part; and no one, I can truly say, has suffered more calumny in his life than I have. She has said the letters contain confirmation of the project for divorce. That is correct, as I shall explain.

She has said they are unimportant from a political point of view. Her memory is at fault. Mine is perfectly clear on the subject. They contain quite a commentary on the electors of my constituency. She has said, and for this I thank her particularly, that what I have written in them is entirely to my honour. I believe so too. Nevertheless it is certain a hostile journalist, director of a newspaper conducting a violent campaign could have made political capital out of certain passages in them; he could also have made political capital out of the whole group of sentimental letters which describe my private life.

You may find it astonishing that Madame Caillaux, after Fate had brought her to the *Figaro* offices to demand these letters, should herself ask for them to be published – a sort of contradiction has been seen in this. In order to understand it one has to bear in mind what my wife has said – that she is a *bourgeoise*. This is the truth. I myself am a *bourgeois*, and that is the basis of my explanations about my private life. Because she is a *bourgeoise*, she was moved in her whole being by the thought that, through the publicity of the newspapers, those hidden things in a woman's life which she wishes to conceal, I mean which she wishes to hide completely, would be known to everyone, to the whole world. When disaster came, when it became necessary to say what these intimate letters contained, then the calumnies, as Madame Gueydan has just admitted, and I thank her for it, the torrent of calumny was unrestrained. It was useless for my wife to protest that what they were saying was untrue – she preferred the letters to be published. It is a perfectly logical attitude.

In reply to attacks which, it has to be admitted today, were without foundation, I was forced here to refer back to my political career – it cost me some pain to do so – beginning with the Prieu Affair, and going on to the others. It seems today I have not yet drunk the cup of sorrow to the dregs ... It is necessary that I should do so. I must, gentlemen of the jury, lay bear my life before you. You will recall the great words of the Latin poet, 'I am a man, and must not be unacquainted with anything that is human.' You too are men. Everything can be said in your presence by one who has never done anything contrary to honour, honesty or right ...

Against a woman who has borne my name I do not wish to say more than is absolutely necessary, a woman to whom I was attached for so many years; but with all my heart, with all my strength, with all my being, I am with the one – who stands there. And I would say, were it not an enormity in the eyes of the law, I would say my place is there beside her, because she is my wife, because I feel and know that she is good, and because she is of my own people, because I have chosen her, and chosen her for that reason.

It was a bitter moment for Madame Gueydan to hear this. It was the cruellest thing that Joseph Caillaux could have said. What less could this man do, torn between cold loyalty to the past and warm loyalty to the present? So they remained, this eternal triangle of one man and two women, both of them destinies in his life. He stood between them, protecting one from the hatred of the other, challenging this other to hate him with his merciless truths of all that had passed between them.

The *Daily Express*, 24th July 1914

CAILLAUX : Ah! *Madame*, allow me to say you have introduced here things that are altogether too much.

I met you in 1900. I was a young Minister of Finance. Life had smiled upon me. Perhaps I was too happy in the early part of my life. A millionaire from my cradle, son of a minister . . . At thirty-five I entered almost triumphantly into the Chamber of Deputies. There was perhaps a certain thoughtlessness, a certain frivolity, in my way of life.

At thirty-seven I met you – Madame Duprè, as you were then. My mistake – I don't want to say anything to hurt you – my great mistake was to marry you, because we were not two beings of the same race, of the same nature. Those whom you have just heard at the bar of the court understood – I assure you I shall say nothing wounding. No one denies I am a man of authority with energy, with will power : you have some of these qualities to excess. It was impossible our association should last. I perceived this almost immediately after our marriage. I perceived this before I had met my present wife; and you know it well. From then on, it was the way of tribulation and sorrow. Ah, you have well said, and your words betrayed your thought, we were admirable friends . . .

BERTHE : Monsieur Caillaux ! You dishonour yourself !

CAILLAUX : I assure you, *Madame*, your violence will do you no good, and that my reticence is understood by all those, friends or adversaries, who are here listening to me. I do not dishonour myself, I tell you the absolute truth.

There was discord between us, almost from the first day, because of our conflicting natures, at once opposed and too much alike, and because I was born in one station of life and you in another. The discord became venomous. Later on I found one whom I had known as a young married woman, and admired. Then one day you took some letters – but we will leave aside the miserable details. Ah! what recriminations, what bitter words, could I address to you also, if I were not a man in the presence of a woman!

One day you took these letters, and you held me . . . yes, that is agreed. There intervened what you do not wish to call a reconciliation, though I do not find in the French language any other word to describe it. You tell me it was not sincere? It was so sincere that some months later . . . I had indeed the thought that the conflict of our two natures would make it impossible for us to live together . . . but there was my word; I had given it to you and I wished to keep it.

Then – it is the only thing I allow myself to say – I told you at the end of June that considerations of personal respect would no longer permit me to remain with you.

BERTHE : Why? Oh, why?

CAILLAUX : That is all I shall say, *Madame*.

BERTHE : No! You cannot go so far without saying precisely what you mean. I challenge you to complete your thought to the end!

CAILLAUX : Let me continue then, if you absolutely demand I should do so, I shall yield to your wishes . . . I shall complete this unhappy story.

In the month of July I began proceedings for divorce. You would not give way, though you knew I was bound to another. Long months went by. In March 1911 you agreed. You have even said pressure had been brought to bear on you. What pressure? . . . you had Maître Duplen as your counsel and Maître Raoul Roussel as your solicitor, and yet you say you have a divorce you didn't want!

*Madame*, let me tell you that in this divorce I wished to pay handsomely for the mistake I had made. No doubt you will say, 'Oh, by pecuniary sacrifices only.' Yes, by pecuniary sacrifices – I don't know if you have ever reckoned it up – to the value of about half my fortune. I was not obliged to give you 18,000 francs a year – you say this has not been paid regularly to you, but you know perfectly well that on the tenth of every month 1,500 francs is paid to you at the *Comptoir d'Escompte*. I gave you at the same time 210,000 francs, and, allow me to remind you, you had not a centime when you came to me. (*Lively protests from the audience.*) But what a little beauty she was (*to himself*).

She who had been abandoned remained impassive, disdainful. One sensed all this was unimportant to her, beside the point. Only the intimate drama still lived in her. She would not come to terms with the past, and a single word about the settlement was sufficient to provoke her to passionate recriminations.

There were writers among the public. What a writer of romances would not give to be able to create a character of this power in one of his books! One saw her in the demi-obscurity of the courtroom withdraw into herself and gather her strength as if to leap forward. Everything she said struck full in the face, or on the heart, of her detested rival or of the man she hated more now, perhaps, than the rival. The avenging breath of the Erinyes passed through the room in which the crime was being judged. It seemed as if one of the Fates had entered it to cut the thread of a destiny.

*L'Illustration*, 1st August 1914

CAILLAUX : What? May I not even announce something which is so greatly to my credit? That I wished the woman who had borne my name be completely sheltered from financial anxiety?
BERTHE : You did it of your own free will, didn't you?
CAILLAUX : Can a statement like this shock you, *Madame*? Can it shock anyone? That was the arrangement I made. What was the only thing I asked you in return? Having learnt that these letters were in the hands of your counsel and your solicitor, letters taken from a whole series that had nothing to do with our disputes – such as the letter about the Income Tax – I stipulated in Article 4 of the settlement that these letters should be burnt. I burnt others of yours.
BERTHE : Which, *Monsieur*?
CAILLAUX : Those addressed from Corfu when you had been to Athens.
BERTHE : What do you mean by that?
CAILLAUX : I shall explain at once because you evidently wish me to.
BERTHE : I ask you to.
CAILLAUX : Then I shall.

But Caillaux made no further reference to her letters from Corfu.*

---

* When they had started out together for their holiday after their reconciliation, she had persistently asked him to take her to Athens – it seems she had been carrying on a flirtation with the King of Greece in 1906 when she entertained him at the Ministry of Finance. She eventually went to Athens alone, and then to Corfu. See Allain, *Joseph Caillaux, Le Défi Victorieux* 81.

From the moment I discovered that the letters which I stipulated should be burnt had not been burnt, considerations of personal respect no longer permitted me to stay with you : unless one believes in supernatural intervention, it is obvious the letter published by *Le Figaro* came from somewhere. Do you wonder at my wife's anxiety, and my own, lest the other two letters should follow? . . . I was told the three letters were shown and offered at the same time. You have given your explanation, but let me tell you, *Madame*, neither Monsieur Vervoort nor Monsieur Desclaux could have invented the detail that the letters they were shown were written under the letter headings of the Prime Minister's official notepaper.

Of one thing I am sure – the three letters were offered together. I am not accusing anybody . . . It was not for me to investigate, neither had I the means to do so. Naturally I believed the others would follow. That is the whole story.

I should like to stop there. I have known happiness in this life, sometimes rising to the heights – but they are so close to the depths. Since November 1911 – I regret having to say this before Madame Gueydan – I have been happy in my private life with a woman of the same mentality as myself, of the same social background, and with whom . . . I don't know why – does one ever know? Both by nature and by character we belong to each other. That is all.

The third character in the drama, the accused, remained silent. While her enemy was speaking, Madame Caillaux kept her eyes fixed on her, only turning away when her glance met that of her rival. More tired, more pale than ever, she nevertheless stood up for a moment. What did she wish to say? . . . her husband replied for her, and the emotion which this *bourgeoise*, the 'lady', had so fiercely controlled, suddenly burst out in tears and sobs. It was the most simple, the most human, the most despairing grief, the grief into which, as the poet says, the worst bitterness enters, the memory of yesterday's happiness.

*Le Matin,* 24th July 1914

CAILLAUX : With you, *Madame*, it was not the same. For long years we lived together : is this the time to throw in each other's faces what we did not wish to say at the time of the divorce? Is this the time to stir up again all the miseries and sorrows of existence? Do you not, all who hear me, feel that if we search a little into our lives, we are like the Spartan with the fox gnawing at his vitals? After the words I have spoken as moderately as possible, after the noble gesture you have made, after the explanation I have given to the gentlemen of the jury in all good faith, showing how these letters weighed upon our spirits – the essential question for the trial – do you really wish me to say more?

BERTHE : Yes, *Monsieur*, I do! (*Caillaux remained silent.*)

ALBANEL : Madame Gueydan, have you something to say?

BERTHE : I do not reply to Monsieur Caillaux's insults – I forgive him.

CAILLAUX : And I forgive you for what you have just said, and I salute you.

Like an antique chorus, the audience reacted in sympathy with the speakers. Though they were partly hostile to Madame Gueydan they gave her a round of applause as she returned to her seat; and the sorrowful, moving confession of the former minister deeply stirred many who did not think of themselves as his friends. Monsieur Caillaux had not inappropriately recalled Terence's verse, 'I am a man, and acquainted with everything that is human.'

*Le Matin*, 24th July 1914

Finally Monsieur Vervoort, whom Berthe had contradicted, asked to be heard again. He submitted a letter-card upon which it was written that she wanted to see him about papers which could be used against Caillaux, and was asking for his address. She protested that it was a forgery; but it had a post mark with the relevant date which both counsel admitted to be genuine: he thus refuted her statement that he had approached her about Caillaux's letters, and established that she had indeed approached him in order to get them published in *Gil Blas*, as he had originally testified.

I cannot imagine scenes more pulsing, more vibrant with human passion than those which were played today during the trial of Madame Caillaux for the murder of Monsieur Gaston Calmette, the editor of *Le Figaro*.

No novelist or dramatist would have dared to conceive such a situation as that into which the principal players in the great human tragedy were thrust today without having to meet the sneer of being melodramatic.

Yet it was not melodramatic. It was life; real, naked life stripped of all its illusions and shams. All the hidden truths were laid bare.

There was a man once Prime Minister, once Finance Minister, and even now the most powerful politician in France ... and here out of the past rose all the intimate life, the private secret things of the man himself. His love affairs and tendernesses, and his passions and intrigues with women were pitilessly exposed before the world in which all these things had happened.

The *Daily Express*, 24th July 1914

Outside in the streets the headlines were announcing the news which staggered Europe – that Austria–Hungary had delivered an ultimatum to Serbia couched in terms impossible for her to accept and still retain her national existence.

CHAPTER SIX

# The Stolen Letters

At the beginning of the session on the following day, Labori reminded the President that Berthe had given him the letters to do with as he pleased. There were eight of them. Two, or three, written by Caillaux, were the so-called 'intimate letters': they had been the subject of so much controversy, he said, of debate and misleading statements, that he felt the only course now was to read them aloud in court. This was necessary so that the motives of Madame Caillaux's action could be discussed. The remaining five were Madame Caillaux's letters to her lover. These he had decided not to read as they had little bearing on the case. To read them in court would be to read them to the public also, and he did not wish to offend the modesty of the writer by doing so. It was unnecessary, and it could have no purpose except to satisfy the unhealthy curiosity of the public.

He wished now to ask Madame Gueydan if she still wished to entrust the letters to him. She gave a sweet smile, in which the earlier melancholy had long given way to triumphant malice, and replied with childlike innocence, 'Oh, I think all the letters should be read.' 'In that case,' Labori said, 'If they were not given to me to do with as I pleased, I decline the gift.' (*He gave them to the usher to take to* Berthe.)

BERTHE : Maître Labori, I should like to oblige you, but I consider that by dividing the letters into two categories you obscure the issue . . . The two letters you wish to read are replies and cannot be understood without the letters which provoked them. I have been covered with calumny . . . In the interests of truth and clarity . . .

Berthe refused to accept the letters. Labori explained again why he wished to read only three. She replied, 'I say all of them, or none !' 'In that case,' he said, 'I shall read none of them.' Chenu intervened to claim the letters, and there was a heated argument, during which the

121

President suspended the session to give them an opportunity to compose their differences. One of the assessory judges, Councillor Dagourie, considering he had done so to help Labori, said, '*Monsieur,* you dishonour us!' *

The suspension of the hearing had the desired effect. It was agreed that Labori should read out only two of the letters, but the rest would be at the disposal of the jury and the officers of the Court to consult if they wished to.

Aware the public were expecting salacious titbits and would be disappointed and ask, 'Is it possible she shot Calmette to prevent these being published?' Labori took care to remind his audience that the basic reason for her anxiety and distress was that her daughter would learn from them her mother was an adulteress:

LABORI : At one time Madame Caillaux feared their publication, and therefore you should hear them. Now she wishes them to be read out, although it will be painful for her; but what is pain of that kind compared to what she has already had to suffer? What will her daughter learn now? Nothing, alas! So the perils of yesterday, and the tortures and anxieties of yesterday, are not those of today.

He took up the letter addressed from the Préfecture of the Sarthe at Le Mans, and dated 19th September 1909:

My Dear Little Riri, – I have read with the attention it merited the letter you sent me which requires a definite answer.
    My dear one, when we met I felt a wave of sympathy surge through the whole of my being. Had I found happiness in my home I should no doubt have resisted it and mastered my feelings for you, but I had not found happiness . . .

Labori's warm and expressive voice held the attention of the audience all through this letter, sixteen pages long, in which Caillaux attempted to describe his embarrassing situation between the two women, and the danger of a scandal which would ruin his career. He reminded her that when their liaison was discovered he had felt it his duty to give her in a letter her entire freedom because he was not sure he would be able to recover his own, but she had gone ahead with her divorce, asking of him only one thing – to love her: He had assured her he

---

* It was rumoured, and afterwards confirmed, that the President had sent his seconds to Dagourie to demand satisfaction for this remark, the Lord Privy Seal intervened, Dagourie apologised, and the incident was closed.

would continue to love her, and that one day he too would be free, but not now : there was an election due in May or June, and the publicity of the divorce proceedings might lose him the support of the Catholic electors of the Sarthe. He described the clash of temperaments between Berthe and himself, and said he was sure the marriage wouldn't have continued, even if he hadn't met Henriette :

> We have everything to fear from the fury of a woman who feels her position is lost and who has not yet had time to get used to the idea . . . What is painful for me, and will be painful for us both, is that for long months we will have to take infinite precautions . . . Life is not easy to manage when one has so many things to consider, and one thing above all, to protect the reputation of the woman I adore. Because you understand, don't you, my dear love, that I love you above everything, beyond everything, that I feel my happiness lies with you, that I wait, that I hope, that I live only in the hope of realising it . . .

It was a rambling repetitive letter with little in it to interest the public. Labori went on to the next one, which had actually been written a day earlier, from Mamers :

> My Riri, dearly loved, – At last I have a moment to write to you . . . On Wednesday morning I intended to go to the funeral . . . but after speaking with Th\* . . . I realised there might be serious consequences, so I gave up the idea . . .
> I slept at the *préfecture* and spent the whole of yesterday and today at the agricultural show to see the 'baests' (I write it as it is pronounced here), allocating tasks to the adjudicators, etc.
> Ouf, here I am back at Mamers this evening whence I shall go tomorrow morning to tasks almost equally interesting . . . so it is not until Tuesday evening the 28th I can spend a day in Paris.
> That is my timetable, my little sweetheart. If I listened only to my heart I should tell my Riri to stop at Mamers or at Mans on Wednesday or Thursday, but we must, alas, be very sensible . . .

There followed a long paragraph in which he attempted to describe the complicated situation with Berthe, then,

> My poor Riri, I see ahead of us many worries and difficulties . . . Sometimes I feel very discouraged, and I am very tired. I sleep little these days. I have hardly had two nights in which I was fairly well rested. What a life I lead ! One consolation, one relief, to think of my little one, to see her in my arms as she was at Ouchy (God ! those

---

\* His lawyer, Thorel.

delicious moments !) and to think of happier days . . . Pity me, my love. Say to yourself or, rather, repeat what you know so well : that I adore you, and that I am yours.

A thousand million kisses all over your adored little body . . .

While Maître Labori was reading the first letter, Henriette bent down and almost disappeared from sight behind the rail,

. . .she wept, her sobs sometimes drowning the voice of her counsel. Then he began to read the second letter. She was still bent almost double, and still she sobbed. Suddenly she was quiet. One of Monsieur Albanel's assessors became anxious and leaned towards her. From his place up at the President's table, he had the best view.

Maître Labori went on reading. The guards round Madame Caillaux rushed towards her. She had fainted.

In the audience, everyone stood up. Monsieur Caillaux, who was sitting in the well of the court, thrust everybody aside, left the court-room and entered the dock. When he reached his wife, the guards had already lifted her up. They carried her outside where doctors hastened to administer first aid.

Maître Labori became aware at last of what had happened. He stood at the bar of the court, pale and deeply moved. He asked for an intermission.

*Le Temps*, 26th July 1914

The rest of the day was taken up in hearing the evidence of the doctors who had attended Calmette, and of other doctors who were extremely critical of the way the case had been handled : they maintained that instead of operating at once, five hours had been wasted in indecision : the patient had not even been given a blood transfusion, nor had he been thoroughly examined, with the result that one wound had not been noticed and it had caused him to bleed to death internally. Dr Doyen, an eminent authority, in the course of his evidence, put on an overcoat similar to Calmette's, upon which he had marked the bullet holes, to demonstrate that the wounds need not have been fatal. It seemed that an unkind fate had left Calmette in the wrong hands, and that he should not have died. Also, he had instinctively crouched down : otherwise he would have been wounded only in the legs.

So far the legal honours rest with Maître Chenu, for in addition to being the goad and prod of the courtroom he has proved to be its most formidable voice as well. His artless way of placing Labori's back to the wall on the question of reading the love letters has also shown his to be the more crafty mind.

*The New York Times*, 26th July 1914

During that evening, and for the whole night until five o'clock in the morning, Labori argued with Caillaux, telling him that if he wanted to save Henriette he must submit the vital evidence that Calmette had been in the pay of the Austro-Hungarian Government. The news of the European Crisis was growing more serious from day to day, from hour to hour, and Caillaux had withheld the most important document supplied to him by Count Károlyi because he was afraid the irrefutable evidence that one of the leading French newspapers was in the pay of a potential enemy would have a harmful effect on the morale of the army, and of the whole country: but for months *Le Figaro* had been accusing him of treachery, and the issue of the trial might very well turn on establishing which of them was the traitor, Caillaux or Calmette.

In the morning of Monday, 27th July, amid the bustle and confusion before the entry of the Court, it was noticed Caillaux was not in his usual place, and the crowds waiting on the steps to demonstrate against him, or in his favour, were disappointed. It was learned he had gone to the Conciergerie and walked with Henriette and her guards along the underground ways to the courtroom: there was a rumour, which was probably true, that he was arranging to rescue her if her case became desperate, by substituting someone else, dressed in similar clothes. When he reached his place among the witnesses, observers thought he looked exhausted, *énervé*, played out. This was the last session in which he could act effectively: next day there would be the speeches by the Public Prosecutor and the various counsel, and then the verdict.

There was more medical evidence, and a eulogy of Calmette by Barthou, who denied he had ever told Caillaux that Berthe had shown him the letters: he complained that the President was not accusing Henriette with sufficient severity. The President referred him to the Act of Accusation.

Monsieur Henri Bernstein, talented and sensitive *avant-garde* dramatist, a gaunt stooping figure with pronounced Jewish features, came to the bar of the court to pay tribute, he said, to his dear and admirable friend, Gaston Calmette, and to protest against Madame Estradère's testimony which he considered to be the point of departure for the campaign to sully Calmette's memory. He thought it was not conceivable that Calmette would have been willing to pay 30,000 francs for the opportunity to converse with Madame Gueydan: it would not have been necessary because both of them, and Henri Bernstein himself, frequented the same *salons*. He could also have met her, had he so desired, through Monsieur Barthou and other politicians. He gave his impressions of Berthe as follows :

BERNSTEIN : During two or three walks on which I had the honour of her company, she told me with infinite dignity the story of her troubles and of her divorce. Be it far from me, gentlemen, to take sides in a matter which I know about only from the words of this unhappy and embittered woman, but I must confess that as an author and an artist I was profoundly moved by the recital of her suffering. With touching simplicity, and with true pathos, she retraced the whole story for me, depicting her helplessness before her all-powerful husband, how she had been deserted, her loneliness, her terror . . . She confided in me that she distrusted the impartiality of the magistrates . . .

Here, the Public Prosecutor protested. Bernstein hastened to reassure him :

BERNSTEIN : It is the story of this woman I am reporting. Far from me be the thought that the magistrates would make the very smallest difference between a minister, or a former minister, and the most humble citizen. (*Laughter.*) I have a most decided opinion about that. I'm sure that in a Court of Justice – to adopt the language I have been hearing for the past two days – a minister, or a former minister, is treated as a simple citizen, such as I am; and if I had had any doubts on that score, the present proceedings would have enlightened me. (*Murmurs in the audience.*)
PROSECUTOR : That is absolutely correct. You are not mistaken.
BERNSTEIN : I think I was at that moment suggesting the difficulties Madame Gueydan might encounter, and I repeat, from the point of view of an artist – the simple point of view of an artist – I found the sombre picture very beautiful. This human being appeared very beautiful to me in her appeal, her smallness, her helplessness, before a wall of hatred and silence.

He said he had told Calmette that as a result of his conversation with Berthe, and her unhappiness, he had found the subject for a new play in which a feeble human being sees descending upon her like rolling waves all the social forces which in the end throw her down and submerge her :

BERNSTEIN: Calmette said, 'You haven't the right to touch that subject. You might wound two women deeply.' I exclaimed that I had always found in real life the source both of the dramatic action and the characters which I presented in the theatre. Without listening to me, and with the gentle insistence his friends so well remember he continued to repeat, 'You would distress two women.' I resolved never to discuss my literary work again with this friend who was really too benevolent: I did not suspect that the day was coming when I should remember his words with a great deal of respect and, I assure you, with profound emotion.

He said he was an independent author; he shared neither Calmette's interests nor ideas, but their friendship was founded on absolute sincerity. On many issues he disagreed with Calmette, whose greatest charm was his love of free discussion: he had told him he didn't like his article on the Prieu Affair, believing that articles of that sort should be fully documented and supported by facts, and he had told him that many of the ideas defended by Caillaux were his ideas also. He said Calmette was the soul of honour and a man of exquisite sensibility: he had delayed the publication of the *Ton Jo* letter by two months because he had not been able to obtain Berthe's consent to its publication: it was unthinkable, therefore, that he would have published the other private letters: he was incapable of violating the intimacy of the sentimental correspondence between a couple as united as Monsieur and Madame Caillaux.

He protested that these proceedings were not the trial of a woman who had killed: Caillaux was conducting before their eyes by a process of defamation, the trial of a dead man, Gaston Calmette, whose body had been pierced by Madame Caillaux's bullets.

The next witness was Dr Albert Calmette. Testifying under oath, he said his brother had told him that although he couldn't produce evidence for some of his allegations in the press campaign against Caillaux, everything published under his signature was true. He said also that apart from the Fabre Report and *Les Verts*, he had no further documents he could publish. Dr Calmette added:

With my other brother I am the executor of the late Gaston Calmette's estate: he cannot defend himself here. It is my duty to his children to announce publicly that his fortune was not acquired under suspicious circumstances. My brother worked all his life. He did not, perhaps, enrich himself progressively by his work because in his profession one scarcely becomes rich, but he had the good fortune to form faithful friendships, touching, grateful friendships, and it is through these friendships his fortune was made.

Everyone in France knows it was as the result of the death of Monsieur Chauchard that my brother's fortune was made : it was not made in any other way. There was nothing to be ashamed of, I can proclaim it here, and his children need not be ashamed.

Caillaux asked to be heard again. He said he had a statement to make of some importance . . .

He began by protesting against the campaign *Le Figaro* was still carrying on to prejudice the case against the accused. Then,

I am a little tired of seeing that no credit is given to me for the moderation we have shown in our statements. I shall not repeat what I have already said about the connections of *Le Figaro* with certain foreign powers, I merely remark to the jury that I shall supply any information they may require, and I deposit these authentic documents, signed by Monsieur Calmette and Monsieur Glaser, which shows most clearly the conditions under which *Le Figaro* has to work with the Hungarian Government – and today every Frenchman can see what the significance of this work may be.

Here are the documents. Let me add they were supplied to me by Count Károlyi, leader of the Independence Party, that is to say, of the Radicals, in Hungary. (*He passed the documents up to the bench.*)

Albanel studied them for a while, and then flushed deep red. He said in a hoarse voice :

It is a contract between the Chief Editor of *Le Figaro* and the Imperial-Royal Government of Austria-Hungary . . . In it Calmette has pledged himself to write for their press office, of the Austro-Hungarian Government, articles which will serve the interests of the Viennese Government.

This produced an extraordinary demonstration, directed this time against Calmette. There were cries of 'Traitor !' 'A bullet was too good for him !' and shouts of anger.

Caillaux followed up his advantage :

CAILLAUX : But what I wish to show you today, in view of the continued attacks by the same journal directed against me to prejudice the case against the accused, is how the late Director of *Le Figaro* acquired in a few years the considerable fortune he has bequeathed to his children. I shall read, with the President's permission, Calmette's will . . .

ALBANEL : How did you get it?

CAILLAUX : The same way that Calmette got the *Ton Jo* letter.

CHENU : Is there really any purpose in reading all that?

CAILLAUX : I shall read only the part which concerns Calmette's fortune, no other detail : 'The greater part of the fortune I leave . . .'

ALBANEL : Before you read the document, don't you think I should consider it first and then, eventually, you can read it . . .

CAILLAUX : *Monsieur le Président*, I bow very respectfully to what you say, but allow me to point out that silence has been observed about this document, as if intentionally . . . I consider it necessary for the defence . . . I ask that it be read to the jury. Whether you do, or I do, is immaterial.

There were murmurs of disapproval from the audience. Maître Chenu complained of the length of the proceedings and said that Caillaux, by continuing his deposition, was taking them back to the beginning.

CAILLAUX : Will you permit me to reply to you, *Monsieur le bâtonnier?*

CHENU : Certainly, *Monsieur*.

CAILLAUX : *Monsieur?*

CHENU : How would you like me to address you? Ah! *Monsieur le Ministre?* Certainly, *Monsieur le Ministre*.

CAILLAUX : I see, *Monsieur le bâtonnier*, you now conform to the customary usage that I myself observe towards you. I am glad to have taught you something.

CHENU : It is to be feared I shall not remember the lesson.

CAILLAUX : I am aware, *Monsieur le bâtonnier*, that you and I have been on opposite sides of the barricade. I know you represented *La Patrie Française*, and in those days you represented Syveton.* I am in the other camp, and shall be always. But I believe none the less

---

* Gabriel Syveton was the Treasurer and one of the most aggressive members of the *Ligue de la Patrie Française* which was formed to prevent Zola and his associates having the Dreyfus Case re-opened. It became so powerful that it secured a majority of the seats on the Paris Municipal Council.

that we can, and must, always observe the courtesies between us, just as we have now.

CHENU : Certainly, *Monsieur le Ministre.*

CAILLAUX : *Monsieur le bâtonnier,* I am glad we agree.

ALBANEL : Kindly continue, Monsieur Caillaux.

CAILLAUX : *Monsieur le Président,* I think it important to indicate why this reading appears to me indispensable. I mentioned in my deposition that Monsieur Calmette left the considerable fortune of thirteen millions . . . Since then certain newspapers have asserted that his fortune consisted solely of gifts from Monsieur Chauchard but, I'll give you a résumé of his will in a few words : eight million were given to him by Madame Maria Bursin, two million he inherited from Monsieur Chauchard – and three million he acquired in a few years. In our *bourgeoise* families it would take twenty years to amass such a fortune.

PRESTAT : All that is incorrect.

CAILLAUX : Is the *partie civile* afraid of my statement?

PRESTAT : We are afraid of nothing after Dr Albert Calmette's statement.

CAILLAUX : I take the responsibility for everything I say – but I think I cannot avoid reading it :

> The greater part of the fortune I leave I had as a personal inheritance which I received on the death of Monsieur Chauchard, and secondly from a personal gift (by a deed deposited with Maître Jousselin, notary) from Madame Boursin (rue de Lisbon, 32) in token of the devotion I showed to Monsieur Chauchard. Together we closed his eyes after his death.
> This personal fortune consists of . . .

PRESTAT : It is in the will?

CAILLAUX : That is what I am telling you.

He read out the list of his investments, the interest he had had to pay to Madame Boursin; and he added that the tax had been evaded. He asked how it had come about that Madame Boursin had parted with eight million francs to Calmette. He said that during the press campaign he had been offered documents very discreditable to Calmette which explained it, but he refused to use them. Now, after 16th March, the same dossier had been sent to a friend, his best friend, Ceccaldi . . .

CAILLAUX : To those who are surprised, I should explain that, very happily for me in the circumstances in which I find myself, I have the support of many people who are unknown to me throughout this democracy. (*Stir in the audience.*) Yes, gentlemen, yes . . . (*Protests.*) Oh, please – I am accustomed to facing more violent storms than this. (*Protests continue.*)

ALBANEL : No more noise, if you please.

CAILLAUX : I have nearly finished, but there are certain things I intend to say, and which no one will prevent me from saying . . .

CHENU : Except the President.

ALBANEL : But I can't know what he is going to say.

LABORI : Besides it is not so. *Monsieur le Président* cannot prevent you from saying what you have to say.

CAILLAUX : That dossier reached my friend Ceccaldi who referred to it in his deposition. The *partie civile* asked for no particulars : perhaps now their curiosity is greater. If not, I take note of it, and I confine myself to saying that it is really ingenuous to oppose to this only the testimony of general morality by Monsieur Bernstein in whose past there are certain circumstances . . . (*Protests.*) *

CHENU : Monsieur Bernstein is not here.

CAILLAUX : I regret it.

CHENU : It is probable that he too will regret it.

LABORI : It is his duty to be here. He has not been excused, and one is not justified in blaming Monsieur Caillaux because he is not here.

CHENU : You should be lenient towards those who are not punctual in their attendance . . .

This provoked an indignant retort from Labori, whereupon Maître Chenu withdrew his remark.

CAILLAUX : I suppose that applies to the remarks which concern me?

CHENU : I have nothing to withdraw, because I have said nothing.

CAILLAUX : You indicated I was wrong to say what I did?

CHENU : Not at all.

CAILLAUX : Then I was mistaken. I simply want to say in conclusion that when it is known to everyone that a man has not fulfilled his duty to his country, it is unbecoming for him to hand out certificates of morality.

Chenu asked if any of the remarks he had just made could explain, excuse or extenuate the crime of which his wife was guilty. Caillaux

---

* Monsieur Bernstein had deserted from the army.

replied, 'There is something worse than losing one's life, and that is to live it while attacking women and enriching oneself at their expense.' (*Applause and protests.*)

The picture of the scene would not be complete if one left out, beside the chivalrous face of Maître Labori, that of Maître Chenu, incomparable courtroom tactician, subtle psychologist skilled in playing with human passions, orator whose voice, rasping, warm, richly nuanced, injecting always at the precise moment the word that flashes like lightning or that pierces like a sword. And what authority in his most simple gesture, what crushing force in his contempt!

*Le Matin*, 24th July 1914

After the intermission, Monsieur Henri Bernstein was again in court. He asked to be heard. On receiving permission, he began :

BERNSTEIN : I have been brought here by a telephone call from a friend . . . Are you there, Caillaux? (*Murmurs from the audience.*) I insult no man in his absence . . . (*Applause.*)

CAILLAUX (*Holding up his hand*) : I am here !

BERNSTEIN : When I deposed, that man said nothing. Now he has spoken.

ALBANEL : Turn towards the jury. That is what you must do first. Then speak only on one particular subject – the deposition that was made in your absence.

BERNSTEIN : I was taking a precaution that I thought consistent with my honour. I thought you would be the last to blame me for it.

ALBANEL : Go on with your deposition.

BERNSTEIN : I am here once more because I was defamed by Caillaux. The man is so insensible he cannot understand that I should come here to express my grief, my immense grief, for the death of a man who was my friend and tenderly loved. The other day I swore to make my deposition without hatred. I assure you I did so, and for that I claim some merit. The spectacle before us here is quite inconceivable — we see a man climbing onto the coffin of his wife's victim to speak more loudly. (*Applause.*)

ALBANEL : That is literature. (*Protests from various parts of the courtroom.*) Confine your remarks to the actual subject.

BERNSTEIN : Let me speak. I speak to defend my honour. You have spoken of yours, *Monsieur le Président*. I too have my honour.

ALBANEL : Stick to the facts.

BERNSTEIN : It is on a precise fact that I depose. I am explaining the reasons for my testimony. I am saying what we, the friends of Calmette, have seen. We have seen the Treasury and the Registry commit this felony without example – the disclosure of a will. Perhaps, gentlemen of the jury, one of you has made a will? Then don't let yourself be assassinated by a minister because next day it will be read out in court. That is what I have to say . . . (*Applause.*)

There is a voice here more authoritative than mine which has cleansed Calmette from all these shameful attacks; that of a man whose generosity and sincerity I have admired for fourteen years; that of Monsieur le Bâtonnier Labori, who said that if Calmette had been here he would have asked for the accused to be acquitted. That I am sure is the most beautiful elegy that could have been spoken. But Calmette is not here. He has been assassinated. He has four bullets in his body.

Now a few words about myself. Caillaux has said I have not the right to come here and make my deposition because I have not observed the military laws of my country. That is one more lie. (*Applause.*) I once committed a folly in my youth for which I publicly expressed my regret, not only because of the odious persecution I suffered at that time, but because my regret was long-standing, sincere and profound. I passionately love my country. In 1911, at the time of the Agadir Crisis, a diplomatic crisis almost as serious as that of today, I asked to be accepted again into the army. I had the honour of having my sentence set aside. During my first term I was in the auxiliary non-combatant service, but in spite of my deplorable state of health I applied for a transfer. Now I am an artilleryman. I leave for the front on the fourth day of the mobolisation, which may be tomorrow. When does Caillaux leave? But I must warn him that in a war one cannot be replaced by a woman. You must do your own shooting! (*Enthusiastic acclamations, cries of 'Bravo Bernstein! Bravo Bernstein!' and prolonged applause.*)

. . . in spite of interpolations of the President and the Public Prosecutor, Monsieur Henri Bernstein, encouraged by the approbation of the audience, continued his protest with extreme violence. There was a storm of acclamation followed by extreme disorder. Everyone stood up, shouting discordantly. The magistrates rose to their feet, hesitated, then withdrew in great disorder.

The court was cleared amidst indescribable tumult. Monsieur Bernstein passed Monsieur Caillaux without turning away his head. Their eyes met. Monsieur Bernstein went out accompanied by the acclamations of the public who were thrust out of the courtroom shouting and singing to the refrain of the *Lampions.*

Those outside pressed forward, asking what had occurred, then, at last, Monsieur Bernstein appeared, bare-headed, pale, dominating the crowd with his tall, rather stooping figure. He was surrounded. Hands were stretched out which he shook. Lawyers, journalists, witnesses, even the guards, questioned and congratulated him. Meanwhile the hearing, which had not been suspended, continued.

A few minutes later, Monsieur Bernstein, accompanied by some friends, escaped from the demonstration of sympathy which had been given to him, and left the *Palais* at about half past four.

*Le Temps,* 18 July 1914

ALBANEL : Now are you going to keep quiet? Yes, or no? (*Silence.*) We'll hear the next witness.

LABORI : Oh, pardon, *Monsieur le Président.* To terminate an incident it is not enough to suspend the hearing. Monsieur Caillaux asks to reply in a few words to what has just been said.

CAILLAUX : I have only a word to say, *Monsieur le Président,* and I shall say it with as much restraint as the previous witness has shown little.

I wish to say only this. A short while ago, in the fullness of my right, I stated a fact and formulated an opinion. The fact I stated, which is not contested and cannot be, is that Monsieur Bernstein during his military service as a medical orderly, took himself off to Belgium and did not return until he could do so under the protection of the general amnesty. Youthful fault, he has said, fault which can be atoned for : but the point I made, and of which I remind all good Frenchmen and good citizens who are here, is that when one has committed so grave a fault one is not in a position to hand out certificates of morality.

Thus Caillaux remained in possession of the field and, in spite of Henri Bernstein's dramatic intervention, it was apparent to all that Calmette was a traitor and also that he had had a strong personal motive to ruin the statesman who, slowly but inexorably, was forcing the Senate to accept the Income Tax Bill which had been passed by the Chamber of Deputies in 1906.

The last important witness was Colonel Aubry, Commandant of the 21st Regiment of Artillery. He explained at some length the difficulty of handling the small Browning automatic pistol. For a nervous or inexperienced person it was almost impossible to fire a single round because the recoil immediately fires the next; or to fire two rounds in the same direct line because the concussion and the reflex action of the palm of the hand automatically raise the barrel unless one expects this and can compensate for it.

Asked if in his opinion Henriette intended to kill Calmette, he answered that most certainly she did not intend to kill him : her first shot showed her intention, and that went into the floor. The pistol automatically did the rest as she was too inexperienced and probably too nervous to control it.

The Caillaux drama shows the whole corrupt world of French politics, finance and journalism in section, as it were, and the unhappy un-balanced woman who was this week tried for the murder of Monsieur Calmette seems only one item in it.

It is still denied by *Le Figaro* that the late Monsieur Calmette held, or sought, or proposed to publish other private letters from Monsieur Caillaux to his wife. The publication of one was a journalistic outrage, which the lowest rag in this country would hesitate to commit, and there seems to be a considerable weight of evidence to show that *Le Figaro* tried to procure other personal letters.

In his vehement evidence, which was rather a counter-attack than a defence of his wife, Monsieur Caillaux, by way of retort to *Le Figaro*'s censures on his patriotism, made some startling allegations about Monsieur Calmette's relations with foreign financial groups . . .

It goes to show that given the present ethics of French journalism and the present state of the French law of libel, there was provocation for a desperate act. A man may call out a traducer or blackmailer. A woman stands outside that code of 'honour'.

The Nation, 25th July 1914

# CHAPTER SEVEN

# Encore

At the opening of the session a crowd, more dense and closely packed than ever, invaded the courtroom which was already three-quarters full. There were no longer any reserved or officially allocated places. Altercations started everywhere – those seated complained loudly of those standing who prevented them from seeing and hearing. The guards cleared a way to the well of the court. A barrister, unable to sit down or to stand up, remained kneeling through most of the day.

The heat was stifling. There were cries from women whose dresses were being crushed. Bottles were passed round. A man, perched high up, took off his false collar and opened his shirt.

*Le Matin*, 19th July 1914

The Commandant of the Law Courts had given new instructions to the attendants to prevent the courtroom from becoming excessively overcrowded. They took these instructions literally. At half past eleven it was announced the courtroom was closed. The great bronze doors were shut. Journalists unable to obtain admittance protested angrily : the Commandant was sent for, and he allowed them to go in. There was a great tumult in the Lemoignon Gallery where law students in great numbers besieged the advocates' entrance. It was the same at the magistrates' entrance : even the Public Prosecutor had difficulty in getting in. At five past twelve Monsieur Caillaux arrived and was conducted straight to his seat : there was nothing he could do now except to let Henriette know he would be there through the long agonising day while her fate was being decided.

The first counsel to address the jury was Maître Seligman for the *partie civile*. He said :

SELIGMAN : I have taken part, silently and sadly, in the doleful debate which you have followed with such exemplary attention. Those who loved Gaston Calmette have passed painful hours here. We have heard the letter read in which, two hours before the crime,

136

Madame Caillaux announced her intention to commit the act, that is, to kill. We have seen the formidable weapon, coldly purchased, minutely tested, carefully dissimulated in a muff during the hour she waited. The pistol was fired at Gaston Calmette six times at point blank range, almost touching. You have had before your eyes the four bullets which caused the four wounds which in a few hours caused his death. A grandfather beside me brings you the complaint of a young man, seventeen years old, and of a little boy of ten, the two sons of the assassinated father.

He described the Calmette family as traditionally dedicated to the service of their country, and how *Le Figaro* under the leadership of Gaston Calmette had become an institution and a centre of Parisian life. He was adored by all who approached him. He described the horror and indignation aroused by his death :

Paris gave him a magnificent funeral : ten thousand people filed past his coffin, manifesting an indignation which anticipates the judgement you are going to pass. In this unanimous concert of respect, affection and sympathy, there was one discordant note : that of Monsieur Caillaux. For long hours you have heard from him that *Le Figaro* is a venal journal, that it has several times treated with Germany, and that Gaston Calmette was a small reporter who had made a fortune out of journalism . . . Monsieur Prestat has replied with nobility to what concerns *Le Figaro*. His lawyers begged him not to reply to what concerns Calmette : they were not able to accept that there should be a dispute before the jury between the grandfather of the orphans and the husband of the murderess.

He asserted that the capital of the financial group which had given Calmette editorial control of *Le Figaro* was entirely French and (ignoring the evidence to the contrary) that the Bank of Dresden had had nothing to do with it. He asserted that the 30,000 francs a year mentioned in the contract signed by Calmette was to advertise Hungarian *Kursaals*, hotels and bottles of mineral water (although it had been proved there was a separate contract for this purpose, and that the contract for 30,000 francs a year was for undertaking to write articles favourable to the Austro-Hungarian Government). He insinuated that Caillaux's relations with the Hungarian Lipscher, who had given Károlyi the documents, made him also suspect.

Thus he defended *Le Figaro* and the discredited Calmette, blandly ignoring the proofs of his traitorous dealings with the Austro-Hungarian Government, the multiple lies of his press campaign and his dishonourable behaviour in publishing a private letter. Seligman concluded :

> Calmette's friends all know, and are ready to affirm, that until his heart ceased to beat at half past midnight in the hospital no thought had ever entered it that was not noble and loyal.

Maître Chenu began his speech for the *partie civile* by saying he would surprise the Court and the jury by speaking of the assassination of Gaston Calmette, and would even promise to speak of nothing else.

He asked the accused who, he said, had spoken so movingly of her daughter, if at the moment when, with a sure and steady aim she shot down the man she had been promising herself all day that she would kill, did she ask herself if that man had children. She knows now he had two sons whom he adored, whose image was always close to his heart and whose photographs he carried in his briefcase. It was in their name he came to demand justice for a crime which, as soon as it was known, rocked Paris and France with a surge of indignant emotion.

He associated himself with everything Maître Seligman had said in praise of Calmette, and added that when one could invoke the testimony of people who were the honour and ornament of their country, bearing witness to Calmette's patriotism, delicacy and loyalty, he could ignore the attacks of a man who could read a will to the applause of his over-zealous friends, over the tomb opened by his wife.

He depicted Henriette as a woman whose head ruled her heart, a woman in complete control of herself, reasoning, discussing, quibbling, defending her position tenaciously, but capable of tenderness – towards herself – when she spoke of her triumphant past and present humiliation and when she spoke of her old father 'imbued with the principles of the *bourgeoisie*.' Here Chenu, protesting that he was not the sort of man who would reply to the reading of a will by the reading of a birth certificate, read out Henriette's birth certificate which showed that her parents married six months after she was born. (*Sensation in the audience.*)

CHENU : Monsieur Caillaux has exceptional qualities of mind, a prodigious memory but with inexplicable gaps and lapses. A high intelligence, with an even higher opinion of his intelligence, ambition without limit or restraint with a curious impatience of obstacles to his ambition; making laws as a legislator, applying them as a minister, but unable to submit to the laws as a citizen . . . Intent upon breaking those who resist him, forcing them to give way, and sweeping from his path those who embarrass or hinder him – in short, one of those men whose power is the result of his own audacity and of the fear he inspires.

And so it happened that Monsieur Caillaux, and the wife so closely associated with his fortunes and, like him, casting envious glances at the highest rungs of the ladder they intended to climb, were most disconcerted and most irritated by what happened in the early months of this year : someone had dared to discuss Monsieur Caillaux and his politics !

He proceeded to justify Calmette's campaign on the grounds that freedom of discussion and the freedom of the press were of the essence of the democracy of their country.

He reminded the jury that both Monsieur and Madame Caillaux had testified that they had found complete happiness in their marriage, and he described it as 'a mutual happiness recalling the sweet innocence of biblical times' :

Be it so. I grant they were happily associated in their sentiments, in their ambition, in their hatred and in their homicidal project openly confessed, and professed, at the bar of this court.

He asserted that when Caillaux went to President Poincaré to ask him to stop Calmette publishing their intimate letters, that was 'pretext, pure pretext'. What they really wanted was to stop the Fabre Report from being published.

Step by step he took Henriette through the whole of the fatal day of 16th March, stressing always her sang-froid, her heartlessness, her visit to the bank, buying the pistol, returning to write a note for her husband 'in beautiful handwriting, calm and tranquil, preparing to commit an assassination between her visits and her afternoon teas . . .' He described the long wait in the *Figaro* offices, a smile on her lips – the death she was bringing was certain, she could afford to wait . . .

He described Calmette's hesitation, then his courteous, 'I cannot refuse to receive a lady', and then the shooting.

Remember, gentlemen, because we have to judge her, we must know her. We shall now try to penetrate into her secret thoughts and motives and discover them . . .

But Henriette had fainted and had to be carried out. The hearing was suspended. When she had recovered, and the hearing was resumed, he said :

Gentlemen of the jury, I simply give you the facts. I don't believe I have any responsibility for these incidents, much as I regret them . . .

Now, the crime has just been accomplished. It is necessary to penetrate into her secret motives and intentions.

The victim lies there bleeding at her feet. He is going to die. Almost in his last agony. He is one metre fifty, or two metres away from her. It may be that her extraordinary presence of mind, the methodical planning, the crime, the sang-froid displayed while committing it – that all this could be the result of nervous tension dominated by her will; but then, it is well known, a reaction should have set in, her body should have stiffened, her chest swelled, her forehead grown moist; there should have been a nervous crisis to which, as we have seen, Madame Caillaux is addicted. But nothing happened. Nothing. All round her there was emotion and consternation, not within her. Within her no chord responded . . .

There was no room for pity in his words. The points dropped from his lips in cold, clear-cut phrases, and each phrase was the knife of a surgeon that cut away all the growth and excrescences of the case and laid bare all the gaping wounds of Gaston Calmette's death.

His voice grew bellicose. No mercy for him. He turned to the bowed figure of the woman in the dock and pitilessly tore down all the fabric of the defence and revealed Madame Caillaux as a blood-stained murderess.

The *Daily Express*, 29th July 1914

He continued in this vein, describing the visible reactions of *La Criminelle*, as he called her, her coldness, her self-possession. The actual motive she gave for the crime was, he said, her fear that the intimate letters would be published :

Then there came to the bar of the court – Madame Gueydan ! I have no intention of recalling to your minds the hour we lived through that day – I believe it is unforgettable for all of you who were present. This woman, coming into the court bowed under the burden of prejudice, alone and, I believe I can say today, splendid in her isolation, searching in vain for a helping hand to be stretched out to her. All drew back. She sought for a starting point for her deposition in a poor little notebook she held in her left hand, and this was denied to her in spite of her and her rights. But then, you remember her slow deposition, hesitant, without order, penetrated by grief; and you know the result. You know how this woman came in, and you know how this women went out drawing after her the sympathy of all generous hearts . . .

And what was the further result? The intimate letters. We have them! So where now is their system of defence? Are they going to try to re-assemble it from the debris?

He challenged Labori to tell him what passage, what phrase, what word, could have been used by the vilest pamphleteer or journalist, from any point of view, in the political battle. There was nothing! Nothing!

Is this what Monsieur Vervoort was invited to publish? Is this what Monsieur Calmette was ready to pay 30,000 francs for? Neither to Monsieur Vervoort nor to Monsieur Calmette were they worth ten *sous.* . . .

Just as Madame Caillaux has lied about her consternation at the time of the crime, she has lied about her motive . . . Once more she has found herself unmasked, and nothing, nothing at all remains of her miserable system of defence she has clung to for so long.

No, no! She did not kill Calmette so that he would not publish her intimate letters which were completely unusable. She killed to avenge herself for what the journalist had already done and for what he was still going to do. He possessed, and he was going to publish in *Le Figaro*, the Fabre Report.

Gentlemen, I believe there are countries where a public figure can regain his position after a fall so low as that which happened to Caillaux in the Chamber of Deputies on 3rd April 1914. I declare, if that country were mine, I should be inconsolable.

In the face of the light that was about to burst forth, they thought they were lost, the audacious minister and his faithful associate. Yes, they truly said there was nothing left to do but smash Calmette's face in.

I understand! Having hoped for everything, dared everything, to have risen so quickly and so high, to be so close to the topmost rank which it was his ambition to reach, to feel the whole edifice shaking, and the more they patched it up the more it cracked and was about to crumble altogether. Oh rage and impotence! There was nothing to be done . . . but one could at least be avenged – but how? They vied with each other in pride and anger, anger and pride! How united they were in their course of action! Kill that man! And as, after all, a woman can shoot as well as a man, and after all runs less risk, she is to be the one to do it. Therefore look no further for motives – they are discovered!

Maître Chenu's speech was listened to . . . with attention but, on the whole, as he proceeded, the very violence of it alienated much of the sympathy it might have aroused. His voice is, at times, a dry, rasping, unpleasant one, and the hearer is disappointed to note that there is too often as much political animosity as love of justice behind the passionate tones in which he indulges. Maître Chenu is too intellectual, too drily combative, to enlist our hearts, and as his speech proceeds it convinces us less and less.

                                    The *Daily Telegraph*, 29th July 1914

He reminded his audience that Caillaux said he had no reason to fear the publication of the Fabre Report because it was without importance . . .

Really! Really! Without importance? That a Prime Minister agrees with his Finance Minister to postpone the trial of a man who has drained away a large part of the savings of the French people, and is known therefore, as the Prince of Crooks, and for this purpose has violated the consciences of two magistrates? Without importance? I have always respected, not, I'm glad to say, the ministers who pass but the magistrates who remain. I am their faithful collaborator; but let me tell you, gentlemen, without emotion, quite calmly, I am compelled to believe it is of importance.

You will recall that Monsieur Caillaux in the witness-box used these words – I don't know if you noticed them, but they made me start, and they made me shudder – and you too, Labori! He faced the Court, his eyes on the eyes of the magistrates, pausing between the words and emphasising them with an imperious finger, 'It was an act of government. I should do it again if necessary.'

Ah! gentlemen, I ask your pardon, but I had at that moment the sensation of a gust of wind from a passing blow not intended for me. Act of Government! Ah, if such doctrines were allowed to pass unchallenged, if they are to become the rule instead of the monstrous exception. Ah! I pronounce it at the top of my voice to all of you who are around me, before all of you who wear this black gown or that red robe, not one of you will deserve to wear the one or the other! Let them bring us the livery of servants and lackeys – though I fear that I, for one, shall never find one which suits me! (*Lively applause and commotion.*)

A VOICE FROM THE AUDIENCE: *Monsieur le Président!* There are people here who insult the barristers! They insult the barristers!

CHENU: Let it pass! The barristers will have their hour of vengeance! Without importance, members of the jury?

He referred to the Commission of Enquiry which had found that the intervention of Clemenceau and Briand, and also that of the Prime Minister Monis and Monsieur Caillaux in the Rochette Case, while it could not be called an act of corruption because both were entirely disinterested and it did not affect the course of justice, constituted a most deplorable abuse of influence. This finding was approved by the Chamber of Deputies by 448 votes to 9. . . . 'Therefore,' Maître Chenu continued, 'there was nothing left for the audacious minister and his faithful associate to do but *'casser la gueule,'* of Monsieur Calmette.

CHENU: Gentlemen of the jury, I have finished. And yet, perhaps, not everything, yes, certainly not everything, has been said . . . I am only the counsel of two poor children whose father has been killed, and whose tears demand justice from you. But in addition to their interests . . . because this crime shakes the foundations upon which rest the honour and the life of the nation, there are other interests which I do not represent, but about which you will be hearing now from the Public Prosecutor in the name of society.

Ah! sir, Public Prosecutor, if you will permit me very respectfully to address myself to you, I shall tell you that, perhaps for the first time in my life, and no doubt the last, I envy you your high functions. You are aware, aren't you, how attached I am to my barrister's robe of light material, but an impenetrable armour which has protected my independence for thirty years, and no doubt will do so till the end? . . . But all the same I should like today to be wearing your red robes and your ermine . . . I should no doubt be unworthy of it, but it seems to me that if I were speaking for the public interest, what force that thought would give me! To feel on this

day, at this moment, that I had all the good people of France behind me, of that France which is so honest, so hard-working, and
which has such reserves of strength that she survives almost intact
the repeated scandals inflicted upon her by her parliamentarians : so
strong, so beautiful, that in spite of them she is at this moment
standing upright, calm, her sword by her side, sure of her children
. . . Ah! of all her children. Seeing without fear the black clouds
gathering on the horizon, but that France which all the same one
must not abuse, and to whom we must demonstrate for once that
we are disposed and ready to heal her from that inner evil which
corrodes her – the ascendancy of politics over justice !

Ah ! never, *Monsieur le Procureur Général*, will you find a better
opportunity to fight this evil. It seems to me I too am filled with
new strength by the idea that I have at this moment by my side the
women of France, those women whom we know and admire, and
love; our daughters, our sisters, our mothers – yours too, gentlemen
of the jury, who have no need to assassinate and to pretend afterwards they wished in that way to prevent revelations, the publication of the letters of their lovers. Ah ! they, rest assured, will not
wish to be confounded with this *criminelle!* They are behind you,
*Monsieur le Procureur Général.*

. . . and you, *Monsieur le bâtonnier* Labori, will you, with your
great and eloquent voice demand impunity for the woman who is
seated behind you? Well, listen once more – and this is all I have to
say. Three months ago, after the elections, a deputy newly elected
addressed his thanks to his electors : he did so with the tranquil
assurance of a man who had indulged in the insensate dream of
taking in hand the government of this honest country, and here is a
phrase taken from these thanks which were displayed on all the
walls of all the town halls of his district : 'More than ever,' he said,
'I shall exert myself to assure to France and the Republic, peace,
order, and stability.'

Mark it well ! One could not say better . . . Peace, order and
stability. But what becomes of all three, if a crime, gentlemen of
the jury, can be committed with impunity? Well, the man who pronounced these three terrible words, peace, order and stability, which
call down upon her head the rigour of our just laws, that man – you
know him ! It is your husband, it is Monsieur Caillaux !

He insinuated that because Caillaux had 'interfered with the course of
justice' in the Rochette Case he had probably interfered also with the

free expression of the jury's opinion :

If he has dared to do that, if he has had the impudence to enquire into your free opinions, then I say very emphatically to the accused, 'So much the worse for you, for the jury will be without pity !'

You will show this man and his associate that this fine institution of the jury, of which I have always been the ardent defender for the guarantees of independence and impartiality it secures, that this jury will not serve anyone, will not surrender to anyone, will not fear anyone – and above all you will not wish, after your verdict, Calmette's two children to say there is no longer any justice in France !

Bursts of applause punctuated Maître Chenu's speech . . . In the name of France, in the name of society, he demanded that the jury should find her guilty of murder with premeditation.

The public applauded and actually cried, *'Bis! Bis!'* (encore) as one would encourage a popular performer.

The *Daily Express*, 29th July 1914

Maître Chenu's speech was awaited with intense curiosity. After Maître Seligman's excellent defence of Calmette and *Le Figaro* against Monsieur Caillaux's accusations, Maître Chenu was looked upon as the true, the only prosecutor, the one who would dare to demand the heaviest possible sentence. He went straight to the point. His speech, in the precision of its arguments, its sombre tone as if clad in mourning, the exaltation and nobility of its thoughts, the purity of its language, its majestic flights, is one of the finest examples of the oratory of our time.

*L'Illustration*, 1st August 1914

Maître Chenu's plea was one of those which mark a date in the history of legal eloquence. It was ardent and courageous, with superb flights and the soaring magnificence which transports crowds.

Those who read the speech in which the phrases have the solidity and brillance of marble, will still be moved by it but will not experience the great thrill that surged through the audience when Maître Chenu, with the beautiful and masculine features of a Gaul, who knows how to look his adversary in the face, spoke of 'the powerful of a day who make and unmake policy' and of the Caesarian hand of Monsieur Caillaux, 'one of those men whose power is created by their own audacity and by the fear they inspire.' It was magnificent ! . . .

Madame Caillaux listened, her head in her hands, stopping her ears so as not to hear the vengeful words, the punishment for the crime.

*Le Figaro*, 29th July 1914

When the applause had subsided, the Public Prosecutor, Herbeaux, began his speech to state the case for the prosecution. His voice was low and quiet, sometimes scarcely audible above the conversation which showed the public were more interested in discussing what had just been said than in anything he might say :

HERBEAUX : As I rise to ask for the condemnation of Madame Caillaux for the killing of Gaston Calmette, my thoughts go out to the victim and those afflicted by his death. I bow with respect to the mourning of two orphans, represented here by the *partie civile*, and I offer my sincere sympathy. I too cannot help feeling emotion and poignant pity for the tragic end of one whom brutal death has mown down, as if in a battle, in the fine flowering of his talent, in his full strength.

Why did it have to happen? How did it come about that the battle degenerated into an implacable conflict in which anger on one side and anguish on the other brought one to the grave and the other to the Court of the Assizes?

It is a melancholy drama indeed we have to trace together. Let us at least fulfil this task as becomes an act of justice, and with no other object in mind but the truth and the just application of the law.

After describing once again the shooting of Calmette, the events of the day leading up to it, and his death six hours later, he concluded that Henriette had killed Calmette, that she had intended to do so, and that it was, therefore, a premeditated crime.

The jury, he said, had not only to know the material facts, they must also understand the motives; certainly not to find excuses for the crime, for there could be no excuse for murder or assassination, but to determine how far one could go in reducing the sentence or its rigorous application.

He considered the question of the intimate letters, and read extracts to show that even those dealing with electoral or political matters could not have been published without divulging that an intimate relationship had existed between Monsieur Caillaux and Madame Rainouard. He described the filching of the letters one night and the catastrophe it represented for the lovers, so much so that Caillaux was prepared to give Henriette up rather than involve her in a scandal. The letters were destroyed, he said, by common consent, but the lovers had no sooner married than disturbing rumours reached them that copies of the letters were being handed round : they were offered to various newspapers who refused to publish them.

The attacks on Caillaux in *Le Figaro* had begun as soon as he became Finance Minister. The articles were signed by Gaston Calmette :

HERBEAUX : I said just now Madame acted not only under the influence of fear but also of anger. She loves her husband. It is a most closely united household, as many witnesses have attested, and now every day her husband was being represented as an exploiter of the people, as a man habitually abusing his authority – all this, of course, on a purely political and financial level, but one has to recognise that the campaign took on a personal character and a degree of bitterness almost unheard of in our annals.

He gave a few examples : that on 8th January Calmette wrote in *Le Figaro* Caillaux had swindled the country out of six million francs on the inheritance of a Frenchman, Prieu, who had died in Brazil; and he commented that it was immediately denied by everybody concerned and proved to be a fabrication : the next accusation was an alleged swindle by Caillaux in connection with the *Société Générale* – also immediately denied by all concerned. The next was that Caillaux had swindled 400,000 francs from the *Comptoir d'Escompte* – even Calmette admitted it was untrue, but,

HERBEAUX : Next day the campaign continued, still just as bitter, just as personal, just as injurious . . . The effect on the mind of the accused was, it goes without saying, to stir the glowing embers of resentment and anger, increasing day by day until it needed, perhaps, only a spark for it to burst into flames. She felt rising about her an atmosphere of distrust and suspicion; she felt herself the object of contempt, and that women were wondering how much stolen money had been expended on the costume she was wearing. All this became an obsession with her, and all this, it seemed to her, was the result of the campaign in *Le Figaro*, the effect of Calmette's 133 articles. She had counted correctly.

He rejected out of hand Chenu's theory that Henriette's motive had been to prevent the Fabre Report from being published – it had nothing to do with it, journalists had already quoted extracts from it, and both Monsieur and Madame Caillaux knew it was going to be published by an evening paper. In any case Calmette had falsified his account of it, repeating in three different articles that the purpose of

the postponement requested by Caillaux had been to allow Rochette
to benefit from the Three Years Immunity Act and thus escape from
justice whereas a simple comparison of the dates showed this could not
have been the case. Calmette continued to assert that it was.

HERBEAUX : Up until 13th March we can understand to what extent
Madame Caillaux was exasperated and embittered. The attacks had
struck home. She has told you how she suffered as a *bourgeoise*
and as a woman with a certain position in society . . . Until now the
campaign had been in the sphere of politics, and she had been
moved to feel more anger than fear, but on 13th March there
appeared in *Le Figaro* the letter which you know, about the income
tax, signed *Ton Jo*.

He described how Calmette had published without authority this
private and intimate letter and had accompanied it with a threat, 'I
feel myself impelled for the deliverance of my country to bring out
from everywhere the corrupted truth . . .' It was known he had been
negotiating for the intimate letters. From three or four different
sources Monsieur and Madame Caillaux had been informed he had
got possession of them and would certainly publish them. The connection in Madame Caillaux's mind, he explained, was that Calmette
would obtain the intimate letters from the same source as the *Ton Jo*
letter, that they would be disclosed to the whole world, and that her
daughter would learn there had been an intimate relationship between
her mother and Monsieur Caillaux. On the morning of 16th March
she read in *Le Figaro* that there would now be a 'comic interlude' and
she had told them of the connection in her mind between this and
what she feared would follow.

HERBEAUX : Now, gentlemen, you know the whole affair. You know
all the elements necessary to judge it. You will do so, not with undue
severity but with, I am sure, a just and sufficient firmness. You are
to apply the law, taking care to do so with humanity but without
weakness. I ask you, gentlemen of the jury, to fulfil your mission
with responsibility.

Assuredly I do not expect from you a pitiless verdict.

Extenuating circumstances are there. I go further : the circumstances provoking the premeditation are absolutely undeniable. If
you go so far as to suppress the premeditation in your verdict, fear-
ing that if you reply in the affirmative to this question the result

will be too serious for the accused, I could only bow before a reply dictated by generosity. But it is on the accessory and entirely secondary point that I must ask you to remember that having sworn to safeguard the rights of society as well as those of the accused, you cannot absolve her.

I ask you insistently not to excuse an act contrary to all law and to all social security. In the name of the respect due to human life, in the name of the sacred interests of society, I direct, and I direct firmly, that you bring in against Madame Caillaux a verdict of guilty.

The hearing was suspended.

In France a jury may return a verdict of 'guilty with extenuating circumstances' and this form of verdict entitles counsel for the defense to introduce into his speeches allusions and intimations which appeal only to the sympathy or passion. He may ask the jury to mitigate the law or to disprove it in its application to the particular case at the bar, thereby putting sentiment above the law.

The result is that while the jury may recognise clearly that a murder has been committed, it may, by the verdict, declare that the particular murder in question ought not to be punished, being influenced momentarily by sympathy or passion.

*The New York Times*, 27th July 1914

# CHAPTER EIGHT

# 'A Shameful Scene'

After a short intermission, Maître Labori rose to put the case for the defence. So great was his reputation as an orator that he was heard with interest and respect: none of the feeling against Caillaux adhered to him. He seemed to be above party. His voice was powerful, but warm and friendly, and he used it with the greatest of ease. Unlike Maître Chenu, whose speech was addressed to the newspapers and the public, he spoke directly to the jury, indeed he seemed at times to be sharing their problem, to be thinking aloud as one of them.

> Maître Chenu in concluding had said he envied – in this affair only, he specified – the right of the Public Prosecutor to call in the name of the people for a condemnation without indulgence. Public Prosecutor Herbeaux did not go so far in the severity of his demands. He recognised criminal intention and premeditation. He admitted extenuating circumstances, and even recommended that the more serious charge, 'absolutely undeniable premeditation', be set aside. That meant throwing a bridge between a sentence of hard labour and an acquittal. Maître Labori, with his admirable eloquence and contagious emotion, took upon himself the task of getting her safely across this dangerous gap.
>
> *L'Illustration*, 1st August 1914

Maître Labori began by saying that the Public Prosecutor, though claiming to be lenient, and no doubt thinking he was being lenient, was in fact asking them to give a verdict of guilty that would condemn Madame Caillaux to hard labour for five to ten years, even if the charge of premeditation were set aside. Monsieur Herbeaux, he said, had done his duty with a sort of objective impassivity, but he might have been more lenient if he had allowed himself to be influenced by the sympathy for the accused which he so obviously felt, and he might have gone further in this direction if she had not been the wife of a cabinet minister.

LABORI: There has been much talk of the favours alleged to
have been shown Madame Caillaux since the beginning of the
investigation . . . but she has suffered all the rigours of common
law imprisonment. A number of other prisoners, either accused
or serving sentences, have been treated with greater leniency . . .
And today, believe me, gentlemen of the jury, her exceptional
position does not give her any exceptional indulgence from the
Public Prosecutor . . . He did one thing, however, which will
strengthen my case – he recognised, with his high authority, the
true motive of the drama.

He alluded to the tragic failure of the doctors to diagnose Calmette's
wounds and quoted the example of Monsieur Ollivier in 1898, Secretary to the Editor of *La Lanterne*, who had been shot by Madame
P . . .* under similar circumstances: he had been operated on by an
inexperienced surgeon, and therefore the Director of Public Prosecutions had dropped the case against Madame P . . . which had many
parallels with the one they were discussing:

She was the wife of a deputy, and she fired on the Secretary to
the Director of *La Lanterne* because of an extremely violent
article about her husband. The affair caused a sensation at the
time. Madame P . . . was treated with an indulgence not accorded
to Madame Caillaux: she was allowed out on bail . . . However,
I am here replying exclusively to the Public Prosecutor – don't
worry, I shall reply later to the *partie civile*. It is to *Le Figaro*,
gentlemen, that I offer this rapid review of the essentials of the
drama I am alluding to: I think it rather appropriate.

This is what, under the headline A PARISIAN DRAMA *Le Figaro*
wrote on 24th September 1898:

A drama, sad consequence of the exaggerations in which polemic
has indulged for some time past, has taken place in the office of
*La Lanterne*. About four o'clock, a young and elegant brunette
wearing white gloves and a black hat with a white veil, got out
of a luxurious car before No 18, rue Richer, went up to the first
floor and asked for Monsieur Millerand, Chief Editor of *La
Lanterne*. She was told he had not yet come in. Without another
word, she left and got into her car again without leaving her
name.
At five twenty she came back and again asked for Monsieur

* Madame Paulmier, wife of the Deputy for Calvados.

Millerand. 'He has not yet come in, Madame,' said the office boy
– 'Then may I see the editor's secretary?' 'Yes, Madame. What
name shall I give?' She wrote it on a card, 'M. Boland.' She was
shown in. No sooner had she entered than she took out a pistol,
levelled it at Monsieur Ollivier and fired six rounds.

You see, I have a right to cite this precedent which is of interest,
and to invoke the law before this court, as we do every day
before the civil and criminal courts. What law? Your law. The
law of the jury. Listen to what follows :

There was general consternation in the publisher's office. One of
the staff, Monsieur Georges Lacour, and the office boy ran out
to find a doctor. While first aid was being administered, the fatal
visitor, who had remained calmly in the editor's office, was
arrested; she then made herself known. She was Madame P . . . ,
wife of the deputy X . . .
    She gave her name and address, and explained her action by
saying she had avenged her honour, outraged by an article in
*La Lanterne.* This article was an appreciation or, rather, a
commentary on a letter written by Monsieur P . . . ,* a letter *Le
Figaro* had published on the previous morning and in which the
deputy had asked the Minister for War to suppress articles written
against the army.

When she read *La Lanterne*'s comments it never even occurred
to her to await the return of her husband, absent at the time in
his constituency. She thought only of her daughter, thinking
these articles might come to her attention. Agitated, exasperated,
with tears in her eyes, she had written to this child to tell her she
was going to obtain justice for herself and for her : and immediately she went and bought a pistol at Gastinne-Renette's in
order to kill Monsieur Millerand, Editor of *La Lanterne*, whom
she considered to be responsible for the injury done her. Not
having succeeded in meeting the Chief Editor, in a paroxysm
of excitement she had shot the editorial secretary.
    That is an example reported by *Le Figaro.* I have compiled a
large dossier – I don't need to read it to you . . . None of the press
representatives listening to me will contradict me when I say that
most of the great newspapers of Paris, and among them our
keenest adversaries of today, treated Madame P . . . with the
greatest consideration, understanding the motive that activated

* Monsieur Paulmier.

her : they saluted her respectfully and anticipated only a verdict of not guilty at the Court of the Assizes.

Listen to what *Le Figaro* wrote – I hope you won't find my extracts indiscreet – they bear directly on the central point of the present case. Listen to what *Le Figaro* wrote on 25th September 1898. 'These new methods ...' *Le Figaro* is speaking of the methods used by the press – these campaigns, fortunately rare, such as that waged for months by *Le Figaro* against Monsieur Caillaux :

> These new methods degrade the French press to a level impossible to describe. They will lead, it is certain, to the press being muzzled, for it is impossible to go on living in this moral stench. If at least we were trying to dishonour only ourselves, the game would be harmless enough, because, after some years in our profession, one is vaccinated against outrage and even finds in it an agreeable savour; but we attack the customers, the politicians above all, and also everyone who passes our door. Some of our victims are silent through contempt, or fear – we shall find them again when laws are proposed against us. Some react, and reply or send their seconds. Others take a pistol and fire at random. That is what Madame P ... did.

There it is, gentlemen. I don't need to plead it because I find in *Le Figaro* of 1898 words which apply so directly to what I have to tell you today. No one has more respect for the press than I have. No one more than I do considers it as perhaps the last guarantee of individual integrity in the present social order, in view of the universal decomposition which we should do well to recognise ... but it is necessary that the press should be worthy of its functions. Generally it is. I salute it when it is. When we see journalists, who should exercise their high functions like a priesthood, disregarding their moral obligations – we can understand how great the peril is.

I have not forgotten, gentlemen, that I mentioned earlier the Director of Public Prosecutions in comparable affairs had been less severe than the Public Prosecutor today.

Speaking on his behalf, the Advocate General Lombard, in the affair of Madame P ... left the decision, without passion and with true moderation, to the conscience of the jury – was not that abandoning the accusation? And, according to *Le Figaro* of 27th December 1898, her counsel pleaded :

... bring Madame P ... before all the juries in France, you would not find a single one to condemn her, neither would you find a single Advocate General to ask for a condemnation.' The jury ... acquitted her, just as their predecessors had acquitted Madame Clovis Hugues who also had defended her honour, killing on the steps of the Palais de Justice the man who had defamed her.

And because I see the name of Madame Clovis Hugues mentioned in all the correspondence about this memorable affair, I come to her case. She had been the victim of odious attacks by a man called Morin who had made lying statements about her and mis-represented the facts ... and what was her attitude? There really seems to be an interesting subject here for study by doctors and psychologists.

You have heard that Madame P ... was perfectly calm. Listen now to what was said about Madame Clovis Hugues. I quote now from the *Gazette des Tribuneaux* ...

*The President:* You said, I believe, 'I should never have imagined that such a crime could be committed with so much calm and sang-froid?' *Witness:* It is true. I was struck by the calmness with which she shot him.

And another witness:

*The President:* What was Madame Hugues' attitude? *Witness:* She held herself erect, grasped the pistol in a sure hand and seemed to take aim with much deliberation at the man she wished to kill.

And yet a third witness:

*The President:* You said at the enquiry that Madame Clovis was as immobile as a statue? *Witness:* Yes, like a statue.

The jury brought in a verdict of not guilty without leaving the courtroom.

He mentioned other similar cases, and said that if he had only the Public Prosecutor to answer he would simply ask the jury to acquit Madame Caillaux, and he was well aware they would not dream of refusing him; but he had other adversaries – the two eminent counsel for the *partie civile.* He had not known with what strange violence they were going to plead, and he would try to answer them.

Maître Seligman had given them a eulogy of Calmette about which
he would have a word to say later.

Maître Chenu, gentlemen, with an admirable talent which I
always acknowledge, and with profound sincerity, but more concerned to continue Calmette's work than to defend his memory,
introduced into this courtroom a political trial. Oh, yes, I have
a right to say so, and I shall demonstrate it. I should be very
surprised myself if that surprises him. He did so simply by associating Monsieur Caillaux, who is here simply as a witness, with
Madame Caillaux whom he constantly alludes to as 'the criminal'
in his cruel repetition of his description of the assassination.

As Maître Chenu has for the magistrates, both standing and
sitting, that admirable respect which just now made the whole
room shake, why does he not bow with equal respect to the dispo-
sitions and decisions of the justices? Monsieur Caillaux is the
prosecution's witness, he is not one of the accused ... has he not
the right to the same respect as the other witnesses? And, I ask
you, if he has been treated thus, and if he has been associated with
Madame Caillaux, is it possible to think it was for any other
purpose than to institute here, in the most complete and absolute
sense, a political trial?

But that is not all. Maître Chenu was not satisfied by making
this before everything else the trial of Monsieur Caillaux, but he
did it in a way that was painful to me. If he had said, 'The guilty
is Monsieur Caillaux – acquit her,' I should have understood the
generosity of such a statement – if he had made it – but to involve
Monsieur Caillaux by saying 'There is not one accused here, there
are two, the husband and the wife, therefore inflict on her a terrible
sentence' – for not the least word of indulgence passed Maître
Chenu's lips – 'as for the other, brand him as a criminal and in
doing so brand French justice which I respect only in appearance.'

He pointed out that Chenu's allegations against Caillaux implied a
serious criticism of French justice for not having put on trial a
minister guilty not only of maladministration but of assassination.
Evidently Maître Chenu's respect for French justice was a mere
pretence.

But that is not all. I swear to you, gentlemen, nothing led me to
foresee so arduous a contention. Maître Chenu told you that the
motive for the drama – he actually said, 'the motive for the crime

of assassination' was not merely the fear of a wife who trembled for her husband, it was the common ambition of a man and wife who had already reached a fairly high position but not as high as they wished : they wanted to reach a higher one, and in their unjust passion counted the life of a man as nothing.

There is the plea of the *partie civile*, the essence of what they say. Is not that a political proceeding? Is this the plea of counsel fulfilling their true role of representing the *partie civile*? of defending the memory of Calmette? No! And I have no word to retract from my previous statement. I have to reply here to Maître Chenu who has made this a political trial.

He said he too had known Calmette, not as an intimate friend, but he could appreciate the pleasantness of his manners and his desire to be obliging in small matters. He thought it would have been better for his memory if the opposing counsel had limited themselves to the facts of the case. He had no wish to sully his memory, and neither he nor his client had forgotten the misfortune that brought them there :

But why, gentlemen, had the *partie civile* to use the language you have heard? Terrible for Madame Caillaux, terrible for the trial, terrible for the unhappy accused to whom no detail has been spared, whom grief has ravaged to the depths of her being, terrible for Monsieur Caillaux. And let it not be said it was Monsieur Caillaux who began it, for the words of the *partie civile* simply continue in this place the attacks of the newspaper.

Open, gentlemen, *Le Figaro*, never mind which number; that of 23rd March, for instance. You will read this sort of thing . . .

They are going to invent a lie to justify the crime. Against those who lie we shall know how to defend the memory of our chief who did not lie.

And on 9th April :

. . . until last month there were two methods to deal with a press campaign : the duel and the injunction. Monsieur Caillaux has found a third : assassination.

The honourable Monsieur Raymond Recouly of *Le Figaro* has published a brochure about the Caillaux Affair. I have it in my dossier. It is in fact a résumé of the polemics of *Le Figaro* :

> It was certainly not with a light heart that this man upon whom fortune had always smiled, who was loyalty, correctness, even gallantry, threw himself into this terrible struggle. He knew the power of the forces he used against an adversary . . .

Now listen to the epithets which follow :

> . . . facing an adversary without scruples, skilful in denying that which should not be denied and, on the contrary, remaining silent when he ought to speak, mingling with unparalleled ability bad faith and cynicism.

It reads like an echo in anticipation of the beautiful and terrible invectives of Maître Chenu . . .

> . . . mingling with unparalleled ability bad faith and cynicism so that nothing touched him, nothing moved him; it was necessary to say things as painful as Gaston Calmette said, it was necessary to speak as he has spoken or he could not have overthrown such an adversary and removed him from power in time.

We'll go on to the final words of the brochure. Listen to what he says of Monsieur Caillaux :

> If the country is liberated in time from the national scourge which is Monsieur Caillaux, it is to Gaston Calmette that we owe it.

No! Monsieur Caillaux did not start it. I understand that *Le Figaro* has experienced immense grief at the loss of a beloved chief, and that it believes itself to be moderate in the passion of its posthumous affection. Listen to what it wrote on Friday, 27th March 1914 – it is like an advance outline of the trial, of this trial where members of the staff chose to appear as witnesses and took the oath to speak without hatred and without fear. Listen to what was written in their name :

> We are carrying on the work of rehabilitation, and we must in the paper, as we shall at the trial, speak without hatred – we shall not be able to – but at least without violence which would weaken and discredit the proofs.

These are the gentlemen who say they cannot speak without hatred. You will decide, gentlemen of the jury, whether at this hearing they have spoken without violence either as witnesses or in the counsels' speeches.

It is not the orphans who have spoken here. It is much more as if, I do not wish to say a political party – Maître Chenu would have the right to protest – but it is at least a political idea which is being expressed. If I wished to reply, gentlemen of the jury, what a mass of mud I could rake up! It would be a natural spontaneous reaction – would it not be justified? But I shall not do so. I shall not stoop to it. Monsieur Caillaux himself has not done so. Let me assure you there is a great deal more he could say, a great deal more he could prove. He struck hard only at the end, because he was driven to extremities.

It is not part of my duty to give Monsieur Caillaux either a testimony or a certificate. I shall not concern myself here with his politics, but I allow myself to say, I who have known him as a colleague in the Chamber of Deputies, but have not known him well until the time of this immense struggle; allow me to say he has made an admirable deposition, and that of all the accusations brought against him not a single one remains.

He commands the respect, even of his adversaries, for his intelligence, his energy, his courage. And, I have the right to add, for his personal integrity . . . (*Applause.*)

Gentlemen of the jury, you are the sovereign judges here, not only as magistrates but as citizens, to judge this case in all its bearings, knowing it in its entirety with all the things they have brought in from the outside : therefore, let us be clear about what they say. What is their theory? It is very simple. It is that the husband has incited the wife, and also that by common accord she has taken his place and, if I have properly understood him, Maître Chenu said, 'If she has struck, if she has killed, it is because they feared the Fabre Report.'

Ah, gentlemen, the Fabre Report. One can understand that an effect was made with it before Parliament where the agitation and the tumult of political conflict often cause right and justice to disappear – and common sense also, I'm afraid. We don't say so officially, of course, but we're ready enough to admit this in our private conversations.

Maître Chenu made a great thing of the Order of the Day which he read to you – I am, gentlemen, in the heart of my subject, on the ground Maître Chenu has chosen – that the conclusions of the parliamentary commission were approved by 400 votes to 0. These are majorities without significance, the result more of circumstances than of the true expression of opinion. The Fabre Report, no one discussed, and no one wished to.

The expression Monsieur Caillaux used, that his intervention was 'an act of government,' yes, had I been in the Chamber I should have subscribed to that . . .

In the Fabre Report I consider we have a document which has not the least importance. It is always referred to as a report or record of proceedings, but it was a one-sided record . . . The prosecutor, Fabre, without any thought of casting a slur on anyone's character, had drafted a little note after an interview with the head of his department, like any of our civil servants might have done. It has no value at all. It was not even submitted for discussion at the time it was written, alone in the silence of his office . . .

But what is more to the point, gentlemen, is to ask if the Fabre Report is itself justifiable? I was very moved just now when Maître Chenu, in his admirable evocation, turned towards the magistrates – for whom I have the same affection and admiration as he does – and when the entire audience broke into applause at the conclusion of his fine words, 'Let us cast off our robes etc., etc.,' Ah, yes. That is splendid, it is very eloquent, it is an admirable evocation, but entirely misplaced. Why? Because a public prosecutor, with all due respect to the eminent magistrate here today, is not a magistrate seated immovable in his place, independent of all authority but his own. The head of the law courts, and of public prosecutions, is the Lord Privy Seal, a member of the government . . . Well then, the Prime Minister, who is the head of the government, and consequently above the Lord Privy Seal, was moved by the Finance Minister, for some reason which we know had nothing to do with any advantage or benefit to himself, or to Monsieur Rochette, to decide that a remission was desirable. Monsieur Rochette is still called a crook, but I defended him and I consider he was to a great extent the victim of a judicial error. (*Murmurs in the audience.*) What? Doesn't the whole world know that at the origin of the Rochette Affair there were scandals a great deal more serious than anything that happened later, when he was arrested and entirely illegal charges were made against him? I am happy to be able to speak of these things before a tribunal of magistrates and lawyers . . . The Fabre Report records a remission without importance.

Of what does Fabre complain? Did he go to his chief, the Minister of Justice, and ask for his support? Not at all. He carried out the order, gentlemen, which would have been humiliating if he had occupied one of those positions in which a magistrate is not answerable to the government but who acts in absolute independence. But he was not . . . He was a law officer of the state.

But what is unforgivable is this : his report was preserved craftily for months, its existence was denied – but hypocritical use was made of it. How? Why? Was it brought out when the spirits of all those servants of the state were indignant and revolting against an injustice? Not at all. Their sentiments slept for as long as was necessary, to awake at the tactical hour for the elections. The Fabre Report is nothing but a political lever by which it was hoped to overthrow the government. . . . That is what I think of the Fabre Report. It caused, as I say, an uproar that was entirely unjustified.

Now I'll come back to the trial and ask myself if the Fabre Report could have motivated Madame Caillaux's act. Evidently not. You have been given the reasons, and I don't need to have to repeat them after what the Public Prosecutor has said. Other newspapers had it, anyone could publish it . . . except Calmette who had given an undertaking not to do so.

He quickly summarised the evidence that both Caillaux and Henriette knew very well that a different paper was about to publish it, 'Therefore,' he concluded, 'it is childish to say that fear of the Fabre Report coming out was Madame Caillaux's motive.'

But also, gentlemen, they have attempted to broaden the accusation, and as I have the habit of not shirking anything, I shall deal with the theses of the *partie civile* however flimsy they may be . . . It is that Monsieur and Madame Caillaux wished to destroy a political rival . . .

Madame Caillaux would have been able to figure as a sort of Charlotte Corday, reacting not against the pamphleteers of the Terror but of the Reaction. Well, if that's it, gentlemen, there's no answer but an acquittal. If Madame Caillaux had in fact done so, I should not have been at a loss for arguments to explain her action . . .

He read a selection of the false charges that had been brought against Caillaux in *Le Figaro*, and demolished and ridiculed them one by one.

Then he turned to Caillaux's divorce from Berthe, and reminded the jury there had been an agreement between them : he was to pay her a large sum and also make her an allowance, and she undertook explicitly to destroy certain letters. Monsieur Caillaux carried out his part of the agreement, Madame Gueydan did not keep her word : therefore Madame Gueydan was the true and only cause of the *Figaro* drama :

> Since the day Madame Rainouard married Monsieur Caillaux she has been constantly threatened that the famous 'intimate letters' would be published. The *partie civile* pretend that these letters contained nothing that Madame Caillaux could be afraid to see published : to believe this, one would have to be very ignorant of what goes on in the soul of a woman, particularly when she is the mother of a daughter who might learn through that publication that she had had a liaison with Monsieur Caillaux while she was married to another. And one such letter was in fact published by Monsieur Calmette. What if he did cut out the intimate passages? Is the signature *Ton Jo* political? That is the question Madame Caillaux asked herself; and then 'Now there follows a Comic Interlude.' What could that portend?
>
> These phrases had a terrible effect on the mind of the accused. She was convinced that other intimate letters were about to appear ...

He recapitulated the testimony of those who had warned her they would be published, notably the minister, Painlevé ... showing she had every reason to believe Calmette would use them. He spoke of the extreme moral sensitivity of his client. He said that from the beginning of their liaison, Monsieur and Madame Caillaux had constantly acted with the greatest delicacy, even with regard to Madame Gueydan, for it was not correct to say that Madame Caillaux took Madame Gueydan's husband from her.

Referring to Henriette's behaviour on the day of the drama, he said that a specialist in mental diseases, who had asked that his name should not be revealed, had given him a diagnosis which he read aloud : it was to the effect that she had obeyed a subconscious impulse with doubling of the personality, a condition which he illustrated by extracts from *Le Figaro*'s reports, and he commented that Henriette herself had said she felt as if she were being driven by an interior force :

A double fatality weighed upon Monsieur and Madame Caillaux :
the rapidity of her automatic pistol, and the fact that Monsieur
Calmette crouched down. Then there was a third fatality – the
error in the diagnosis. Three doctors have testified that Monsieur
Calmette was operated on too late. We have the right to ask if he
could have been saved. If so, the case presents a very different
aspect.

He implored all who heard him to give up political hatreds, party
strife and internal quarrels because they needed a vast movement of
integration to enable them to face the dangers that threatened the
country from outside; and he appealed to the jury to bring in a
verdict of not guilty which this evening everyone would accept.

Maître Labori's face was singularly handsome. His eyes reflected
the gentleness and mercy of which he spoke. The dignity and dis-
tinction in his broad figure and the memory of old associations and
past triumphs marked him out as one of the world's greatest
leaders ... It was a magnificent appeal to the hearts of the jury.
He played on their sentiments with the power of one who knows
his fellow countrymen. His deep voice now boomed in passages of
splendid and illuminating rhetoric, now sank to low and tremulous
tones, as he pleaded for an acquittal.

The *Daily Express*, 29th July 1914

It was a few minutes to eight when Maître Labori sat down. The
questions to the jury were quickly put. They were two. The President's customary advice was quickly given. The jury went up to
their room. A quick verdict was expected ... but an hour passed.

At a quarter to nine, word went round that the jury had sent for
the President. Preceded by the court usher, he went up the stairs
to the second floor, followed by the Public Prosecutor, the Attorney
General, Maître Labori and Maître Chenu.

Soon it was known that the jury had asked if the sentence demanded could be mitigated by application of the Beranger Law :
they were informed that this lenient law could not be applied to
actions designated 'criminal'. They again deliberated ...

Nine o'clock. A bell sounded. The twelve men returned. Then
the magistrates came in again.

*Le Matin*

The scene when the verdict was brought in to-night was the culmi-
nation of a series of thrilling scenes and incidents, which had kept
the Court in a state of tense excitement all day, as much, perhaps,

as in any *cause célèbre* ever tried by a French and a Parisian jury.
... the president of the jury stood up to read the verdict. Two
questions ... had been given them to answer, and he read them
out slowly one by one. First, is Madame Caillaux guilty of voluntary homicide? On our soul and conscience we reply No. The
principal juryman had hardly time to read the second question and
its negative reply. The first was already sufficient. His voice was
drowned in one sudden, irrepressible outburst of cheers. The courtroom, which hitherto seemed to have been full of an overwhelming
majority against Monsieur Caillaux, seemed suddenly, as by the
waving of a magic wand, to have been transformed into ardent
Caillauxists.

'*Vive Caillaux!*' was shouted from every bench and corner of the
courtroom. Men and women in a wild outburst of enthusiasm
jumped on the tables and chairs to be higher still and to vociferate
more loudly their cheers for Caillaux. '*Vive Caillaux!*' everyone
shouted at the top of his lungs. Men waved their hats and women
their handkerchiefs for fully ten minutes.

## EX-PREMIER'S TRIUMPH

Madame Caillaux was presented at once with the court register, on
which she signed her name, and from being pale, haggard, and
drawn with tense emotion before, relaxed and became flushed, but
there was no smile, no expression of pleasure, except when she
looked in the direction of her husband, who was vainly trying to
make his way towards her through the shouting and cheering crowd.
He finally had to move towards a side exit whilst men and women
almost screamed '*Vive Caillaux!*' into his ears.

He was actually raised off the ground and lifted out of the door,
a happy, satisfied-looking man, and he had a thousand reasons to
feel happy, for it was he who had conducted the whole defence, he
who had shown such devotion and fidelity through thick and thin
to his wife that even his opponents at the end forgave him, for he
deserved the victory.

The *Daily Telegraph*, 29th July 1914

It seemed that the powerful Nationalist faction had been overwhelmed and silenced by the enthusiasm for Caillaux when suddenly
a single cry dominated the tumult: it came from a young man in
barrister's gown, Maître Viven, who had climbed onto a desk and
was shouting at the jury, *Vive la France! A bas les vendus!* meaning
they had sold their verdict. His supporters began chanting, '*Caillaux
Assassin! Caillaux Assassin!*'

Then, oh then! After applause had broken out at the back of the courtroom, there was a shameful scene of indescribable violence. Never in the memory either of journalist or lawyer have the walls of the Court of Assizes echoed to a clamour equal to this. Powerless to maintain order, aware that in the uproar of voices he could not pronounce the judgement of acquittal, President Albanel ordered the court to be cleared and retired with his assessors.

Standing on the Court Usher's table, Lieutenant Fontan of the Municipal Guard – an officer who deserves less uncongenial duties – directed the long and difficult operation.

*Le Matin*, 29th July 1914

In the courtroom the uproar continued, irresistible, implacable, '*Hou! Hou! Caillaux Assassin! Assassin!* and there were curses and whistles directed against him.

It was a scene impossible to describe, a ferocious mêlée of shouts, howls, applause, raised fists, distorted features, and mouths shouting angry cries, all the passions unleashed, a sort of revolutionary fury possessing the excited crowd, a monstrous upsurge of all the lusts, of all the hatreds.

It was a dramatic session, agonising, a date in history. The roar of the crowd echoing like thunder in the long corridors of the Palais already suggested the roar of distant gunfire.

*Le Figaro*, 29th July 1914

At a quarter past nine the Court re-entered and the trial was formally concluded. Henriette embraced Labori – her hat with the black spreading wings fell off and rolled out of the dock. The *partie civile* were awarded the classic one franc damages and ordered to pay the costs of the trial. The jury had remained throughout as impervious to the violence and uproar of the Nationalist factions as the peasants of the Sarthe: this was highly creditable because, according to *Le Bonnet Rouge* which quoted an interview with one of them, 'they were harassed by letters, telegrams, visits, bribes and threats, and terrible reprisals if Madame Caillaux was acquitted.'

A group of Caillaux's friends was waiting outside the courtroom in the Vestibule de Harlay. As soon as he appeared there was a demonstration of sympathy; it provoked cries of '*Vive l'Assassin!*' and ironical cheers, but his friends surrounded him and acclaimed him. Outside there were hostile shouts from a crowd massed on the steps. He was almost carried to his car which moved off accompanied by *Vivats!* and by hoots and jeers. The crowd barred its way to the Place Dauphin but the *gendarmes* cleared the way and he reached the Conciergerie where the formalities for Henriette's release were immediately put in hand. At ten o'clock she was free and he took her home.

> The counsels' speeches were magnificent, as had been expected. Maître Chenu was clear and great : he spoke to the country. Maître Labori was moving and resourceful : he spoke to the jury. One addressed the public conscience, the other the uneasy sensibility, the frayed nerves of a few men. The acquittal of Madame Caillaux by the jury of the Seine was not a defeat for Maître Chenu. As soon as the verdict became known the almost universal protest was the victorious justification of the victorious *bâtonnier*.
>
> *L'Illustration*, 1st August 1914

The boulevards were kept in an uproar by the organised bands, the *Camelots du Roi*, led by Maurice Pujo of the newspaper *L'Action Française*, parading and shouting '*Caillaux Assassin!*' An opposition group demonstrating in favour of Caillaux was attacked, and others demonstrating against the war were driven off with derisive hoots. Successive charges by the police, who were pelted with bottles and glasses from the cafés and by tables thrown from the first floor windows, failed to disperse the demonstrators. They were in control of the boulevards for several hours :

> At various points our friends got up onto the benches and harangued the crowd. Mounted police charged several times with sabres drawn, other policemen drew their revolvers and threatened to fire. Then, at a quarter to twelve, the demonstration ceased upon a signal from our leader.
>
> *L'Action Française*, 29th July 1914

A reporter from *Le Matin* found Monsieur and Madame Caillaux at home in their luxurious apartment :

> Candelabra with a thousand lustres scattered light over the Persian carpets and brought their marvellously variegated designs to life ... On a Louis XVI couch with soft cushions a white fox stole had been left, staring with great eyes of jade ...
>
> It is eleven o'clock at night. We are in the long room adjoining Madame Caillaux's apartments. Everywhere there are busy servants, and electric bells ring : one is more insistent than the others – the telephone. Relieved voices reflect, briefly, disjointedly, excitedly, the anxieties of the past few days, 'Is it you, *chère amie*? Oh, thank you. Thank you ... ' Letters are brought in, visiting cards pile up, the first flowers arrive. An intimate dinner party 'round the family lamp', as one used to say.

A group surrounds Madame Caillaux . . . in a dress of embroidered blue net, airy and sparkling. The anguish of weeks seems to have fled away, and the long ordeal does not seem to have left any deep mark on her features. She is again a woman of the world and mistress of her household. She has regained possession of herself, gracefully receiving her guests with smiles and enveloping charm. 'I'm not quite myself yet,' she says, 'which is not surprising. My recollection of today which has been so long that it seemed it would never end, is confused, bewildered. Resounding phrases ring in my ears, Monsieur Labori's moving phrases as he was pleading my cause with so much ardour and faith. In a daze I learned I was acquitted, then I was in the open air, then home, as in a dream.'

The former Prime Minister, rather pale, leaning on the back of the Empire armchair upon which she is seated, listens to her in silence, his eyes straying over the little Egyptian gods and scarabs that crowd the window ledges of his *salon*.

*Le Matin*, 29th July 1914

# CHAPTER NINE

# Les Responsables

In the morning newspapers, sharing the headlines with the result of the trial, was the news that Austria had invaded Serbia : so the latest European Crisis had overtaken Caillaux while he was out of office and occupied with Henriette's defence, whereas he should have been presiding over the destinies of France and, through France, Europe; and he would have been, but for Calmette's unscrupulous press campaign.

The Nationalist papers continued to attack him with unabated fury. *Le Figaro* asserted that he had bribed or terrorised the President of the Court, the Public Prosecutor and the jury, that it was the most enormous scandal of the epoch and that the editors felt obliged to continue Calmette's 'patriotic' work relentlessly and without fear :

> It is possible to seduce twelve jurymen, one can seat an Albanel under the picture from which the Christ has been banished, one can engage fifty criminals to shout *'Vivats'* and carry a felonious minister on their shoulders which should be branded. One can count on the trembling *camaraderie* of ministers and the obedience of the police, all the treasons, all the complicities, all the lapses. But one cannot seduce the crowd. One could not force it to acclaim the assassin or dishonour the tomb. Yesterday if the jury, as a relaxation from their duties, had attempted to walk in the seething town they could have learned the true verdict, the only one that restores, encourages and comforts us, the voice of the people, and learn that the true trial has opened.
>
> *Le Figaro* 29th July 1914

*L'Action Française* was equally abusive, under headlines such as JUSTICE ASSASSINATED and PERMISSION TO KILL; and under PARIS VERSUS THE ASSASSINS they reported at great length details of the riots on the boulevards which their gangs had organised.

> European tension has just made it easier for a scandalous verdict to absolve an assassin. Caillaux can thank Germany whose politics he has served so well.

The need to consider the defence of the country before everything else has made more than one citizen hesitate to take the punitive action they had planned. Is it only adjourned? That depends on Caillaux, and on Caillaux alone.

'Madame Caillaux, wounded and stricken for ever . . .' Maître Labori said. . . . We shall abandon *La Criminelle* to her remorse, to her regrets – and to her husband.

But there is one condition – that the two assassins make it possible for us to forget them. Let them disappear completely. Let Monsieur Caillaux renounce not only his intention to preside over this Republic, which once again he has succeeded in dishonouring, but also let him abstain from soliciting any ministry, from speaking under any pretext in the name of France. We give him this definite advice.

If he ignores it, he can only blame himself for the consequences. We shall reiterate his title of assassin for as long and as often as necessary. We are not sure if we shall be able to restrain the many good men whom the breakdown of justice has exasperated. Caillaux, accomplice of his wife, has succeeded, like her, in escaping a prison sentence : much good may it do him! But it is on himself alone that the anger of the patriots will descend if he fails to understand that retirement and silence are all that he has left him.

Their leader writers turned the attack on Caillaux into an attack on the Republican form of constitutional government, reminding their readers that for the past three centuries they had been accustomed to listen absent-mindedly to the roar of cannon fire in Europe, knowing that not one of these rounds could have been fired without His permission, without the consent or the command of France personified by the great king installed in majestic peace in Versailles. Now this great people had been reduced to waiting to learn from decisions taken in Peterhof or London whether the troops were to march, or whither, or how. But, for the moment, there was only one question – were they prepared for the war which seemed imminent?

In Paris today there is only one answer : we can hope one day to be prepared, provided we can get rid of the political system under which we have seen a former Prime Minister, accomplice in an assassination, freely defy the apparatus of justice solely because he has remained *persona grata* with the most insolent and brutal enemy of our country.
*L'Action Française*, 29th July 1914

Caillaux didn't control any newspapers. *L'Humanité*, the official organ of the Communist Party, did not attack him and Henriette as members of the *bourgeoisie*, probably because of the influence of Jaurès. The unimportant *Bonnet Rouge*, which Caillaux subsidised during the trial, commented that the jury had dealt justly with the abominable press campaign and the scandalous proceedings which if they became general would dishonour the press. The trial aroused considerable interest in Great Britain and the USA.

The unhappy woman who stood in the dock engaged our sympathy in so far as she had acted under the spur of an intolerable provocation, but it was impossible to pass from pity to admiration. To shoot down a defenceless man without a word of warning is a cowardly act at best, and no generous concern for any high human end redeemed it . . .

Why was it that a fashionable conservative newspaper like *Le Figaro* pursued its resentments by methods which the lowest 'rag' in this country would shrink from using? . . . The jury decided the issue by the light of nature, and it was the witnesses and not the advocates who supplied the real eloquence of the debate. They harangued; they stormed; they made epigrams; they revealed their inner emotional life with a power of statement and self-revelation which in England may be seen only on the stage, and only there in a translated play . . .

Painful and disorderly as it was, it is quite arguable that this natural debate is preferable to our own frigid professional trials. The Capulets and the Montagues came into court, not with swords, but with ringing speeches, and the jury had before it not the abstract fact of an isolated 'crime', but the whole feud of mingled and mutual wrong which issued in the murder . . . Nor can we in all the circumstances profess to regret the result. The real criminal was the whole of this envious, hating, blackmailing world. The real offender was the social code which tolerates the stealing and publication of private letters. The real mischief is that no law of libel restrains a venal and dishonourable press . . . If an editor may steal a woman's private love-letters and publish them to the world, if this offence leads neither to social ostracism nor to any legal penalty, it is folly to expect that private vengeance will stay its hand.

*The Nation*, 1st August 1914

The great murder trial in Paris, in the course of which intrigues of politics, finance, and love have been woven with subtle ingenuity . . . into the main theme of the proceedings, has come to an end; Madame Caillaux has been acquitted. For eight long days of anguish the wife of one of the most prominent statesmen of France has sat in the dock charged with causing the death of Monsieur Calmette, the editor of *Le Figaro* . . .

The case was the outcome of a newspaper campaign, conducted with the object of bringing about the ruin of Monsieur Caillaux, formerly the Chief Minister of the French Republic . . . He is a man of great for of character, whose domestic life has been no less stormy than his public career . . .

The wife had fought in defence of her husband's honour, and in a moment of passion had fired a weapon with which she intended, so she declared, only to threaten. The husband, from the hour of her arrest, stood by her side, determined by every means in his power to save her from condemnation. The proceedings provided one of the most pathetic and moving spectacles ever presented in a court of law . . .

The Court has acquitted her of the crime : it has not been prepared to condemn a beautiful and courageous woman who struck in defence, as she believed, of her own and her husband's honour. It is not for us to draw any deductions from the verdict. The case admits of no generalisation; it stands in a class by itself . . . It is the mission of justice to temper the punishment not only to the crime but to the temperament and circumstances of the prisoner. It may be that in this instance – remarkable as the verdict may appear – substantial justice has been done.

The Daily Telegraph, 29th July 1914

Jaurès, on the final day of the trial, 28th July, had had to leave Paris to attend a meeting of international socialist leaders he had convened at their headquarters in Brussels. As soon as he arrived at his hotel he ran to the telephone to learn the verdict.[1] His anxiety about Henriette's acquittal astonished his colleagues who did not know of his purpose to take office under Caillaux. Thus he learned that one obstacle to peace had been removed – even Poincaré had admitted that Caillaux would have to be entrusted with the government if his wife were acquitted. It meant, if they could stave off the present crisis, they would be able to form a government with a large enough majority to force Poincaré's resignation and reverse his foreign policy.

His great hope, like Caillaux's, lay in the fact that the peoples themselves had no desire to fight each other. He thought a concerted general strike of Socialist workers, in every country threatened by war, might force the military leaders to accept Britain's proposal for an immediate conference of the great powers to settle their differences.

At the meeting with the other leaders he was assured by Haase, head of the German Socialist Party, six million strong, that they would refuse their government's demand for war contributions. They listened to reports on the anti-war strikes in Russia, on protest meetings in industrial towns in Germany, on a demonstration of workers dispersed by the police on the Unter den Linden in the centre of Berlin. Jaurès recognised the necessity for the German workers to resist a Pan-Slav invasion, just as the French workers would have to resist a Pan-German one: it would be necessary to act before the situation became more acute. They approved plans for an international general strike.

In the evening Jaurès addressed a crowd of 8,000 in the vast arena of the Cirque-Royale and was given a rapturous welcome. He appealed to the workers of all nations to refuse to march against each other, assured his audience that the French Government didn't want war, and supported the appeal of the British Government for a conference. He concluded:

> If mechanical force and the intoxication of the first battles prevails; if the absolute masters succeed in inflaming the masses until death and misery show their hideous faces everywhere, and typhus rounds off the work of the guns, then all the armies will turn against their rulers and ask, 'Where are your reasons for these heaped up corpses?' Then the Revolution unleashed will say to them: 'Be gone and pray to God and man for mercy!'
>
> But if we succeed in abating the storm, then will not the people cry, 'Let us forbid this spectre to rise every six months from the grave to afright the world!'?
>
> I thank our German comrades in the name of the French, and I swear we will continue to support them like brothers against the warmongers' Attila campaign, true till death![2]

Before leaving for Paris he wrote a manifesto for the French news-papers:

> The Socialist Party proclaims aloud that only France can dispose of France's fate; that in no circumstances must she be involved through the more or less arbitrary exploitation of secret treaties and obligations in a frightful conflict . . . We know only one treaty, the treaty which binds us to the human race.

He was not very hopeful that war could be avoided, but he consoled one of his companions, Vandeleere, by reminding him of the prolonged crisis of Agadir which nevertheless had finally been resolved.

On the 30th he spent a couple of hours in the museums, and when he boarded the 1 p.m. train for Paris he was tired out and promptly went to sleep. A fellow member of the French delegation, Lonquist, remarked, 'He looks as if he were dead.'[3]

Poincaré had returned from Russia on the 29th. He conferred with his ministers, and a Cabinet meeting was held that afternoon. On the

following day at about 6 p.m., Malvy, Minister for the Interior, telephoned Caillaux and asked him if he could come at once to his office :
Caillaux thought he had done so on Poincaré's instructions in order to
get his reactions to their latest policy decision. His account of the meeting is recorded in his memoirs :

'I have asked you to come, my dear President,' Malvy began, 'to
inform you of the grave decision which has been taken in Council,
and to have your opinion.' 'I am listening.' 'Russia has asked us if
she can mobilise.' 'And what have you replied?'
'We have replied "Yes." We are committed to support her. 'Hell!'
I said. 'You are exceeding the terms of the Treaty of Alliance, but,'
I added immediately, 'you are acting in accord with England?'
'Ah,' Malvy replied, 'there was no question of England.' 'Miscre-
ants!' I cried, jumping up from my armchair, 'You have just unleashed the war . . .

He told Malvy that if they had had the assent of Britain, he did not
believe either Germany or Austria would incur the huge risk of attacking a solid alliance of three powers; and if Britain refused her assent,
France would have every reason to discourage Russia's warlike de-
signs : in either case, war would be avoided. He insisted, he says, with
all his strength, that they should try to withdraw the fatal dispatch to
Russia under the pretext of the necessity of discussions with Britain,
and that they should immediately try to engage Britain to adopt a
common policy with them.[4]

As soon as he left Malvy he contacted all the members of the
government he thought he could influence, and impressed on them the
seriousness of what they had done. He added that in any case it was
a crime to court war while they were unprovided with heavy artillery
– for, unhappily for France – Poincaré and the succeeding Prime
Ministers had failed to exercise control over their experts and generals,
with the result that Caillaux's orders for the heavy howitzers to be put
into production had been cancelled. Experiments had been carried on
with a different type, but only one or two pieces had been completed,
and there were no shells for them, nor had the firing tables been calculated.

Poincaré now sent a courier to King George V, asking him to declare publicly that his country would support France – but of course
the decision lay not with the king, and he could only send a non-
committal reply. Indeed the majority of the cabinet and of the British

people were not prepared to go to war about the situation in the Balkans. The *Daily News* published letters from religious leaders and from other men of importance protesting against intervention, and the Governors of the Bank of England called on Lloyd George at the Treasury to state that financial and trading interests were totally opposed to it. As in other countries, there were mass meetings of protest organised by the Socialists.

A 5.15 p.m. on the 30th, Jaurès arrived at the Gare du Nord in Paris, old brown portmanteau in one hand and a large yellow poster in the other bearing a manifesto against war. He was greeted by head-lines in *Le Temps* that Russia had mobilised twenty-five divisions – but all was not lost, he told the other delegates, for Britain was still con-tinuing her efforts for reconciliation. At seven in the evening he went with a delegation to the Prime Minister, Viviani, and insisted that the government should speak forcibly to Russia, tell her to halt mobilisa-tion and refrain from interfering in Serbia, or France would not sup-port her. Viviani was at pains to reassure Jaurès of the government's peaceful intentions by informing him they had ordered all French troops to withdraw ten kilometres from the frontiers to avoid incidents – but he didn't mention the telegram he had sent to St Petersburg con-firming France's solidarity with Russia.

In the ante-room, Isvolsky passed them : Jaurès remarked in a loud voice, 'That dog of an Isvolsky.' The insult was ignored, and Jaurès went back to the offices of *L'Humanité* of which he was political correspondent.

The general strike against war was announced at mass meetings in Paris and other towns, but Jaurès was careful to make it clear that it was an international protest, and if it didn't take place in countries that were potentially their enemies, it wouldn't take place in France either.[5] He sent telegrams to the Socialist and Democratic leaders in Germany, Austria, Russia and Belgium, calling on them to declare a strike also. Not one of them was delivered.

Next day he was with Malvy, insisting Russia must be categorically informed France was associating herself with Britain's peace moves and would not follow her into war. He tried to see Viviani again, but could only get to Abel Ferry, Under-Secretary for Foreign Affairs, who told him war could not be avoided.

All that day, 31st July, Henriette was so ill as the result of her long ordeal that Caillaux dared not leave her : therefore a pale young man, vaguely wandering among the crowds in the streets and along the corridors of the Palais-Bourbon, failed to find him.

Jaurès, like Caillaux, had been execrated in the Nationalist press. On 18th July Charles Maurras in *L'Action Française* had called him an infamous traitor, and 'everyone knows Jaurès is Germany'. He added, 'Our politics are not of words,' which seemed to imply a threat. Maurice de Waleffe in *Paris-Midi* wrote that a general who ordered Jaurès to be shot would only be doing his duty. Others were equally abusive in the same vein, Léon Daudet, Gohier – and Charles Péguy who wrote, 'In time of war there is only one policy, that of the National Convention * . . . Jaurès in a tumbril and a roll of drums to drown that great voice.'[6]

In the *Café du Croissant* at the corner of the rue Montmartre, on the evening of 31st July, Jaurès dined with several of his friends : they discussed the situation and found only one gleam of hope – that the six million strong German Socialist Party would protest, together with the French, against the war. He was expecting a messenger from Brussels . . .

He had his back to the window which was screened from the street by a curtain. It was very hot. Several times the curtain was raised from the outside, finally by a tall man with a soft-brimmed hat pulled well down over his eyes who peered in and then hurried away. The editor of *Le Bonnet Rouge*, Dolié, was in the café with his young wife : he brought out a photograph of their baby daughter. Jaurès asked her age, and smiled . . . 'She is sweet . . .' Again the curtain was lifted and a hand carrying a revolver appeared. A shot crashed out, and then another. A woman's piercing scream, 'They have killed Jaurès !' He had fallen sideways onto the cushioned seat, the smile fading from his lips. In a few minutes he was dead.

His assailant, Villain (the pale young man), was pursued, arrested, and saved with difficulty from the crowd. He told the police his mission was to kill Caillaux and Jaurès, the enemies of France, who had opposed the Three Years Service Act. He had two pistols; on the butt of one he had carved a C for Caillaux, and of the other a J for Jaurès.[7] He was an active member of a Nationalist group called *Les Jeunes Amis d'Alsace-Lorraine*.

As news of the crime spread to the suburbs, there were demonstrations, riots, police charges and arrests.

News of the assassination spread rapidly through the town. Paris was stunned by grief through which indignation forced its way.

* The National Convention was the Assembly of Deputies from 1792–1795 during which time the King and Queen were guillotined, and also Danton, Lavoisier and many others – and finally Robespierre himself.

Towards eleven o'clock in the evening, when the 13th edition of *Le Bonnet Rouge* came out, carrying the announcement of the death of Jaurès, an imposing crowd appeared on the boulevards and moved down through the *Faubourg Montmartre* with immense clamour and loud cries. It halted in front of *Le Petit Journal* and *Le Figaro*. Here it was dispersed by a brigade of police. The people turned solemnly away. There were sobbing men and women round the notices posted by the Government paying homage to the great man who had passed on.

*Le Bonnet Rouge* 2nd August 1914

Outside the *Humanité* offices there were extraordinary emotional scenes, hundreds of people stood calling 'Jaurès! Jaurès!' like an incantation, as if he could still help them. As his body was being carried away, Captain Gerard, who had collaborated with him on his book, *La Nouvelle Armée*, pinned his own Legion of Honour onto his breast. It was not yet known whether the assassination was the work of a lone gunman or part of a widespread conspiracy, so the Chief of Police went to Caillaux and warned him to get out of town as quickly as possible.[8]

*L'Action Française* with its *Camelots du Roi* was thought to have been responsible for the crime, but the editor, Charles Maurras, denied this. He wrote, 'I should have liked to see Jaurès executed, but I would not have approved of the assassination, even if it had been Caillaux.' Anatole France wrote, 'One day in July, ignoble calumnies transformed an imbecile into an assassin.'

Many people saw in the death of Jaurès a sign that the world catastrophe was upon them —and they were right. On the previous evening the first general mobilisation order – which makes war inevitable because it forces your opponent to do the same – had been issued by Russia. It was followed by that of Austria-Hungary on the 31st, and of France on 1st August. According to the treaties, Russia and France should only have mobilised if Germany had done so, but German mobilisation came only after that of France, but also on 1st August.

Caillaux and Henriette, because of the general mobilisation, were not able to leave Paris on the morning of 1st August without a pass. For hours, the car waiting at the door, they paced up and down their *salon* while one was being obtained for them, and every few minutes the phone rang with anonymous threats or with warnings from friends that they were about to be assassinated. The crowd, inflamed by the Nationalist papers, had tasted blood.

For the first time in his life, Caillaux says, he felt fear, not only for

himself but for Henriette. Until then, knowing that he had a great
following in the country, he had felt secure; but now, with the onrush
of events and the death of Jaurès, his plans to lead France along the
way of conciliation with the rest of Europe had crumbled to dust, and
both he and his policy were out of favour. Ever since he had learned
from Malvy of the telegram from the French Government supporting
Russian mobilisation he had had no hope that peace could be preserved; and in fact the news that three million Russians were massing
on their eastern frontier had turned even the most peace-loving German into an ardent defender of the Fatherland, and the Socialist
deputies who had applauded Jaurès in Brussels, voted the war contributions demanded by their government.

Germany's answer to Russia's mobilisation was to declare war on her
on 1st August. Isvolsky brought the news to Poincaré who declared
categorically that the Cabinet, like himself, were firmly decided to im-
plement the Treaty of Alliance and to carry out in full their obligations
to Russia – he had made secret agreements, which he was allowed to do
under the constitution, to back Russia whether she was invaded or not,
but he didn't wish this to be known or discussed until Germany could
be proved to be the aggressor : therefore the Chamber was not sum-
moned until 3rd August. When the deputies arrived they found the
doors closed and a notice postponing the session until the following
day : the reason being that although the invasion of Belgium had begun, the Kaiser had not yet declared war on France. On the following
day the deputies were faced with a *fait accompli*. The Government
had declared war without their consent, and then Germany had
declared war on France. Viviani announced, 'We have done everything to avoid war, but we are the victims taken by surprise of an
odious and traitorous aggression . . .'

In Britain the whole situation was changed by the news of the
German invasion of Belgium, and the crowds who had demonstrated
against war on 3rd August demonstrated in favour of it on the 4th:
it was felt that the invasion of Belgium threatened the existence of independent nations and that a German victory would mean the destruction of democracy and liberty in Europe.

During the opening weeks of the war Caillaux watched with a kind
of despair the disasters to the French arms brought upon them by the
mistakes of the high command, for alas! it was not only the orders he
had placed for heavy artillery while he was Prime Minister that had
been countermanded but, which was even more serious, his orders had
not been carried out that the French armies were to concentrate on the

Acquitted! Henriette embraces Maître Labori.

Jaurès, the great tribune.

north-eastern frontier in the event of war in order to oppose an attack through Belgium.[10] His orders had been superseded by Joffre's Plan Seventeen, which was not so much a plan as a mystical idea : 'Attack! Attack!'

The French Government, so far from giving orders to its army, was not even informed of what the high command was doing.[11] Under Plan Seventeen, thousands and thousands of French lives were thrown away on futile attacks on German prepared positions farther to the south while Von Kluck was advancing in strength through Belgium and the industrial regions of Northern France.[12]

When Joffre had lost a third of his army – more than 300,000 men in six weeks, he went to the opposite extreme and began to carry out a new plan – a withdrawal to defensive positions in the Central Massif of France, abandoning Paris and Verdun – it was the reverse face of the 'Attack! Attack!' mystique. Von Kluck turned to pursue him, ignoring Paris, and in doing so exposed his flank. Gallieni, still in command of the garrison of Paris, saw his opportunity, persuaded Joffre to support him, and launched an attack which threw the Germans back in confusion.

From the day of this victory, the famous Battle of the Marne, fought on both sides with near-exhausted troops and won by a general he himself had appointed, Caillaux never doubted France would win through in the end. He thought Poincaré should have sent for him to form a government as he was the leader favoured by the majority of the electorate; but Poincaré did not send for him. He formed an emergency government, on 27th August 1914, without him, and without reference to the Senate or to the Chamber of Deputies. It was a *coup d'état*.

Because it was so well known that Caillaux was opposed to his Nationalist policies, Poincaré was obsessed by the idea that he would continue to work against him. In this he was entirely wrong. Once the die was cast and France was fighting for her life, he placed his services at the government's disposal and supported them in the Chamber. He reserved his advice and criticism for private conversation and committee work. After a short spell as Paymaster General to the Army with the rank of colonel – during which he was frequently insulted, indulged in fisticuffs with a British officer and nearly lost his life in a fast car thoughtfully provided for him without brakes or lights – he was sent, in November 1914, to Brazil on a trade mission and to enlist sympathy for France. He was so successful that the German Government sent 300,000 marks to their representative there to counteract the effects of his visit, and the Naval Attaché sent a telegram to the German Admiralty asking for the ship in which he was returning, the *Araguaya*, to be intercepted, saying, 'capture most desirable.'[13] He got safely back to France and was officially thanked for the success of his mission.

He was much embarrassed at this time by articles praising him in the German Press. The *Gazette of Frankfurt* represented him as the incarnation of parliamentary government against the domination of an oligarchy. The *Rheinische Westphalische Zeitung* of 23rd July, said, 'The band Raymond Poincaré-la-conscience Barthou & Co., tremble in secret before the popularity, growing from day to day, of Caillaux, the true, the only statesman of France.' And the *Kölnische Zeitung* of 16th April 1915, said, 'If Monsieur Caillaux had remained in office, if Madame Caillaux's gesture had not been made, the plot against the peace of Europe . . . would not have succeeded.' It maintained that Henriette's 'gesture' was the decisive incident which led to the outbreak of the war, not the assassination at Sarajevo which was merely a pretext and, had it not occurred, another would have been found. All of which, however true, did not exactly endear him to his fellow countrymen. It was even worse when the Germans published documents they had seized when they entered Brussels, among them the pre-war reports of the Belgian ambassadors to the Allied courts, to the effect that they believed Caillaux's return to power would diminish international rivalries and provide the basis for an understanding between France and Germany.

Henriette had volunteered as a nurse, but she was hissed out of the wards and had to resign. In the summer of 1916, Caillaux took her to Vichy for her health. Two days after their arrival, while walking in the gardens, they were set upon by an angry crowd and had to take refuge in a nearby house. Here they underwent a regular siege, a howling mob shouting, 'Death to Caillaux!' bombarding the house with bricks and stones and trying to force the doors and shutters which fortunately held until the police arrived. Caillaux had disguised Henriette as a housemaid and hidden her under a bed. The crowd had been joined by convalescing soldiers who, it seems, had been told Caillaux was one of those responsible for the war.

After an official investigation it was announced it was a spontaneous attack, but this was immediately contradicted by *L'Action Française* who claimed the credit for it in an article by Charles Maurras on 26th August 1916.

Caillaux then booked accommodation for himself and Henriette at Biarritz; the local Police Inspector begged him to cancel their visit as the *Camelots du Roi* had got wind of it and had organised an anti-Caillaux demonstration which he had not sufficient force to control.

Towards the end of 1916, Sir Edward Grey, British Foreign Minister, sent a journalist to ask Caillaux how he envisaged an eventual peace. He replied he didn't know when peace would come, but he thought it would be of paramount importance for Britain and France to work together for an undivided Europe.

As Henriette was evidently not safe in France, Caillaux took her to Italy. They were cold-shouldered by the French Embassy officials in Rome, but they found congenial companions with whom they could relax and talk as much as they pleased, which was important to Caillaux as it helped him to formulate his ideas.

On 29th December 1916 an article appeared in *The Times* insinuating that he had gone to Rome to engage in peace propaganda :

> ... he is reported to have recommended in Italian 'neutralist' quarters, where pro-German feeling is still strong, a France-Italy policy of startling boldness. Germany, he is understood to have said, is disposed to accord the most generous treatment to France, and is prepared to compel Austria to grant Italy terms that would fulfil all, or nearly all, her national aspirations . . . It is said that Monsieur Caillaux failed to obtain an audience of the Pope, though Madame Caillaux paid her respects to some members of the Sacred College . . .
>
> In Rome the ideas he has ventilated are thought to be not unconnected with the peace manoeuvres in which international high finance has lately been indulging.

Caillaux immediately sent an indignant denial, calling upon the editor to prove his allegations, or withdraw them. On 4th January 1917, *The Times* published his telegram with the comment : 'We are not accustomed to "justify" our "assertions" but to satisfy ourselves of their accuracy before publication. In the present instance we followed our usual practice.'

This was not sufficient for Caillaux. He wrote a long letter to Lord Northcliffe, asking him by what right he published this libellous accusation against a French deputy which was calculated to sow dissension in the councils of Britain's ally and thus weaken their combined war effort. He stated emphatically that neither in Rome nor anywhere else had he brought forward, presented or suggested peace negotiations, that he had had no dealings with representatives of the German Government since the negotiations of 1911, and as for international finance, he didn't know if it still existed, but he had had no contact with it.

'I am ready today,' he wrote, 'as I was yesterday and shall be tomorrow, to submit my entire life, my every act, even my every thought, to investigation by an impartial tribunal.'

The rest of his letter consisted of a denunciation of what he called 'The Dictation of Calumny' exercised by small groups working on the masses through their control of the most important newspapers which could defeat the purposes of democracy by discrediting the people's elected representatives who didn't suit them. He again demanded that the original statement be withdrawn or substantiated, and he challenged Northcliffe to publish his letter.[14] His letter was not published, neither could Northcliffe substantiate the original statement because, wherever his correspondents raked it up from, it was complete nonsense, with no truth in it whatsoever. The Vatican categorically denied that Caillaux had approached them or that any discussion with him had taken place.

The story that Caillaux had tried to contact enemy peace envoys through the Vatican was seized upon by the Nationalist papers : they labelled him 'defeatist' although throughout the war he had shown himself to be a staunch patriot. The damage to France's prestige and morale caused by the deliberately propagated belief that one of her leading statesmen desponded of her cause was so great that Caillaux seriously wondered if the ultra-Nationalists wanted the war to be lost so that the Republic would be ruined and they might be able to set up a Royalist Government in its place.

On 22nd July 1917 Clemenceau accused Malvy, Minister of the Interior, of acting contrary to the national interest. Malvy had no difficulty in clearing himself but, finding he was unsupported by the Prime Minister, Painlevé, he resigned a month later. This affair gained for Clemenceau the support of *L'Action Française*, a combination that was fatal for Caillaux. The collapse of Russia as an ally, and major disasters on the Western Front – particularly the offensives of General Nivelle and his Chief of Staff of the 'Attack! Attack!' school – had created an atmosphere of depression which might have led to a demand for a change of government, and Caillaux was the obvious alternative.

On 16th November 1917 Poincaré called upon Clemenceau to form a government. This seems surprising as the two men detested each other, and there was no parliamentary support for the move, but they had in common their hatred of Germany and their fear of Caillaux's influence in the country. Clemenceau had been writing a series of articles in his paper, *L'Homme Enchaîné*, attacking the government and the military leaders, articles which were regularly reproduced in the *Gazette des Ardennes*, the newspaper which the Germans circulated in the five occupied French departments. According to Monsieur Capus, Director of *Le Figaro*, who effected the reconciliation and brought Clemenceau to the Elysée, Poincaré's first words after the conventional greetings were, 'Then it is understood, dear friend, that we'll imprison Caillaux . . .'[15]

# CHAPTER TEN

# Guilty of Innocence

When Clemenceau had been in office for only three weeks he placed before the Chamber a letter from General Dubail, Governor of Paris, accusing Caillaux of having worked for the destruction of France's alliances while military action was in progress, and of having seconded the progress of the enemies' armies. He moved that diplomatic immunity be withdrawn from Caillaux. It transpired that the letter had been written by an obscure politician, Ignace, in the employ of the government, and that General Dubail had been 'invited' to sign it.

For the first time in three years, Caillaux stood at the rostrum to reply to his adversaries. He said he didn't want diplomatic immunity because there was nothing in the entire record of his public life he wished to conceal. He protested that never at any moment had he tried, directly or indirectly, to deal with the enemy. He described the policy of peace and conciliation he had always pursued, the policy which had been overturned by the events of 1914: to illustrate this he quoted Jaurès, 'If the people are not on their guard, violent or cunning minorities bring disaster upon us.'

Now that the Great War had broken out, he continued, and the country was in danger, he didn't want to embarrass the Government, so he would confine himself within the limits necessary for his defence. He regretted that a Government of the Right had been formed without the support of the majorities of the Left, relying only on so-called 'public opinion'. It was likely, therefore, to be dominated by sterile retrograde forms:

CAILLAUX: If one cannot remedy their overall political control and direction of the war effort, is one at least permitted to ask that it should be better organised at every level of work and responsibility to prevent the waste of human life and of the country's resources?

And is it forbidden also to raise the problem of the peace? We need not only a better direction of the war, we must at the same time lay the foundations of peace, I mean a durable peace, a humane peace. I cannot, and I shall not, recognise any other . . .

I understand the Prime Minister stated recently . . . that one must not talk while fighting. . . . Are we permitted to have a different opinion? May we not agree with President Wilson that it is singularly dangerous to allow our enemies hypocritically to adopt the formula, 'No annexations, no penal indemnities, the right of free determination of peoples to decide their own future'? We should adopt these great words and substitute them for our present varying war aims . . .

Many of us think we cannot enclose our country's destiny within the space of a few years, however divine the tragedy may be that we are living now. We are the depositories of the life of France and we have the duty to conserve it. We have to take a wide view of the future, we have to think of reconstituting and of maintaining a free and independent nation, to think of its economy, rudely tested in this war, and which requires that urgent measures should be taken.

Can it be . . . that when one asks oneself what is best for the country, when one ponders with agony on the spectacular vicissitudes of the war, when one scans the horizon on the look out for the best solutions, that one should be called 'defeatist'? There is not a Frenchman, I am certain, who has ever wished for the defeat of his country, who has ever dreamed of it! Just as there isn't a Frenchman – and I speak here for myself – who has ever dreamed of breaking the treaties of alliance in time of war, who has ever dreamed, particularly, of separating his country from a country such as Britain to whom goes out spontaneously the admiration of all democrats brought up under the influence of her great tradition! Defeatist! Ignoble word, coined by those trying to create scandal and exploit it! By those who organised against me the incidents of Vichy . . .

Monsieur Clemenceau! Against the calumniators of Dreyfus you waged an admirable campaign with generosity and courage: now you cancel it out by attacking me as Dreyfus was attacked! You are waging a Dreyfus campaign against me! (*Shouts of agreement from the deputies: 'With the same people!' 'With the same methods!' 'The same general staff!'*)

He said he had been accused, among other things, of being imprudent, but for those who dare at great moments to take their responsibilities seriously, imprudence was almost inseparable from action; for those who dare, for example, to preserve their country from a threatening war . . . Sometimes they are forced to actions that could be called imprudent.

He concluded with a quotation, explaining that the words had been spoken by his accuser, Clemenceau himself, before the jury of the Seine in 1895 :

'Gentlemen it is time we made an end of all this unworthy play acting. We have not the right to play with the highest sentiments in a man, his patriotism. By suspicion and calumny we disseminate hatred and cause disturbances among the citizens, we weaken our country and leave it wide open to the enemy !'[1]

His speech was received with tremendous applause, and deputies crowded round him, offering congratulations. Again there was talk that he would take over the government. Poincaré, who had initiated the plot against him, was uneasy at the sucecss of his defence. He wrote :

His speech produced a very powerful effect . . . it influenced even his opponents. Ignace, however, is counting on the investigation bringing interesting results quickly.[2]

It was obvious the Dubail letter was based on no evidence, and that the purpose of the investigation was to find something to support the accusations.

This attempt to ruin Caillaux having failed, agents were sent abroad to contact as many people as possible to whom he might have spoken on his travels, to South America, Spain, Switzerland, Italy, to see if an indiscreet action or some unguarded word could be found that might be used against him.

On the demand of the French Ambassador to Italy, his safe-deposit box in a bank in Florence was seized and opened without any representative of his being present .The Ambassador, Barrère, reported that it contained two million francs in securities and 500,000 francs worth of jewelry besides political documents. Where could so much money come from? From the enemy, of course! The news was given to the press, and Caillaux was informed that he would be arrested: it was hoped, no doubt, he would take to flight and thus confirm his guilt, but he had no such intention. The Countess Greffuhle, invited him, as a gesture of sympathy, to her *salon;* and he, although he rarely attended social functions, accepted – it was a situation that appealed to Proust: the Countess was popularly supposed to be one of the models for his character of the Duchesse de Guermantes. For this action she was reviled in the columns of *L'Action Française* by Léon Daudet to whom Proust had dedicated *Le Côté de Guermantes.* Next morning the police arrived and arrested Caillaux in his bathroom. The poetess, Anna de Noailles, who had mounted guard outside the house, obstructed the police and tried to prevent them taking him away.

It was discovered almost immediately – and Caillaux was able to prove it – that the safe-deposit box contained only a reasonable amount of securities to provide for Henriette and himself in case of need, her family jewels and some notes for articles and speeches, for it was his constant habit to note down ideas as they occurred to him. The wealth in the box was as chimerical as the crown of diamonds supposed to have been given to Henriette by the Kaiser as a wedding present.

In spite of this, Caillaux was not released. He was divested of watch, tie, all toilet articles, even of braces, and shut up in a cell in the wing reserved for the most dangerous criminals and murderers awaiting execution. He was kept under constant observation, and the bright electric light in his cell was never extinguished. The punishment cells were opposite his, where the wretched inmates howled and screamed, sometimes all night, and hurled themselves against the walls.

He reflected that France had never been generous to those who loved and served her, and that he ought to be content to follow in the footsteps of those who had been wrongfully persecuted – Malesherbes, Danton, Jaurès . . . but in the anguish of sleepless nights he was haunted by the thought that not all those who are wrongfully persecuted are afterwards redeemed to glow in the pages of history, and he feared he might go to his tomb with the Nessus shirt of calumny still clinging to him. When the interminable interrogations started, he felt it as a relief to have an adversary to pit his wits against, an adversary whose business it was to find a pretext to send him to a traitor's death in the ditch of the Château de Vincennes.

A Parliamentary Commission was appointed to consider the charges against Caillaux: its members were astonished at their flimsiness and told Clemenceau there was nothing in them but idle gossip more suitable for the newspapers than for a Parliamentary Commission, and that they refused to deliver up anyone to private vengeance.

Clemenceau replied it was his duty to maintain the high morale of the people, both those at home and those serving in the forces. He insisted it was necessary that the troops who were sacrificing their lives at the front should have confidence in the government's determination that they should not be betrayed at home. Already they were saying, 'They don't make such a fuss about sending one of us to face the firing squad.' A Member of the commission, Viollette, retorted that they would not manufacture evidence of guilt, even to satisfy public opinion. They extorted a guarantee from the government that Caillaux would not be tried by court martial unless there was clear evidence of intelligence with the enemy.[3]

When he had been in prison for nine months and had been submitted to more than fifty interrogations there was still not the shadow of a piece of evidence that he had communicated with the enemy, so the intention to bring him before a court martial had to be abandoned. He was transferred to another prison while new charges were being prepared against him. The war ended. The statesmen gathered at Versailles to make a treaty of peace – and Caillaux's voice was not heard. His antagonists knew he would have been totally opposed to the policy they were pursuing, that his over-riding thoughts were that the peace treaties must lead to the reorganising of Europe as one economic unit, and that terms must not be imposed on the vanquished that must inevitably lead to another war – the mistake that Germany had made in 1871.

The French Government were aware of his plans for the future, not only from his undeviating policy but from the papers, written in 1915, which they had seized in his safe-deposit box. They contained the thoughts of a man who might have been called upon at any time to take over the government of his country, perhaps in a state of emergency which could have made it necessary for him to have governed, for a limited time, by decree.

What would he have done? First he would have superseded Joffre and the other generals of the 'Attack! Attack!' school and appointed Sarrail Commander-in-Chief; he would have created a Council for National Defence to direct operations; a Council of State, in which industrialists, merchants and the trade unions would be represented, to advise on technical matters. To prevent war being declared in future by any government without consultation with the people, he envisaged an association of nations each of which would have to undertake to introduce a law making it illegal for a general mobilisation to be ordered without a public referendum. There was an essay recording the events leading to the outbreak of the war. It was entitled *Les Responsables.* His *responsables* were the governments of Austria, Germany and Russia – and Poincaré. He gave it as his opinion that the Kaiser wanted the war 'with a will at the same time so vacillating and so passionate that if he had come up against a proud and dignified determination on the part of France to maintain peace, he would have given way.' He would have had the direct and the indirect authors of the war brought to trial.

The papers included a draft law with penalties for libels in the press, as in Britain; for the nationalisation of the railways, for raising the compulsory school age to seventeen : he had plans for improved housing, for old age pensions and unemployment insurance, and measures to fight tuberculosis and infant mortality. There was also a plan 'to eliminate from the ante-chambers of power the staffs of *Le Figaro* and *L'Action Française.*'

Prolonged attempts were made to find in all this something treasonable, without success.

When the Treaty of Versailles had been signed, he was arraigned before the Senate, the High Court of Justice, held within the painted and panelled walls of the Chambre des Séances of the Palais du Luxembourg. He stood again at the rostrum from which he had so often justified his policy as a minister. The Senators, his judges, robed in purple and ermine, sat before him in a hemicycle flanked and half encircled by large marble statues of earlier legislators. He was charged with intelligence with the enemy and with plotting against the external security of the state, under articles 77 and 79 of the criminal code. When the charges had been read out on behalf of the government, the senators who were members of the government took their places among his judges.

The Prosecutor's line of argument was that because his attitude at the time of the Agadir Crisis had been one of accommodation with Germany he was not likely to have changed it after the outbreak of war. Therefore everything he had done, and every conversation he had held must be interpreted in this sense. Consequently Caillaux had once more to defend his policy of 1911 when he had prevented war from breaking out by exercising his constitutional authority to override de Selves and the Quai d'Orsay. As the proceedings went on he began to dominate the Senate, as so often in the past, and the questions of the President of the Court sounded like interpolations which he answered and took in his stride. At the end of the first session, the moderate newspapers thought he had won, but the Nationalists said, 'Wait till you have heard the witnesses!'

The first witnesses were de Selves and the officials of the Quai d'Orsay, and the next few sessions were purely political discussions. The bitterness with which they attacked Caillaux for the Agadir Settlement amply demonstrated how necessary it had been to override them. He was accused of having attempted, under cover of the negotiations to seek a *rapprochement* with Germany and to modify France's other alliances. Jules Cambon, however, the French Ambassador in Berlin, testified he had worked in perfect accord with Caillaux who had concealed nothing from him, and that none of the accusations was true. Messimy, Caillaux's Minister for War, also spoke for him and described their common effort to put the country into a state of defence and to supply the army with heavy artillery, and he reminded the Senate that the reversal of their plans had caused the disasters of 1914. So far the Prosecution had established nothing.

Then they started on the old accusations that had been gone over again and again in so many interrogations. First the visit to Italy. The staff of the French Embassy in Rome repeated the gossip about Caillaux, but they could not produce a single witness to testify that he had ever said or done anything disloyal. The stories about him having tried to negotiate for peace through the Vatican were shown to be nonsense.

Next the Prosecution brought up the Lipscher Affair, the double agent who had given Count Károlyi the documents which proved Calmette had been working for the Austro-Hungarian Government. A police commissioner had been sent to Switzerland to persuade him to come to Paris to testify against Caillaux: he had replied he would do so for 31,800 francs. An ingenuous police secretary, Nicolle, had solemnly copied that item into his official report, so Lipscher had to be dropped: the senators might have thought evidence bought at such a price might not be exactly reliable. They had had no better luck with a man called Bolo who was under sentence of death for having received a large sum from the Germans to buy a French newspaper (but had simply pocketed the money). He was told that the only way he could prolong his life would be to incriminate Caillaux. He replied he knew nothing against Caillaux, and was shot.

Then there was the affair of the leftist newspaper *Le Bonnet Rouge*, which Caillaux had subsidised during Henriette's trial, being grateful for its support. Two years later, in 1916, one of its directors, Duval, was caught on the Swiss frontier with a cheque of allegedly German origin – but that was long after Caillaux had ceased to have anything to do with the newspaper. He neither knew Duval nor had had any dealings with him, and all attempts to prove the contrary were in vain.

There were other futile accusations – that in voting against the Three Years Service bill he had tried to demoralise France, that he had tried to finance a German *coup d'état* in Switzerland, that in introducing the Income Tax he had introduced a German system of taxation into France – whereas in fact he had modelled it more upon the British system. And then there was Calmette's old calumny that he had given public money to the Radical Party funds, though prolonged investigation had already shown that there had never been the least irregularity in his accounts.

Finally the Prosecution brought up again the question of his visit to South America : a witness was produced, named Rosenwald, who testified he had warned Caillaux in Buenos Aires that the American representative of the New York Guarantee Trust, Minotto, was a German agent, and that Caillaux had replied, 'I know, but he gives me interesting information.' Unfortunately for the Prosecution, Caillaux was not in Buenos Aires at the time the alleged conversation was supposed to have taken place, neither had the US Government considered Minotto to be a German agent. A member of the League for Human Rights came forward and disclosed that Rosenwald was an imposter, named Cahen : 'Rosenwald' disappeared before he could be charged with giving false evidence.

Nowhere, in any of the anti-Caillaux documents – there were 40,000 or more – which the Prosecution had collected with all the resources of the state behind them, was there the slightest evidence that he had at any time behaved in a dishonourable or unpatriotic manner. So little of all the accusations remained that the Prosecutor, Lescouve, in his final speech, at the thirty-second session of the trial, admitted that he doubted his guilt.

The Counsel for the Defence made effective replies which refuted all the charges from a legal point of view, and then Caillaux himself addressed the senators. He again defended his policy during the Agadir Crisis which had made him the symbol of peace with their neighbours, a symbol which could not be changed, but it was no proof that he had attempted negotiations with the enemy after the outbreak of hostilities. Nothing at all had been proved against him, and in fact he had had no dealings with German representatives since the negotiations of 1911.

He justified the economic and political views he had expressed in his papers seized in his safe-deposit box in Florence which in any case were only private thoughts which he had a perfect right to record – the Prosecutor had made great play with them, saying that they explained the true motives of his conduct, particularly the one headed *Les Responsables* describing the events leading to the outbreak of the war.

Because he had made peace with Germany in 1911, he said, all sorts of intrigues and campaigns had been directed against him – his words, his thoughts, his actions, even his inactions, were all supposed to be proofs of guilt – 'He hides,' they say, 'Therefore he is intriguing!' He gave as an example plots against him which had originated in Clemenceau's newspaper, *L'Homme Enchaîné.*

CAILLAUX : Diderot tells us there are two kinds of laws – those which are the expression of pure equity, and those born of blind opinion and circumstance. 'He who infringes the latter is treated with ignomiy, but in the future this ignominy is reflected not only upon his judges but upon the mob who applauded them.' (*Prolonged disturbance among the senators. Caillaux crumpled up the piece of paper upon which he had written the quotation and threw it disdainfully away from him.*)

Of Socrates who drank the hemlock, and those who made him drink it, which is dishonoured today? (*Renewed disturbance.*)

Gentlemen, you will excuse one final plea . . . Answer me! Does not my innocence radiate from my whole being? From my words, from my attitude – which is arrogant if you like. If I were guilty, would I use such language? (*Prolonged acclamations.*)

Never, never, never have I had the least dealings with an enemy agent! Never, never, never have I harboured a thought disloyal to my country! I have had only a single thought – the welfare and greatness of France!

I may be speaking for the last time to this assembly. (*He lowered his voice and spoke in tones of infinite sadness*) I bequeath to History all my political past. I believe I have rendered great services to my country. It is those services which have brought me here.

Tomorrow, if I could live my life again, I would take up the same causes. I should insure to this country a democratic system of taxation, even if I should once more incur the hatred of the plutocracy. Yes, I introduced the Income Tax. That was for the benefit of France.

(*After a short pause.*) Gentlemen, I have suffered. I have endured – and particularly during these past years while I was deprived of my common rights as a citizen. I am still ready to submit to everything which is in store for me, because I have nothing to reproach myself with. I would swear this on the tomb of my parents. But I cannot believe that a monstrous iniquity can triumph in the Senate of the Republic!

Gentlemen – Judge me!⁴

There was a storm of applause with repeated shouts of *Vive Caillaux!* A unanimous vote for his acquittal seemed a foregone conclusion.

Following the usual procedure, the President of the Court should then, without intermission, have put the question, was Caillaux guilty or not guilty? He declined to do so, making the excuse that he had not yet framed his question, and adjourned the session until the following afternoon. This gave the senators the opportunity to ask each other in the corridors, and to be asked, 'What will happen if Caillaux is acquitted?' An awkward question. The Left would again have an effective leader, and if he left the Court without a stain on his reputation he might soon become Prime Minister again, and would he not then get his own back on his persecutors? It would certainly be a vote against Poincaré and Clemenceau, the sponsors of the trial, who were still walking about with haloes for having led France to victory. Was it to be known that they had kept an innocent man in prison for two years and three months and that absolutely nothing could be found against him? That they had, in fact, attempted the judicial murder of the opposition leader?

Next day the Senators who had applauded his speech sat silent with averted eyes: but he was acquitted by the enormous majority of 231 votes against 28. No intelligence with the enemy! No plot against the external security of the state!

Then came a complete surprise. Instead of ordering Caillaux to be released, the President of the Court read out supplementary charges under article 78* of the criminal code, an article which had not been mentioned by the Prosecutor or in any of the interrogations. It read, 'If the correspondence with the subjects of an enemy power . . . (was

---

* It had been introduced during the Continental Blockade in the Napoleonic War to deal with merchants who unwittingly gave away important information in their business correspondence.

without criminal intent) . . . but was nevertheless detrimental to the military or political situation of France or her allies . . . he shall be punished.'

Caillaux had not corresponded with any enemy subject, nor had any witness testified that he had. The President of the Court himself did not allege that this had occurred : his charges were vague compilations based on gossip which had already been shown to be without foundation. Nevertheless, Caillaux was declared guilty and sentenced to three years in prison (which he was deemed to have already served.) He was deprived of civil rights for ten years and debarred from entering Paris or any other large town except Toulouse for five years – a punishment usually reserved for notorious criminals.

Perhaps the most perfidious of the accusations was that he had been in touch with enemy agents without being aware of it : perfidious because it could have been said of almost any leading politician of the time. Bolo, for instance, had been fêted by 'all Paris' and warmly recommended to Caillaux by Monier, President of the Seine Court of Civilian Assizes : he had been received by Poincaré at the Elysée Palace and entrusted with a diplomatic mission to the King of Spain.

The charges against Caillaux could have been disposed of as easily as all the others, but neither he nor his counsel were allowed to answer them, on the pretext that he was being tried not by a court of justice but by a tribunal – a proceeding which eminent jurists and members of the League for Human Rights have found to be not in accordance with the law. Zola was no longer there to write another *J'Accuse!* but Anatole France wrote on 23rd April :

> My Dear Caillaux, – A Party which knew neither how to prevent the war, nor how to terminate it before the country was ruined, wished to remove from power by the most iniquitous of condemnations the great citizen who vanquished Germany in 1911 without spilling a drop of blood. The hatred of your enemies makes you greater. I shake your hand.
>
> (Signed) Anatole France.[5]

> The indictment was narrowed down to the charge that M. Caillaux had been in contact with the agents of Germany, and he was left to prove that the contact had not been of a guilty nature. But there is little or no doubt as to the principal characteristics of the case. It was, in the first place, a political prosecution, and it was decided before a political court. . . . he represented the school which before the war would have made an accommodation with Germany.
>
> *The Manchester Guardian* 24 April 1920

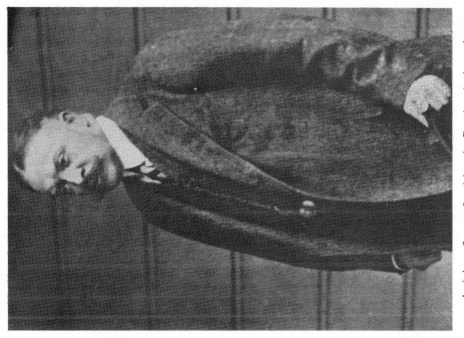

A sinister figure—Isvolsky, the Russian Ambassador.

President Poincaré taking the oath to tell 'the truth, the whole truth . . .'

Caillaux's electors never doubted his integrity.

Caillaux's home in Mamers.

It was found later that the government had suppressed a report from the French Ambassador in Brazil which should have been made available to the Counsel for the Defence :

. . . during the whole of his stay in Brazil Caillaux's attitude was most correct, he always expressed the most patriotic views and he never saw anyone who was suspect . . .

In order to prejudice his case with the public, the government issued to the press the intercepted telegram from the German Naval Attaché, that Caillaux's capture was most desirable, but with the words changed to read that his capture was 'not desirable,' as if to imply that the Germans considered him to be their man and they wanted him left alone.

There was an exultant article by Latzarus in *Le Figaro* claiming that justice had been done at last, and that the judgement on Caillaux was a reversal of the jury's verdict after Henriette's trial.

Henri Barbusse, whose brutally realistic war novel *Under Fire* had caused a sensation, wrote :

All free spirits without exception must defend Joseph Caillaux to-day . . .

Because, with great wisdom and unattackable ability, he conducted our foreign policy in a situation inherited from previous governments which was fraught with danger . . . and yet avoided war . . . Because he conducted with great courage his personal campaign for the more equitable distribution of wealth . . . infamous legends were fabricated about him, and an *intrigue du cinema* has been mounted regardless of expense with faked evidence.

They have condemned him to unpopularity, hoping to do more, and everyone who took part in it knows that he is innocent. He is the most outstanding victim of the enormous militarist and capitalist machine of which the French Government has been the tool and accomplice . . .

The French people cannot allow these persecutions to continue. They are a shameful stain on our national life and on the progress of ideas.[6]

However well it may have been understood in France at the time that the trial was purely a political manoeuvre, the stigma of his imprisonment and sentence ruined Caillaux's reputation abroad.

Monsieur Caillaux heard the sentence almost unmoved. He appeared jaunty and smiling . . .

An old man sits alone tonight in a small flat in Passy. He was the only French statesman who had the moral courage to have Caillaux arrested. I wonder what that old man, Clemenceau, is thinking?

The *Daily Express*, 24th April 1920[7]

The last act of Caillaux's political life has been played.

*Le Journal des Débats*, 24th April 1920

The British Military Historian, Captain Cyril Falls, wrote :

France faced an assault undreamed of in Great Britain, a defeatist campaign against her spiritual vitals. A series of treason trials disclosed a horrifying state of affairs. They involved a former Prime Minister, (Caillaux) . . . sentenced to imprisonment.

*The First World War*, page 210

Captain Falls might have been more horrified if he had known what really happened. Caillaux was guilty, as he said himself, only of being innocent, and this his enemies could not bear, for it proved to all the world their hatred and injustice.

# CHAPTER ELEVEN

# The Undefeated Leader

Caillaux retired to his home at Mamers where Henriette was waiting for him – she had visited him in prison whenever she was allowed to. His career was apparently at an end. In ten years, when his civil rights were to be restored, he would be sixty-eight. His enemies had nicely calculated that his working life would be over. The inevitable journalists came and asked him what were his projects, now he was at liberty. He would only say that he was going to have his teeth seen to – he had suffered from toothache during his imprisonment, and for two years had not been allowed the services of a dentist.

His faithful peasants had not changed their opinion of the Parisians : they treated him with great respect. The Sarthe regiments during the war had been known as 'Caillaux's Electors' as distinct from 'The Real French'. It was a title which pleased them, though it wasn't meant to.[1] The only rudeness he met with was from local officials who were not 'of the country'. Wherever he went, two detectives followed him.

At first he spent most of his time in his garden or his study, reading and writing. To justify himself, and to get the horrors he had suffered out of his mind, he wrote a book, *Devant L'Histoire: Mes Prisons*, in which he described what his life had been like 'inside', the efforts of the government to have him shot as a traitor, the traps set for him, the methods of the interrogators; and he again refuted all the charges which had been brought against him. Then he felt ready to turn to the future, and he wrote *Où va La France? Où va l'Europe?* in which he traced the evolution of European economy, claiming that the onward march of humanity had been encumbered by the blind rivalries of nationalist captains of industry entrenched behind ridiculous customs barriers. Then he examined the social and economic disorders resulting from the Great War, including the vexed questions of reparations, and called upon all the nations of Europe to unite and reorganise their industry. He addressed himself particularly to

'Men of disinterested mind . . . the source of all human progress on earth.'

He never reproached Henriette for her rash act which had ruined his career and brought so much misery in its train : 'She was only defending her honour,' was always his explanation. A visitor, the Comte de Fleurieu, expecting to meet a virago, was astonished to find her a modest and amiable hostess.

In the intervals of work they toured France together by devious ways to avoid the big towns he was not allowed to enter. They were frequently insulted in hotels and restaurants, but they found temporary refuge with their staunch friends Anatole France in Touraine, and Anna de Noailles in Haute Savoie : she had been awaiting him with flowers when he was released, and she refused to receive anyone who would not receive him. He greatly admired her delicate romantic verses and thought her the equal of Leopardi.[2]

Towards the end of 1921 he was invited to speak at a Socialist meeting in Grenoble, and he gladly accepted. He made it clear in his speech that although he was an exile he was neither a Socialist nor a Communist:[3] that he had not changed his political ideas. In spite of this he was generously applauded – but a gang of rowdies invaded his hotel armed with bricks and stones, and caused a riot.

'They may kill me,' he had written in 1914, 'but they shall not defeat me.' Now they nearly did kill him. He was attacked while walking along a street in Toulouse to visit his dentist, and felled by the truncheons of the *Camelots du Roi*. He narrowly escaped with his life; but he bore remarkably little resentment against his assailants. It was only aspersions on his honour he never forgave. He didn't condemn legitimate Nationalist aspirations. 'Traditional attitudes,' he wrote, 'and new impulses react upon each other, clash and mingle – that is the ferment of progress. Everyone who engages in politics from the highest motives and with a true conscience, whatever his beliefs, serves his country.'[4]

At the beginning of 1922, the League for the Rights[5] of Man began campaigning, though without success, for his sentence to be annulled. He was already addressing meetings in the small towns he was allowed to enter, trying once more to gain support for his policy of moderation, and to oppose the government's Versailles policy because it was intensifying the hatreds and resentments of the war instead of working for a peaceful solution of their common problems and the reconstruction of Europe. He told his audiences they must understand that every German labourer and farmer was not a criminal, neither were the women and children criminals. They had not wanted war, and never wanted it. A vindictive attitude merely played into the hands of the militarists and piled up new horrors for the future. He was obsessed with the idea that the war would break out again. He begged his countrymen to form an accord with the ordinary people across the frontier, to work with them to repair the enormous waste and havoc of the war. While it was right, he admitted, that Germany should pay for the destruction wrought in Belgium and Northern France, it was ridiculous to expect the huge reparations promised by Poincaré, for Germany was ruined and her economy destroyed. He agreed that Clemenceau's energy and determination had contributed to victory, but the aggressive patriotism of which he was the symbol and embodiment was destructive not only of their enemies but in the long run of France herself, for it was destroying the economy of Europe of which France too was a part.

Few were prepared to listen. The post-war boom was still on. France was victorious. It wasn't until the winter of 1923–4 that he began to get favourable reactions, particularly in the industrial regions: he was acclaimed at Denain, Montpellier, Agen, Bergerac . . . Tattered posters were still visible on the walls, put up by the Royalists; they predicted that each soldier returning to his own fireside would be provided, thanks to *L'Action Française,* with a handsome sum of money supplied by Germany. 'Shameful misrepresentation!' Caillaux exclaimed, 'that neither the crass ignorance of economic questions, nor indeed of human possibilities, can explain or justify.'[6]

At last, in the elections of May 1924, the *Bloc National* was swept from power: Poincaré, who had been Prime Minister for two years, was forced to resign, and so was the President, Millerand. Steps were immediately taken to have the judgement on Caillaux reversed.

In October he was given permission to go to Paris, for the first time since his trial, to attend the funeral of Anatole France. To his great surprise, his old colleagues greeted him as a friend. Where were the people who had condemned him? They were the same people, but the psychological climate had been transformed and he now seemed to have been the one man who had retained his sanity in a world of madmen. In January 1925 an amnesty annulled his sentence and all charges against him.

The Radical Party gave a banquet at Magic-City to welcome him back to public life. The streets in the neighbourhood were cleared, but there was no attempt at a demonstration. Toasts were drunk to 'The Martyr for Peace', but he would have none of this. He wouldn't dwell on his past suffering: he had turned the last page of that chapter, and closed the book. The theme of his speech, which was addressed as much to the late government as to the present one, was, 'You who have had the power, what have you done with France?'

Among the questions he asked on this occasion, and in his other speeches and writing of the time were :

Why had they allowed the war to go on for so long? Why had the German peace overtures in 1916 been rejected? The Germans then, realising that no quick victory was possible, were anxious to make peace.[7]

And why had Austria's offer to change sides been rejected in 1917?

And after the Armistice, why had the Socialist parties, who had no responsibility for the outbreak of the war, not insisted that there should be an equitable peace treaty upon which the economy of Europe could be reconstructed? This should have taken precedence over their doctrinaire quarrels among themselves. A peace treaty implies concessions on both sides. One that is imposed is merely a continuation of the war. Nothing durable could be founded on hatred.[8]

Why had the question of inter-Allied debts not been taken up and settled immediately after the cessation of hostilities, before differences had arisen between the Allies?

Why had the government, instead of attempting to balance their budgets, raised huge loans, both during and after the war, proclaiming, 'Germany will pay!' whereas it was obvious that Germany, in order to pay, would have to make herself the greatest industrial power in the world, which was precisely what the Allies wished to prevent?

Among the worst effects of the war, he said, was the legacy of corruption and demoralisation. They needed a complete overhaul of government departments, and they needed a firm administration to curb unfair trading and profits at the expense of the less favoured income groups.

France had lost between a third and a quarter of her national wealth. Now the day of *La Grande Pénitence* had come, and all must work and make sacrifices to repair the losses and destruction of the war.

His hearers were uncertain of what all this portended, and some were apprehensive about where his ideas might lead them to, but it was abundantly clear that he had become, almost over night, a force to be reckoned with.

In May 1925, on the fall of Herriot, Painlevé having been asked to form a government invited Caillaux to be President of a Commission of Experts. He refused, and was offered his old post of Finance Minister. He hesitated to accept it because, as he told Painlevé, it was both too soon and too late. He would be expected, like a magician, to clear up the situation created by the Nationalists' ten years of irresponsible finance, and to repair the losses of a war that had been entered into in spite of him, and unnecessarily prolonged. But, as to be Finance Minister again meant complete rehabilitation, he ended by accepting. Painlevé sent a car to fetch him and Henriette from Mamers. It broke down on the return journey to Paris, and they arrived during the night. As they had no home in the city, they moved straight into the familiar apartments in the Ministry which he had known from his childhood when his father had been Minister of Finance. 'What are you crying for?' he asked Henriette. 'I told you the future belonged to us.'[9]

It was still necessary for Painlevé to face the deputies with his selected ministers and secure a vote of confidence. When Caillaux entered the Chamber there were protests from a group of Nationalist deputies, and their spokesman, Taittinger, read out the Supreme Court's judgement, adding that Caillaux had confessed to treason. This false statement recalled the scandalous methods of the Prosecution and aroused so much resentment that the new government was enthusiastically approved. It had not even been necessary for Caillaux to speak in his own defence.

Now that he was firmly established again, his ante-room was thronged with Senators wanting to excuse themselves for having voted for his condemnation, knowing him to be innocent. Some said they had had to bow to public opinion, others that they had promised their electors to find him guilty. He brushed all their explanations aside and behaved as if he had just returned from a long holiday. He blamed no one. Even Barthou came, bringing him a present. Once again, after a ten-year interval, Henriette presided at receptions and banquets, and had tea at the Ritz. She also joined the Ecole du Louvre as an art student.

Caillaux no longer had to fight for the Income Tax – it had been accepted in principle by the Senate in July 1914 – but his situation as Finance Minister was extremely difficult. The public expected him to stabilise the franc, but there was no balance sheet of national credits and debits; recent budgets, still being audited, were not available; government bonds amounting to fifty thousand million francs, and widely distributed among the public, were about to mature; and France's war debts would amount to about twice as much as this unless they could be reduced by diplomatic negotiation. Successive governments had withheld the true state of the country's affairs from the public : they were not ready to make real sacrifices, they wanted him to find ingenious solutions to their problems. He went to London and made a pact with Churchill, then Chancellor of the Exchequer, for a reduction of the French debt to Britain of 50% to 60%, contingent on a similar pact being made with the USA. He went to Washington and submitted a plan which the New York bankers pressed their government to accept, but President Coolidge refused to make any concession.

On his return to Paris he had to content himself with preparing the ground for measures he knew would eventually be necessary, and he was forced to resign after holding office for only six months. This time he was not an exile. In July he had been elected Senator for the Sarthe, so he was still able to have a voice in his country's affairs.

In 1926, when the franc fell disastrously, he was brought into the Briand Government, again as Finance Minister. He submitted to the Chamber his plan to retrieve the situation – it entailed voting the government special powers to rule by decree for five months. Herriot objected to this, joined with Poincaré and the Nationalists and succeeded in overthrowing the government. Herriot in his turn was immediately overthrown and Poincaré became Prime Minister. Fortunately he adopted Caillaux's plan, every part of which he had opposed, and the franc was saved – only he introduced certain exaggerations of his own which had a bad effect later on European economy. The special powers denied to Caillaux were granted to Poincaré : 'Thus Caillaux's thesis served him twice over, first as a target, then as a programme : it was the biggest conjuring trick of modern times.'*

Caillaux again retired and devoted himself to writing his memoirs, but in 1931 he became President of the Finance Commission of the Senate where he exercised very great influence. In 1932 he was invited to give the Richard Cobden lecture in London. Here he paid tribute to the great Free Traders of the Manchester School who had inspired so much of his own work. He told his audience that for thirty decisive years the Continent had accepted Britain's doctrine of Free Trade which was a great force for peace; and its effect was decisive because, through it, industries had been established where they were most

* A. Febre-Luce, *Caillaux*, page 242.

useful. In unfortunate contrast, the new countries created by the Treaty of Versailles, instead of being brought into a European Customs Union, had been allowed to set up their own customs barriers behind which new industries had been established and artificially protected where they were not needed while vigorous industrial entities which should have been maintained had been broken up, thus perpetuating and intensifying the economic conditions out of which the war had come – unlimited and uncontrolled productivity unrelated to the needs of the consumer, resulting in international rivalry for dwindling markets.

The rapid development of technical appliances, he said, had brought new problems : we had an incredible pile of products and manufactured articles on one side, and on the other the masses of humanity, including the thousands deprived of the means of purchasing owing to unemployment, who couldn't absorb all the goods offered for sale. He suggested that if the great Free Traders had been alive today they would have met this challenge with new methods. Unbridled licence, allied to a misunderstanding of the elementary laws of economics, was the cause : the solution was voluntary discipline. The authorities must intervene, encouraging and controlling employers, financiers and merchants to rationalise and co-ordinate the use of their technical appliances in such a way that individual enterprise, which would always be the motive force in human progress, was not diminished. The great question was how to act so that mankind should reap all the benefits of science without being overwhelmed by them.

In 1934 he campaigned for the proposed Four Power Pact between France, Germany, Britain and Italy. In order to have a government that would support it, he tried to form an alliance with Léon Blum, the cultured intellectual who was leader of the Socialist party which had grown up under the influence of Jaurès. He failed, and the Four Power Pact failed also. The shadows of coming events were becoming darker. He did not hold office against except in the short-lived Bouisson Government in 1935 which was opposed by the whole of the Left and lost a vote of confidence by two votes. It was overthrown by Laval.

Meanwhile Henriette was quietly going on with her work in the Ecole du Louvre. While she was receiving her diploma, anti-Caillaux demonstrators interrupted the proceedings, but he bore down on them with such fury that they left the hall. It was the last attempt of the kind, the final flicker. Henriette brought out a book, which was highly esteemed, on the sculptor Dalou, who had died in 1902. She also catalogued his works in the Ecole des Beaux Arts.

At the beginning of 1938 Mussolini informed the Blum Government that Hitler had offered him a 'total' alliance, and that he would reject it in favour of a close friendship with France. Blum rejected this offer. Caillaux, believing Blum had sacrificed his country's interests on doctrinaire grounds, overthrew his government: but it was too late. Mussolini had turned to Hitler. The Axis was formed. President Lebrun, according to the usual interpretation of the constitution, should now have sent for Caillaux, but he ignored him and sent for Chautemps.

After the defeat of the French armies in 1940, Laval went to see Caillaux who was at Royat: he was evidently hoping to get his support for an accommodation with Germany. They met on 14th June. Caillaux urged him to continue the war against the Nazis and to fight them 'anywhere and everywhere'. 'But Britain is already defeated,' Laval objected. 'Is the British Fleet defeated?' Caillaux asked. 'If we go on fighting, Hitler will lose in the end.'[10] Two days later the French Government asked for an armistice.

After the surrender, Caillaux supported Pétain on the grounds that there had to be someone to deal with the Germans to lighten as far as possible the burden of the occupation, and why not the Defender of Verdun? But when Pétain sent a telegram of congratulation to Hitler on the occasion of the British repulse at Dieppe and announced his co-operation with the Germans, he resigned all his offices and once more retired to Mamers. In January 1943 Henriette, his inseparable companion, died, and he was left alone. He had already lost all his close friends and near relations.

In 1944, after the liberation, a visit from General de Gaulle restored his prestige in the eyes of his countrymen, but he was then too old to play any further part in his country's affairs. He died in the following year, aged eighty-one. A contemporary historian, Alfred Fabre-Luce, suggested posterity might consider him to be the one statesman of the time whose story was worthy to be told.

Throughout his public career he pursued a clear undeviating policy of sound finance, control of the basic necessities of life and, as a long term policy, the control of production through the control of credit, geared to the needs of the consumer, first in Europe and then throughout the world: he thought that the internationalisation of all basic materials for war industries would eventually be necessary.[11]

He did not believe in any political doctrine rhyming with ism which offered an escape from reality and the inexorable march of time by promising some impossible paradise such as his friend Jaurès used to talk about. In spite of the prolonged abuse and false accusations of his adversaries who wielded the full power of the venal press, his career stands out as a model of integrity and honourable dealing. In Foreign Affairs he believed in a firm dignified, patient and non-aggressive policy, working always towards the unification of Europe which had to begin with the reconciliation of France and Germany. He lamented that when the government of one country held out the hand of brotherhood it was always rejected by that of the other because aggressive patriotism happened to be in the ascendant there; and that next time it was the other way round.

At last, four years after his death, after two world wars, after millions of lives and hopes had been destroyed, there was a change. On 9th May 1950, when Chancellor Adenauer of Germany was presiding over a Cabinet meeting, an urgent letter was brought to him from the French Minister for Foreign Affairs, Robert Schuman, proposing that the entire French and German production of iron and steel should be placed under a common authority within the framework of an organisation which should be open to other European countries as well.[12] The proffered hand was taken. The tragic chapter that had opened in January 1912 when Caillaux's Government was overthrown for having made an enlightened peace with Germany, was brought to a close, and a new chapter began in the history of Europe.

# Source Notes

*Chapter One:*

1. Clemenceau's *Grandeur and Misery of a Victory*, p. 343.
2. *Whither France? Whither Europe?* pp. 20–21.
3. Caillaux thought these misleading telegrams, one at least sent in a code von der Lancken knew had been broken, were intended to sow dissension between him and the Quai d'Orsay – a view which seems to have been correct. See J-C Allain, *Joseph Caillau, le Défi Victorieux*, p. 395.
4. Caillaux, *Mes Mémoires, II*, p. 205.
5. Churchill, *The World Crisis, I*, p. 63.
6. Tardieu, *Le Mystère d'Agadir*, p. 583.

*Chapter Two:*

1. Captain Dreyfus, a Jew, was convicted of espionage by a court martial and condemned to serve a life sentence on Devil's Island. Evidence of his innocence was suppressed by the military authorities, but they were forced by the novelist, Emile Zola, and others, to re-open the case. The sentence was eventually annulled and Dreyfus was reinstated in the army. The case now symbolises liberal versus reactionary ideas.
2. Fabre-Luce, *The Limitations of Victory*, p. 132.
3. Loreburn, *How the War Came*, pp. 90, 131.
4. Bernhardi, *Germany and the Next War*, p. 14.
5. At the beginning of his career Jaurès determined not to be 'the prisoner of a party.' He thought all those seeking in good faith to find a solution to their common problems would eventually be united.
6. See Prolo, Jacques, *Une Politique . . . Un Crime!* p. 121.
7. Messimy said before a Commission of Enquiry in 1919: 'It is beyond all doubt that the high command in 1912 and 1913 did not wish to use reservists. It must be clearly stated that it was a grievous fault. They preferred to resort to the over-simple solution of the Three Years Law which no one would defend

today in the light of our war experience.' Margueritte, *Au Bord du Gouffre*, pp. 104–5.
8. Hannah, *Jung, his Life and Work*, p. 107.
9. Caillaux, *Mes Mémoires*, III, 130 ff., and Gheusi, *Cinquante Ans de Paris*.
10. Emil Ludwig, *July 1914*, p. 80, and Stieve, *Isvolsky and the World War*, 114 ff. Le Clère, *L'Assassinat de Jean Jaurès*, p. 89.
11. Paix-Séailles, *Jaurès et Caillaux*, p. 93. Fabre-Luce, *Caillaux*, p. 72. Caillaux, *Mes Mémoires*, III, p. 153. Pease, *Jean Jaurès*, p. 85.
12. Caillaux, *Mes Prisons*, pp. 121–2.
13. Pease, *Jean Jaurès*, pp. 15–16.
14. Caillaux, *Mes Prisons*, p. 140.

*Chapter Four:*
1. Captain Cyril Falls doubted if France would have survived the 1914–18 war without her colonial troops, specially those from North and Central Africa.
*The World War*, XX.

*Chapter Five:*
1. Poincaré, *Au Service de la France*, IV, p. 132.
2. Le Clère, *L'Assassinat de Jean Jaurès,* p. 89.

*Chapter Nine:*
1. Rabaut, *Jean Jaurès et son Assassin*, p. 50, quoting Rappoport, *Mémoires Inédite.*
2. Emil Ludwig, *July 1914*, p. 116.
3. Rabaut, p. 52.
4. Fabre-Luce, *Caillaux*, p. 116. Caillaux, *Mes Mémoires*, III, pp. 170–1, 353.
5. Rabaut, 43.
6. Le Clère, pp. 119–120.
7. Caillaux, *Mes Mémoires*, III, pp. 104–5. Calvet, *Visage d'un Demi-siècle*, p. 59.
8. The Villain enquiry was swept under the carpet. After the war, in March 1919, he was tried and acquitted. With inherited money he built a villa in Majorca and was shot during the Spanish Civil War.
9. Margueritte, *Debout les Vivants!* 141N. 161 ff. Among the papers seized in Caillaux's safe-deposit box was the following note among his future projects: 'The Peace Treaty must, in

every case, carry the interdiction upon making war, and even of issuing a decree of mobilisation, without a referendum.' And again, 'All mobilisation, total or partial, only with the approval of the public.

10. Margueritte, *Au Bord du Gouffre*, p. 109. Caillaux, *Mes Mémoires*, II, p. 213.
11. Margueritte, *Au Bord du Gouffre*, p. 94.
12. Margueritte, *Au Bord du Gouffre*, 122 ff.
13. Caillaux, *Mes Prisons*, p. 134.
14. Caillaux, *Ma Doctrine*, 189 ff.
15. Bredin, *Joseph Caillaux*, p. 172.

*Chapter Ten:*
1. Caillaux, *Ma Doctrine*, p. 205 ff.
2. Fabre-Luce, *Caillaux*, p. 155. Emile Roche, pp. 55, 57.
3. Bredin, p. 178. Fabre-Luce, *Caillaux*, p. 154. Caillaux, *Mes Prisons*, pp. 65–6.
4 *Journal des Débats*, 23rd April, 1920.
5. Caillaux, *Mes Mémoires*, III, p. 208.
   Anatole France (Jacques Anatole François Thibault) was for many years the most eminent literary figure in France. He was also a passionate campaigner for liberal ideas and a committee member of the League for the Rights of Man. In 1926 he was awarded the Nobel Prize for Literature.
6. Introduction to Paix-Séailles, *Jaurès et Caillaux*.
7. It seems Clemenceau didn't really believe the charges against Caillaux. He wrote to Poincaré on October 5th, 1918, 'Have confidence. The war will end. We shall pass together under the *Arc de Triomph*, and then we shall liberate Caillaux who will follow us.' Emil Roche, p. 82.

*Chapter Eleven:*
1. Fabre-Luce, *Caillaux*, p. 191.
2. See Emile Roche, pp. 55, 57.
   La Comtesse Anna de Noailles, Caillaux's 'incomparable friend in time of trouble,' died in 1913.
3. Caillaux said in an interview with Martin du Garde: Do you think the Marxists have understood? They are still living in 1850. There is excellence in Marx, and he should be read. But do you think he would be a Marxist today? The sour little authoritarian men who have slipped into the prophet's discarded mantle today would make him laugh. They repeat a formula

which had its value when Marx announced it, but how could he know what the modern industrial world would be like?... *Le Revue des Deux Mondes*, 1st Oct. 1963.

4. Fleurieu, p. 241.

5. The League for the Rights of Man was founded in 1888 to combat the threat of a dictatorship under General Boulanger, and again in 1898 during the Zola Trial, 'to oppose every kind of arbitrary action or militarism.'

6. Caillaux, *Mes Prisons*, p. 296.

7. Caillaux thought Alsace-Lorraine could have been regained at this time. To judge by the Crown Prince's letter to the Kaiser written in July 1917, he was probably right. An extract was published in *Le Matin* of 14th August, 1920, under the heading, *Le document le plus Sensationnel de la Guerre* :

> Certainly we are much weaker than our enemies (in military supplies and munitions) but this is nothing in comparison with the morale situation. The morale of the people, after the immense sacrifices that all German families have had to accept, is deplorable. Misery increases, despair is shown more openly. It is always disturbing in periods heavy with revolution, to see the women lose hope; that is the case with the German women, usually so heroic. Infant mortality is on the increase to a terrifying extent, contagious diseases are rampant.
>
> If Germany does not obtain peace before the end of the year there will be imminent danger of revolution ...
>
> Austria is in the same situation, or, rather, life in Austria is more insupportable than in Germany. The Emperor Charles is certainly one of our faithful friends, but if he has to choose between the complete ruin of Austria and saving her by abandoning us, his duty to his people would constrain him to abandon us. Bulgaria and Turkey cannot continue the struggle.
>
> The hope founded on the submarine war is vain. The Admiralty repeat continuously 'In a few weeks we shall be saved.' Let those few weeks pass, and look at the results. If this does not justify our holding on, let us resolutely seek to obtain peace.
>
> There is no longer any question of victory, of the increased greatness of Germany, or of glory. The only question is the life of the German people. No cause must be dearer to us. Our dynasty will be in danger? Of course for you and for me that is a great misfortune, but it is nothing in comparison to the disaster which menaces the German people ...

Written from Charleville, July 1917.

8. Caillaux said in an interview with Martin du Garde: 'All the disorders come originally from the war, the absurd pre-historic

war which at all costs we should have avoided instead of allowing ourselves to slide into it.

'But if we couldn't avoid it, at least we must understand it! And the even stupidier peace which followed it! Versailles! A peace of another age, whereas all that mattered was the economic re-organisation and the advance of the workmen's circumstances which the Industrial Revolution had been awaiting for years. All could have been brought about without drama . . .

'An exhausting war for France which laid her low for half a century. A Glorious Peace – Oh, really? in which Clemenceau behaved like a bear petrified in dead ideas. Courageous, determined, the good fellow. A magnificent Jacobin! 'But blind. For him the realities of the 20th Century didn't exist. He had in his head the defeat of 1870 and The Revenge! But beyond that? Nothing . . .' *Le Revue des Deux Mondes*, 1st Oct. 1963.

9. Proust brings Caillaux in, though not by name, to the de Guermantes *salon* in the final volume of his great novel of the period, *Remembrance of Things Past*. The Narrator returns to Paris after a long absence and finds everyone a generation older. He describes the former Prime Minister who once had been execrated by the public and society, and who had been the object of criminal proceedings, now lauded by the newspapers and sought after by duchesses. No humiliations, however great, he comments, should cause us to lose heart, knowing that within a certain term of years everything will be changed by the renewal of society at all levels and the extinction of individual passions. Only, this is the work of time. . . Thus turns the wheel of the world. *Le Temps Retrouvé*, p. 110.

10. Emile Roche, *Caillaux que j'ai connu*, p. 300.

11. Emile Roche, p. 39.

12. Adenauer Memoirs, pp. 195–53, 257–8.

# Bibliography

Adenauer Memoirs, 1945–53. Trans. B. R. von Oppen, 1960.

Alexander, E., *Adenauer and the New Germany*, 1957.

Allain, Jean-Claude, *Agadir 1911*, 1967.

———————— *Joseph Caillaux, le Défi Victorieux*, 1978.

Augstein, R., *Konrad Adenauer*. Trans. W. Walich, 1964.

Bainville, Jacques, *Les Conséquences Politiques de la Paix*, 1920.

Bernhardi, General F. von, *Germany and the Next War*. Trans. A. H. Powles, 1914.

Binion, R., *Defeated Leaders*, 1960.

Bogićević, M., *Causes of the War*, 1919.

Borely, M. *L'Émouvante Destinée d'Anna de Noailles*, 1939.

Bredin, Jean-Denis, *Joseph Caillaux*, 1980.

Burdick, W. L., *Bench and Bar of Other Lands*, 1939.

Caillaux, Henriette, *Aimé-Jules Dalou*, 1935.

Caillaux, Joseph, *Agadir, Ma Politique Extérieure*, 1919.

———————— *Devant L'Histoire, Mes Prisons*, 1921.

———————— *Où va La France? Où va l'Europe?* 1923.

———————— *Whither France? Whither Europe?* Trans. K. M. Armstrong, 1923.

———————— *Ma Doctrine*, 1926.

———————— *The World Crisis*: the lessons which it teaches and the adjustments of economic science which it necessitates. The Richard Cobden Lecture for 1932.

———————— *D'Agadir à la Grande Pénitence*, 1933.

———————— *Mes Mémoires*, 3 Vols., 1942–7.

Calvet, J., *Visage d'un Demi-Siècle*.

Chenu, C. M., *Le Procès de Madame Caillaux*, 1960.

Churchill, Winston, *The World Crisis*.

Clemenceau, Georges, *Grandeurs et Misères d'une Victoire*, 1930.

Demartial, Georges, *Patriotism, Truth and War Guilt*, 1920.

———————— *Le Mythe des Guerres de Légitime Défence*, 1931.

———————— *La Haine de la Vérité*, 1939.

Drou, Alexandre, *Péguy*, 1956.

Du Garde, Martin, *Caillaux en Liberté. Revue des Deux Mondes,* 1st October, 1963.

Falls, Captain Cyril, *The First World War.*

Fleurieu, le Comte Roger de, *Joseph Caillaux au cours d'un demi-siècle de notre histoire,* 1951.

Gaston-Martin, *Joseph Caillaux,* 1931.

Germain, André, *Les Clefs de Proust,* 1953.

Gheusi, P.-B., *Cinquante Ans de Paris,* 1939–42.

Habe, Hans, *Gentlemen of the Jury,* 1967.

Hannah, Barbara, *Jung, his Life and Work,* 1977.

Hausleiter, L. *The Machine Unchained,* 1933.

Heppenstal, R., *A Little Pattern of French Crime,* 1969.

Jäckh, E. (Editor), *Alfred von Kiderlen-Wächter, der Staatsmann und Mensch.* Brief-wechsel und Nachlas. 1925.

Lancken, Freiherr von der, *Mein Dreissig Dienstjahre,* 1931.

Larnac, J., *La Comtesse de Noailles,* 1931.

Le Clère, *L'Assassinat de Jean Jaurès,* 1969.

Letellier, Albert, *Joseph Caillaux, l'Empereur des Crédules,* 1922.

Loreburn, the Earl, *How the War Came,* 1919.

Ludwig, Emil, *Kaiser Wilhelm II.* Trans. E. C. Mayne, 1926.

——— *July 1914.* Trans. C. A. Macartney, 1929.

Manevy, *La Presse de la IIIe Republique.*

Margueritte, Victor, *Au Bord du Gouffre. Aug–Sept 1914,* 1919

——— *Debout les Vivants!* 1932

Monnerville, G., *Clemenceau,* 1968.

Murray, Gilbert, *The Foreign Policy of Sir Edward Grey, 1906–15.* 1915.

Nicolson, Harold, *Peacemaking 1919,* 1933.

Noailles, La Comtesse Anna de, *Le Livre de ma Vie,* 1932.

Paix-Séailles, Charles, *Jaurès et Caillaux,* 1920.

Pease, Margaret, *Jean Jaurès,* 1916.

Poincaré, R., *Au Service de la France. Neuf Années de Souvenirs.* 10 Vols., 1926–33.

Prolo, Jacques, *Une Politique . . . Un Crime!* 1916.

Proust, Marcel, *Le Temps Retrouvé,* 1927.

Rabaut, Jean, *Jaurès et son Assassin,* 1967.

Raphael, John, *The Caillaux Drama,* 1914.

*Revue des Deux Mondes,* Oct. 1963.

Ribot, Alexandre, *Journal,* 1936.

Roche, Emile, *Caillaux que j'ai connu,* 1949.

Ségur, Nicolas, *Conversations avec Anatole France,* 1925.

Stieve, Friedrich, *Isvolsky and the World War*. Trans. E. W. Dickes, 1926.

Tardieu, André, *Le Mystère d'Agadir.*

Vergnet, Paul, *Joseph Caillaux*, 1918.

Walton, C. C. *Kiderlen-Wächter and the Austro-German Problem*, 1940.

# Index

# Index